A Theory of Jerks

and Other Philosophical Misadventures

A Theory of Jerks

and Other Philosophical Misadventures

Eric Schwitzgebel

The MIT Press
Cambridge, Massachusetts
London, England

This book was set in Stone Serif and Stone Sans by Jen Jackowitz.

Library of Congress Cataloging-in-Publication Data is available.

ISBN: 978-0-262-04309-0

In memory of my father,
psychologist, inventor, parent, philosopher, and giver of
strange objects

Contents

Preface

I enjoy writing short philosophical reflections for broad audiences. Evidently, I enjoy this immensely: Since 2006, I've written more than a thousand such pieces, published mostly on my blog *The Splintered Mind*, but also in the *Los Angeles Times*, *Aeon*, and elsewhere. This book contains fifty-eight of my favorites, revised and updated.

The topics range widely—from moral psychology and the ethics of the game of dreidel to multiverse theory, speculative philosophy of consciousness, and the apparent foolishness of Immanuel Kant. There is no unifying thesis.

Maybe, however, there is a unifying theme. The human intellect has a ragged edge, where it begins to turn against itself, casting doubt on itself or finding itself lost among seemingly improbable conclusions. We can reach this ragged edge quickly. Sometimes, all it takes to remind us of our limits is an eight-hundred-word blog post. Playing at this ragged edge, where I no longer know quite what to think or how to think about it, is my idea of fun.

Given the human propensity for rationalization and self-deception, when I disapprove of others, how do I know that I'm not the one who is being a jerk? Given that all our intuitive, philosophical, and scientific knowledge of the mind has been built on a narrow range of cases, how much confidence can we have in our conclusions about the strange new possibilities that are likely to open up in the near future of artificial intelligence? Speculative cosmology at once poses the (literally) biggest questions that we can ask about the universe and reveals possibilities that threaten to undermine our ability to answer those same questions. The history of philosophy is humbling when we see how badly wrong previous thinkers have been, despite their intellectual skills and confidence.

Not all of my posts fit this theme. It's also fun to use the once-forbidden word "fuck" over and over again in a chapter about profanity. And I wanted to share some reminiscences about how my father saw the world—especially since in some ways I prefer his optimistic and proactive vision to my own less hopeful skepticism. Other of my blog posts I just liked or wanted to share for other reasons. A few are short fictions.

It would be an unusual reader who enjoyed every chapter. I hope you'll skip anything you find boring. The chapters are all freestanding. Please don't just start reading on page 1 and then try to slog along through everything sequentially out of some misplaced sense of duty! Trust your sense of fun (chapter 47). Read only the chapters that appeal to you, in any order you like.

Riverside, California, Earth (I hope)
October 25, 2018

I Jerks and Excuses

1 A Theory of Jerks

Picture the world through the eyes of the jerk. The line of people in the post office is a mass of unimportant fools; it's a felt injustice that you must wait while they bumble with their requests. The flight attendant is not a potentially interesting person with her own cares and struggles but instead the most available face of a corporation that stupidly insists you stow your laptop. Custodians and secretaries are lazy complainers who rightly get the scut work. The person who disagrees with you at the staff meeting is an idiot to be shot down. Entering a subway is an exercise in nudging past the dumb schmoes.

We need a theory of jerks. We need such a theory because, first, it can help us achieve a calm, clinical understanding when confronting such a creature in the wild. Imagine the nature documentary voice-over: "Here we see the jerk in his natural environment. Notice how he subtly adjusts his dominance display to the Italian-restaurant situation . . ." And second—well, I don't want to say what the second reason is quite yet.

As it happens, I do have such a theory. But before we get into it, I should clarify some terminology. The word "jerk" can refer to two different types of person. The older use of "jerk" designates a chump or ignorant fool, though not a morally odious one. When Weird Al Yankovic sang, in 2006, "I sued Fruit of the Loom 'cause when I wear their tightie-whities on my head I look like a jerk" or when, in 1959, Willard Temple wrote in the *Los Angeles Times*, "He could have married the campus queen. . . . Instead the poor jerk fell for a snub-nosed, skinny little broad," it's clear it's the chump they have in mind.[1]

The jerk-as-fool usage seems to have begun among traveling performers as a derisive reference to the unsophisticated people of a "jerkwater town," that is, a town not rating a full-scale train station, requiring the boilerman to pull on a chain to water his engine. The term expresses the traveling troupe's disdain.[2] Over time, however, "jerk" shifted from being primarily a class-based insult to its second, now dominant, sense as a moral condemnation. Such linguistic drift from class-based contempt to moral deprecation is a common pattern across languages, as observed by Friedrich Nietzsche in *On the Genealogy of Morality*.[3] (In English, consider "rude," "villain," and "ignoble.") It is the immoral jerk who concerns me here.

Why, you might be wondering, should a philosopher make it his business to analyze colloquial terms of abuse? Doesn't the Urban Dictionary cover that kind of thing quite adequately? Shouldn't I confine myself to truth, or beauty, or knowledge, or why there is something rather than nothing? I am, in fact, interested in all those topics. And yet I see a folk wisdom in the term "jerk" that points toward something morally important. I want to extract that morally important thing, isolating the core phenomenon implicit in our usage. Precedents for this type of philosophical work include Harry Frankfurt's essay *On Bullshit* and, closer to my target, Aaron James's book *Assholes*.[4] Our taste in vulgarity reveals our values.

I submit that the unifying core, the essence of "jerkitude" in the moral sense, is this: *The jerk culpably fails to appreciate the perspectives of others around him, treating them as tools to be manipulated or fools to be dealt with rather than as moral and epistemic peers.* This failure has both an intellectual dimension and an emotional dimension, and it has these two dimensions on both sides of the relationship. The jerk himself is both intellectually and emotionally defective, and what he defectively fails to appreciate is both the intellectual and emotional perspectives of the people around him. He can't appreciate how he might be wrong and others right about some matter of fact, and what other people want or value doesn't register as of interest to him, except derivatively upon his own interests. The bumpkin ignorance captured in the earlier use of "jerk" has become a type of moral ignorance.

Some related traits are already well-known in psychology and philosophy—the "dark triad" of Machiavellianism, narcissism, and psychopathy; low "Agreeableness" on the Big Five personality test; and Aaron James's conception of the asshole, already mentioned. But my conception of the jerk differs from all of these. The asshole, James says, is someone who allows himself to enjoy special advantages out of an entrenched sense of entitlement.[5] That is one dimension of jerkitude, but not the whole story. The callous psychopath, though cousin to the jerk, has an impulsivity and love of risk taking that needn't belong to the jerk's character.[6] Neither does the jerk have to be as thoroughly self-involved as the narcissist or as self-consciously cynical as the Machiavellian, though narcissism and Machiavellianism are common jerkish attributes.[7] People low in Big Five Agreeableness tend to be unhelpful, mistrusting, and difficult to get along with—again, features related to jerkitude, and perhaps even partly constitutive of it, but not exactly jerkitude as I've defined it. Also, my definition of jerkitude has a conceptual unity that is, I think, theoretically appealing in the abstract and fruitful in helping to explain some of the peculiar features of this type of animal, as we will see.

The opposite of the jerk is the *sweetheart*. The sweetheart sees others around him, even strangers, as individually distinctive people with valuable perspectives, whose desires and opinions, interests and goals, are worthy of attention and respect. The sweetheart yields his place in line to the hurried shopper, stops to help the person who has dropped her papers, calls an acquaintance with an embarrassed apology after having been unintentionally rude. In a debate, the sweetheart sees how he might be wrong and the other person right.

The jerk's moral and emotional failure is obvious. The intellectual failure is obvious, too: No one is as right about everything as the jerk thinks he is. He would learn by listening. And one of the things he might learn is the true scope of his jerkitude—a fact about which, as I will explain shortly, the all-out jerk is inevitably ignorant. This brings me to the other great benefit of a theory of jerks: It might help you figure out if you yourself are one.

৵৹

Some clarifications and caveats. First, no one is a perfect jerk or a perfect sweetheart. Human behavior—of course!—varies hugely with context. Different situations (department meetings, traveling in close quarters) might bring out the jerk in some and the sweetheart in others.

Second, the jerk is someone who *culpably* fails to appreciate the perspectives of others around him. Young children and people with severe cognitive disabilities aren't capable of appreciating others' perspectives, so they can't be blamed for their failure and aren't jerks. ("What a selfish jerk!" you say about the baby next to you on the bus, who is hollering and flinging her slobbery toy around. Of course you mean it only as a joke.

Hopefully.) Also, not all perspectives deserve equal treatment. Failure to appreciate the outlook of a neo-Nazi, for example, is not a sign of jerkitude—though the true sweetheart might bend over backwards to try.

Third, I've referred to the jerk as "he," since the best stereotypical examples of jerks tend to be male, for some reason. But then it seems too gendered to call the sweetheart "she," so I've made the sweetheart a "he" too.

❧

I've said that my theory might help us assess whether we, ourselves, are jerks. In fact, this turns out to be a strangely difficult question. The psychologist Simine Vazire has argued that we tend to know our own personality traits rather well when the traits are evaluatively neutral and straightforwardly observable and badly when the traits are highly value laden and not straightforward to observe.[8] If you ask people how talkative they are, or whether they are relatively high-strung or mellow, and then you ask their friends to rate them along those same dimensions, the self-ratings and the peer ratings usually correlate well—and both sets of ratings also tend to line up with psychologists' attempts to measure such traits objectively. Why? Presumably because it's more or less fine to be talkative and more or less fine to be quiet, okay to be a bouncing bunny and okay instead to keep it low-key, and such traits are hard to miss in any case. But few of us want to be inflexible, stupid, unfair, or low in creativity. And if you don't want to see yourself that way, it's easy enough to dismiss the signs. Such characteristics are, after all, connected to outward behavior in somewhat complicated ways; we can always cling to the idea that we've been misunderstood by those who charge us with such defects. Thus, we overlook our faults.

With Vazire's model of self-knowledge in mind, I conjecture a correlation of approximately zero between how one would rate oneself in relative jerkitude and one's actual true jerkitude. The term "jerk" is morally loaded, and rationalization is so tempting and easy! Why did you just treat that cashier so harshly? Well, she deserved it—and anyway, I've been having a rough day. Why did you just cut into that line of cars at the last moment, not waiting your turn to exit? Well, that's just good tactical driving—and anyway, I'm in a hurry! Why did you seem to relish failing that student for submitting his essay an hour late? Well, the rules were clearly stated; it's only fair to the students who worked hard to submit their essays on time—and that was a grimace not a smile.

Since probably the most effective way to learn about defects in one's character is to listen to frank feedback from people whose opinions you respect, the jerk faces special obstacles on the road to self-knowledge, beyond even what Vazire's theory would lead us to expect. By definition, he fails to respect the perspectives of others around him. He's much more likely to dismiss critics as fools—or as jerks themselves—than to take the criticism to heart.

Still, it's entirely possible for a picture-perfect jerk to acknowledge, in a *superficial* way, that he is a jerk. "So what, yeah, I'm a jerk," he might say. Provided that this admission carries no real sting of self-disapprobation, the jerk's moral self-ignorance remains. Part of what it is to fail to appreciate the perspectives of others is to fail to see what's inappropriate in your jerkishly dismissive attitude toward their ideas and concerns.

Ironically, it is the sweetheart who worries that he has just behaved inappropriately, that he might have acted too jerkishly, and who feels driven to make amends. Such distress is impossible if you don't take others' perspectives seriously into account. Indeed, the distress itself constitutes a deviation (in this one respect at least) from pure jerkitude: Worrying about whether it might be so helps to make it less so. Then again, if you take comfort in that fact and cease worrying, you have undermined the very basis of your comfort.

❧

Jerks normally distribute their jerkitude mostly *down* the social hierarchy and to anonymous strangers. Waitresses, students, clerks, strangers on the road—these are the unfortunate people who bear the brunt of it. With a modicum of self-control, the jerk, though he implicitly or explicitly regards himself as more important than most of the people around him, recognizes that the perspectives of others above him in the hierarchy also deserve some consideration. Often, indeed, he feels sincere respect for his higher-ups. Maybe deferential impulses are too deeply written in our natures to disappear entirely. Maybe the jerk retains a vestigial concern specifically for those he would benefit, directly or indirectly, from winning over. He is at least concerned enough about their opinion of him to display tactical respect while in their field of view. However it comes about, the classic jerk kisses up and kicks down. For this reason, the company CEO rarely knows who the jerks are, though it's no great mystery among the secretaries.

Because the jerk tends to disregard the perspectives of those below him in the hierarchy, he often has little idea how he appears to them. This can lead to ironies and hypocrisy. He might rage against the smallest typo in a student's or secretary's document while producing a torrent of typos himself; it just wouldn't occur to him to apply the same standards to himself. He might insist on promptness, while always running late. He might freely reprimand other people, expecting them to take it with good grace, while any complaints directed against him earn his undying enmity. Such failures of parity typify the jerk's moral shortsightedness, flowing naturally from his disregard of others' perspectives. These hypocrisies are immediately obvious if one genuinely imagines oneself in a subordinate's shoes for anything other than selfish and self-rationalizing ends, but this is exactly what the jerk habitually fails to do.

Embarrassment, too, becomes practically impossible for the jerk, at least in front of his underlings. Embarrassment requires us to imagine being viewed negatively by people whose perspectives we care about. As the circle of people the jerk is willing to regard as true peers and superiors shrinks, so does his capacity for shame—and with it a crucial entry point for moral self-knowledge.

As one climbs the social hierarchy it is also easier to *become* a jerk. Here's a characteristically jerkish thought: "I'm important and I'm surrounded by idiots!" Both halves of this proposition serve to conceal the jerk's jerkitude from himself. Thinking yourself important is a pleasantly self-gratifying excuse for disregarding others' interests and desires. Thinking that the people around you are idiots seems like a good reason to dismiss their intellectual perspectives. As you ascend the social hierarchy, you will find it easier to discover evidence of your relative importance (your big salary, your first-class seat) and of the relative stupidity of others (who have failed to ascend as high as you). Also, flatterers will tend to squeeze out frank, authentic critics.

This isn't the only possible explanation for the prevalence of powerful jerks. Maybe the precociously jerkish tend to rise swiftly in government, business, and academia. The truest sweethearts often suffer from an inability to advance their own projects over the projects of others. But I suspect the causal path runs at least as much in the other direction. Success might or might not favor the existing jerks, but I'm pretty sure it nurtures new ones.

༄

The *moralistic jerk* is an animal worth special remark. Charles Dickens was a master painter of the type: his teachers, his preachers, his petty bureaucrats and self-satisfied businessmen, Scrooge condemning the poor as lazy, Mr. Bumble shocked that Oliver Twist dares to ask for more food, each dismissive of the opinions and desires of their social inferiors, each inflated with a proud self-image and ignorant of how they are rightly seen by those around them, and each rationalizing this picture with a web of moralizing "shoulds."

Scrooge and Mr. Bumble are cartoons, and we can be pretty sure we aren't as bad as they are. Yet I see in myself and all those who are not pure sweethearts a tendency to rationalize my privilege with moralistic sham justifications. Here's my reason for dishonestly trying to wheedle my daughter into the best school, my reason why the session chair should call on me rather than on the grad student who got her hand up earlier, my reason why it's fine that I have four hundred library books in my office . . .

Philosophers appear to have a special talent in concocting such dubious justifications: With enough work, we can concoct a moral rationalization for anything! Such skill at rationalization might partly explain why ethicist philosophers seem to behave no morally better, on average, than do comparison groups of nonethicists, as my collaborators and I have found in a long series of empirical studies on issues ranging from returning library books, to courteous behavior at professional conferences, to rates of charitable giving, to membership in the Nazi Party in 1930s Germany (see chapters 4 and 53). The moralistic jerk's rationalizations justify his disregard of others, and his disregard of others prevents him from accepting an outside corrective to his rationalizations, in a self-insulating cycle. Here's why it's fine for him, he says, to neglect his obligations to his assistants and inflate his expense claims, you idiot critics. Coat the whole thing, if you like, in a patina of business-speak or academic jargon.

The moralizing jerk is apt to go badly wrong in his moral opinions. Partly this is because his morality tends to be self-serving, and partly it's because his disrespect for others' perspectives puts him at a general epistemic disadvantage. But there's more to it than that. In failing to appreciate others' perspectives, the jerk almost inevitably fails to appreciate the full range of human goods—the value of dancing, say, or of sports, nature, pets, local cultural rituals, and indeed anything that he doesn't personally care for. Think of the aggressively rumpled scholar who can't bear the thought that someone would waste her time getting a manicure. Or think of the manicured socialite who can't see the value of dedicating one's life to dusty Latin manuscripts. Whatever he's into, the moralizing jerk exudes a continuous aura of disdain for everything else.

Furthermore, *mercy* is near the heart of practical, lived morality. Virtually everything that everyone does falls short of perfection: one's turn of phrase is less than perfect, one arrives a bit late, one's clothes are tacky, one's gesture irritable, one's choice somewhat selfish, one's coffee less than frugal, one's melody trite. Practical mercy involves letting these imperfections pass forgiven or, better yet, entirely unnoticed. In contrast, the jerk appreciates neither others' difficulties in attaining all the perfections that he attributes to himself nor the possibility that some portion of what he regards as flawed is in fact blameless. Hard moralizing principle therefore comes naturally to him. (Sympathetic mercy is natural to the sweetheart.) And on the rare occasions where the jerk is merciful, his indulgence is usually ill tuned: The flaws he forgives are exactly the ones he sees in himself or has ulterior reasons to let slide. Consider another brilliant literary cartoon jerk: Severus Snape, the infuriating potions teacher in J. K. Rowling's novels, always eager to drop the hammer on Harry Potter or anyone else who happens to annoy him, constantly bristling with indignation, but wildly off the mark—contrasted with the mercy and broad vision of Dumbledore.

Despite the jerk's almost inevitable flaws in moral vision, the moralizing jerk can sometimes happen to be right about some specific important issue (as Snape proved to be)—especially if he adopts a big social cause. He needn't care only about money and prestige. Indeed, sometimes an abstract and general concern for moral or political principles serves as a substitute for concern about the people in his immediate field of view, possibly leading to substantial self-sacrifice. He might loathe and mistreat everyone around him, yet die for the cause. And in social battles, the sweetheart will always have some disadvantages: The sweetheart's talent for seeing things from the opponent's perspective deprives him of bold self-certainty, and he is less willing to trample others for his ends. Social movements sometimes do well when led by a moralizing jerk.

ↄ

How can you know your own moral character? You can try a label on for size: "lazy," "jerk," "unreliable"—is that really me? As the work of Vazire and other personality psychologists suggests, this might not be a very illuminating approach. More effective, I suspect, is to shift from first-person reflection (what am *I* like?) to second-person description (tell me, what *am* I like?). Instead of introspection, try listening. Ideally, you will have a few people in your life who know you intimately, have integrity, and are concerned about your character. They can frankly and lovingly hold your flaws to the light and insist that you look at them. Give them the space to do this and prepare to be disappointed in yourself.

Done well enough, this second-person approach could work fairly well for traits such as laziness and unreliability, especially if their scope is restricted—laziness-about-x, unreliability-about-y.

But as I suggested earlier, jerkitude is probably not so tractable, since if you are far enough gone, you can't listen in the right way. Your critics are fools, at least on this particular topic (their critique of you). They can't appreciate your perspective, you think—though really it's that you can't appreciate theirs.

To discover one's degree of jerkitude, the best approach might be neither (first-person) direct reflection upon yourself nor (second-person) conversation with intimate critics, but rather something more third-person: looking in general at other people. Everywhere you turn, are you surrounded by fools, by boring nonentities, by faceless masses and foes and suckers and, indeed, jerks? Are you the only competent, reasonable person to be found? In other words, how familiar was the vision of the world I described at the beginning of this essay?

If your self-rationalizing defenses are low enough to feel a little pang of shame at the familiarity of that vision of the world, then you probably aren't pure diamond-grade jerk. But who is? We're all somewhere in the middle. That's what makes the jerk's vision of the world so instantly recognizable. It's our own vision. But, thankfully, only sometimes.

2 Forgetting as an Unwitting Confession of Your Values

Every September 11, my social media fill with reminders to "never forget" the Twin Towers terrorist attacks. Similarly, the Jewish community insists that we keep vivid the memory of the Holocaust. It says something about a person's values, what they strive to remember—a debt, a harm, a treasured moment, a loved one now gone, an error or lesson.

What we remember says, perhaps, more about us than we would want. Forgetfulness can be an unwitting confession of your values. The Nazi Adolf Eichmann, in Hannah Arendt's famous portrayal of him, had little memory of his decisions about shipping thousands of Jews to their deaths, but he remembered in detail small social triumphs with his Nazi superiors. The transports he forgot—but how vividly he remembered the notable occasion when he was permitted to lounge beside a fireplace with Reinhard Heydrich, watching the Nazi leader smoke and drink![9] Eichmann's failures and successes of memory are more eloquent testimony to his values than any of his outward avowals.

I remember obscure little arguments in philosophy articles if they are relevant to an essay I'm working on, but I can't seem to recall the names of the parents of my children's friends. Some of us remember insults and others forget them. Some remember the exotic foods they ate on vacation, others the buildings they saw, others the wildlife, and still others hardly anything specific at all.

From the leavings of memory and forgetting we could create a map, I think, of a person's values. Features of the world that you don't see—the subtle sadness in a colleague's face?—and features that you briefly see but don't react to or retain are in some sense not part of the world shaped for you by your interests and values. Other people with different values will remember a very different series of events.

To carve David, simply remove everything from the stone that is not David.[10] Remove from your life everything you forget; what is left is your reduction of the world to the parts you care about.

3 The Happy Coincidence Defense and The-Most-You-Can-Do Sweet Spot

Here are four things I care intensely about: being a good father, being a good philosopher, being a good teacher, and being a morally good person. It would be lovely if there were never any trade-offs among these four aims.

It is highly unpleasant to acknowledge such trade-offs—sufficiently unpleasant that most of us try to rationalize them away. It's distinctly uncomfortable to me, for example, to acknowledge that I would probably be a better father if I traveled less for work. (I am writing now from a hotel room in England.) Similarly uncomfortable is the thought that the money I will spend this summer on a family trip to Iceland could probably save a few people from death due to poverty-related causes, if given to the right charity.[11]

Below are two of my favorite techniques for vanquishing such unpleasant thoughts. Maybe you'll find these techniques useful too.

The Happy Coincidence Defense

Consider travel for work. I don't really need to travel around the world giving talks and meeting people. No one will fire me if I don't do it, and some of my colleagues do it much less. On the face of it, I seem to be prioritizing my research career at the cost of being a somewhat less good father, teacher, and global moral citizen (given the pollution of air travel and the luxurious use of resources).

The Happy Coincidence Defense says, no, in fact I am not sacrificing these other goals at all. Although I am away from my children, I am a better father for it. I am a role model of career success for them, and I can tell them stories about my travels. I have enriched my life, and I can mingle that richness into theirs. I am a more globally aware, wiser father! Similarly, though I might cancel a class or two and deprioritize lecture preparation, since research travel improves me as a philosopher it improves my teaching in the long run. And my philosophical work, isn't that an important contribution to society? Maybe it's important enough to justify the expense, pollution, and waste: I do more good for the world jetting around to talk philosophy than I could do by leading a more modest lifestyle at home, working within my own community.

After enough reflection, it can come to seem that I'm not making any trade-offs at all among these four things I care intensely about. Instead I am maximizing them all. This trip to England is the best thing I can do, all things considered, as a philosopher *and* as a father *and* as a teacher *and* as a citizen of the moral community. Yay!

Now that *might* be true. If so, it would be a happy coincidence. Sometimes there really are such happy coincidences. We should aim to structure our lives and societies to enhance the likelihood of such coincidences. But still, I think you'll agree that the pattern of reasoning is suspicious. Life is full of trade-offs and hard choices. I'm probably just rationalizing, trying to convince myself that something I want to be true really is true.

The-Most-You-Can-Do Sweet Spot

Sometimes trying too hard at something ruins your performance. Trying too hard to be a good father might make you
overbearing and invasive. Overpreparing a lecture can spoil your
spontaneity. And sometimes, maybe, moral idealists who push
themselves too hard in support of their ideals collapse along the
way. For example, people moved by the arguments for vegetarianism who immediately attempt the strictest veganism might be
more likely to revert to cheeseburger eating after a few months
than those who set their sights a bit lower.

The-Most-You-Can-Do Sweet Spot reasoning runs like this:
Whatever you're doing right now is the most you can realistically, sustainably do. Were I, for example, to try any harder to
be a good father, I would become a worse father. Were I to spend
any more time reading and writing philosophy than I already
do, I would only exhaust myself, or my ideas would lose their
freshness. If I gave any more to charity, or sacrificed any more
for the well-being of others in my community, then I would . . .
I would . . . I don't know, collapse from charity fatigue? Bristle
with so much resentment that it undercuts my good intentions?

As with Happy Coincidence reasoning, The-Most-You-
Can-Do Sweet Spot reasoning can sometimes be right. Sometimes you really are doing the most you can do about something
you care intensely about, so that if you tried to do any more it
would backfire. Sometimes you don't need to compromise: If
you tried any harder or devoted any more time, it really would
mess things up. But it would be amazing if this were reliably
the case. I probably could be a better father if I spent more time
with my children. I probably could be a better teacher if I gave
more energy to my students. I probably could be a morally better
person if I just helped others a little more. If I typically think

that wherever I happen to be, that's already the Sweet Spot, I am probably rationalizing.

೧

By giving these ordinary phenomena cute names, I hope to make them more salient and laughable. I hope to increase the chance that the next time you or I rationalize in this way, some little voice pops up to say, in gentle mockery, "Ah, lovely! What a Happy Coincidence that is. You're in The-Most-You-Can-Do Sweet Spot!" And then, maybe, we can drop the excuse and aim for better.

4 Cheeseburger Ethics (or How Often Do Ethicists Call Their Mothers?)

None of the classic questions of philosophy is beyond a seven-year-old's understanding. If God exists, why do bad things happen? How do you know there's still a world on the other side of that closed door? Are we just made out of material stuff that will turn into mud when we die? If you could get away with robbing people just for fun, would it be reasonable to do it? The questions are natural. It's the answers that are hard.

In 2007, I'd just begun a series of empirical studies on the moral behavior of professional ethicists. My son Davy, then seven years old, was in his booster seat in the back of my car. "What do you think, Davy?" I asked. "People who think a lot about what's fair and about being nice—do they behave any better than other people? Are they more likely to be fair? Are they more likely to be nice?"

Davy didn't respond right away. I caught his eye in the rearview mirror.

"The kids who always talk about being fair and sharing," I recall him saying, "mostly just want you to be fair to them and share with them."

ɞ

When I meet an ethicist for the first time—by "ethicist," I mean a professor of philosophy who specializes in teaching and researching ethics—it's my habit to ask whether they think that ethicists behave any differently from other types of professor. Most say no.

I'll probe further. Why not? Shouldn't regularly thinking about ethics have some sort of influence on one's behavior? Doesn't it seem that it would?

To my surprise, few professional ethicists seem to have given the question much thought. They'll toss out responses that strike me as flip or as easily rebutted, and then they'll have little to add when asked to clarify. They'll say that academic ethics is all about abstract problems and bizarre puzzle cases, with no bearing on day-to-day life—a claim a few examples easily shows to be false: Aristotle on virtue, Kant on lying, Singer on charitable donation. They'll say, "What, do you expect epistemologists to have more knowledge? Do you expect doctors to be less likely to smoke?" I'll reply that the empirical evidence does suggest that doctors are less likely to smoke than nondoctors of similar social and economic background.[12] Maybe epistemologists don't have more knowledge, but I'd hope that specialists in feminism were less biased against women—and if they weren't, that would be interesting to know. I'll suggest that the relationship between professional specialization and personal life might play out differently for different professions.

It seems odd to me that philosophers have so little to say about this matter. We criticize Martin Heidegger for his Nazism, and we wonder how deeply connected his Nazism was to his other philosophical views.[13] But we don't feel the need to turn the mirror on ourselves.

The same issues arise with clergy. In 2010, I was presenting some of my work at the Confucius Institute for Scotland. Afterward, I was approached by not one but two bishops. I asked them whether they thought that clergy, on average, behaved better, the same, or worse than laypeople.

"About the same," said one.

"Worse!" said the other.

No clergyperson has ever expressed to me the view that clergy behave on average better than laypeople, despite all their immersion in religious teaching and ethical conversation. Maybe in part this is modesty on behalf of their profession. But in most of their voices, I also hear something that sounds like genuine disappointment, some remnant of the young adult who had headed off to seminary hoping it would be otherwise.

෴

In a series of empirical studies starting in 2007—mostly in collaboration with the philosopher Joshua Rust—I have empirically explored the moral behavior of ethics professors. As far as I know, Josh and I are the only people ever to have done this in a systematic way.[14]

Here are the measures we've looked at: voting in public elections, calling one's mother, eating the meat of mammals, donating to charity, littering, disruptive chatting and door slamming during philosophy presentations, responding to student emails, attending conferences without paying registration fees, organ donation, blood donation, theft of library books, overall moral evaluation by one's departmental peers, honesty in responding to survey questions, and joining the Nazi Party in 1930s Germany.

Obviously, some of these measures are more significant than others. They range from trivialities (littering) to substantial life decisions (joining the Nazis) and from contributions to strangers (blood donation) to personal interactions (calling Mom). Some of our measures rely on self-report (we didn't ask ethicists'

mothers how long it had *really* been), but in many cases we had
direct observational evidence.

Ethicists do not appear to behave better. Never once have we
found ethicists as a whole behaving better than our comparison
groups of other professors by any of our main planned measures.
But neither, overall, do they seem to behave worse. (There are
some mixed results for secondary measures and some cases in
which it matters who is the comparison group.) For the most part,
ethicists behave no differently from other sorts of professors—
logicians, biologists, historians, foreign-language instructors.

Nonetheless, ethicists do embrace more stringent moral
norms on some issues, especially vegetarianism and charitable
donation. Our results on vegetarianism were especially striking.
In a survey of professors from five US states, we found that 60
percent of ethicist respondents rated "regularly eating the meat
of mammals, such as beef or pork" somewhere on the "morally
bad" side of a nine-point scale ranging from "very morally bad"
to "very morally good." In contrast, only 19 percent of professors
in departments other than philosophy rated it as bad. That's a
pretty big difference of opinion! Nonethicist philosophers were
intermediate, at 45 percent. But when asked later in the survey
whether they had eaten the meat of a mammal at their previous
evening meal, we found no statistically significant difference in
the groups' responses—38 percent of professors reported having
done so, including 37 percent of ethicists.[15]

Similarly for charitable donation. In the same survey, we
asked respondents what percentage of income, if any, the typical professor should donate to charity, and then later we asked
what percentage of income they personally had given in the
previous calendar year. Ethicists espoused the most stringent
norms: their average recommendation was 7 percent, compared
with 5 percent for the other two groups. However, ethicists did

not report having given a greater percentage of income to charity than nonphilosophers (4 percent for both groups). Nor did adding a charitable incentive to half of our surveys (a promise of a $10 donation to their selected charity from a list) increase ethicists' likelihood of completing the survey. Interestingly, the nonethicist philosophers, though they reported having given the least to charity (3 percent), were the only group that responded to our survey at detectably higher rates when given the charitable incentive.[16]

∽

Should we expect ethicists to behave especially morally well as a result of their training—or at least more in accord with the moral norms that they themselves espouse?

Maybe we can defend a "no." Consider this thought experiment:

An ethics professor teaches Peter Singer's arguments for vegetarianism to her undergraduates.[17] She says she finds those arguments sound and that in her view it is morally wrong to eat meat. Class ends, and she goes to the cafeteria for a cheeseburger. A student approaches her and expresses surprise at her eating meat. (If you don't like vegetarianism as an issue, consider marital fidelity, charitable donation, fiscal honesty, or courage in defense of the weak.)

"Why are you surprised?" asks our ethicist. "Yes, it is morally wrong for me to enjoy this delicious cheeseburger. However, I don't aspire to be a saint. I aspire only to be about as morally good as others around me. Look around this cafeteria. Almost everyone is eating meat. Why should I sacrifice this pleasure, wrong though it is, while others do not? Indeed, it would be unfair to hold me to higher standards just because I'm an ethicist. I am paid to teach, research, and write, like every other professor. I am paid to apply my scholarly talents to evaluating intellectual arguments about the good and the bad, the right and the wrong. If you want me also to live as a role model, you ought to pay me extra!

"Furthermore," she continues, "if we demand that ethicists live according to the norms they espouse, that will put major distortive pressures on the field. An ethicist who feels obligated to live as she teaches will be motivated to avoid highly self-sacrificial conclusions, such as that the wealthy should give most of their money to charity or that we should eat only a restricted subset of foods. Disconnecting professional ethicists' academic inquiries from their personal choices allows them to consider the arguments in a more evenhanded way. If no one expects us to act in accord with our scholarly opinions, we are more likely to arrive at the moral truth."

"In that case," replies the student, "is it morally okay for me to order a cheeseburger too?"

"No! Weren't you listening? It would be wrong. It's wrong for me also, as I just admitted. I recommend the avocado and sprouts. I hope that Singer's and my arguments help create a culture permanently free of the harms to animals and the environment that are caused by meat eating."

"This reminds me of Thomas Jefferson's attitude toward slave ownership," I imagine the student replying. Maybe the student is black.

"Perhaps so. Jefferson was a great man. He had the courage to recognize that his own lifestyle was morally odious. He acknowledged his mediocrity and resisted the temptation to paper things over with shoddy arguments. Here, have a fry."

Let's call this view *cheeseburger ethics*.

ↄ

Any of us could easily become much morally better than we are, if we chose to. For those of us who are affluent by global standards, one path is straightforward: Spend less on luxuries and give the savings to a good cause. Even if you aren't affluent by global standards, unless you are on the precipice of ruin, you could give more of your time to helping others. It's not difficult to see multiple ways, every day, in which one could be kinder to those who would especially benefit from kindness.

And yet most of us choose mediocrity instead. It's not that we try but fail, or that we have good excuses. We—most of us—actually aim at mediocrity. The cheeseburger ethicist is perhaps only unusually honest with herself about this. We aspire to be about as morally good as our peers. If others cheat and escape unpunished, we want to do the same. We don't want to suffer for goodness while others laughingly gather the benefits of vice. If the morally good life is uncomfortable and unpleasant, if it involves repeated painful sacrifices that aren't compensated for in some way, sacrifices that others aren't also making, then we don't want it.

Recent empirical work in moral psychology and experimental economics, especially that by Robert B. Cialdini and Cristina Bicchieri, seems to confirm this general tendency.[18] People are more likely to comply with norms that they see others following and less likely to comply with norms they see others violating. Also, empirical research on "moral self-licensing" suggests that people who act well on one occasion often use that as an excuse to act less well subsequently.[19] We gaze around us, then aim for so-so.

What, then, is moral reflection good for? Here's one thought. Maybe it gives us the power to calibrate more precisely toward our chosen level of mediocrity. I sit on the couch, resting while my wife cleans up from dinner. I know that it would be morally better to help than to continue relaxing. But how bad, exactly, would it be for me not to help? Pretty bad? Only a little bad? Not at all bad, but also not as good as I'd like to be if I weren't feeling so lazy?

These are the questions that occupy my mind. In most cases, we already know what is good. No special effort or skill is needed to figure that out. Much more interesting and practical is the question of how far short of the ideal we are comfortable being.

Suppose it's generally true that we aim for goodness only by peer-relative, rather than absolute, standards. What, then, should we expect to be the effect of discovering, say, that it is morally bad to eat meat, as the majority of US ethicists seem to think? If you're trying to be only about as good as others, and no better, then you can keep enjoying the cheeseburgers. Your behavior might not change much at all. What would change is this: You'd acquire a lower opinion of (almost) everyone's behavior, your own included.

You might hope that others will change. You might advocate general social change—but you'll have no desire to go first. Like Jefferson maybe.

ℰↄ

I was enjoying dinner in an expensive restaurant with an eminent ethicist, at the end of an ethics conference. I tried these ideas out on him.

"B+," he said. "That's what I'm aiming for."

I thought, but I didn't say, *B+ sounds good.* Maybe that's what I'm aiming for too. B+ on the great moral curve of white middle-class college-educated North Americans. Let others get the As.

Then I thought, most of us who are aiming for B+ will probably fall short. You know, because we fool ourselves. Here I am away from my children again, at a well-funded conference in a beautiful two-hundred-dollar-a-night hotel, mainly, I suspect, so that I can nurture and enjoy my rising prestige as a philosopher. What kind of person am I? What kind of father? B+?

(Oh, it's excusable!—I hear myself saying. I'm a model of career success for the kids, and of independence. And morality isn't so demanding. And my philosophical work is a contribution to the general social good. And I give, um, well, a little to charity, so that helps compensate. And I'd be too disheartened if I couldn't do this kind of thing, which would make me worse as a father and as a teacher of ethics. Plus, I owe it to myself. And . . . Wow, how neatly what I want to do fits with what's ethically best, once I think about it! [See chapter 3 on Happy Coincidence reasoning.])

A couple of years later, I emailed that famous ethicist about the B+ remark, to see if I could quote him by name. He didn't recall having said it, and he denied that that was his view. He is aiming for moral excellence after all. It must have been the chardonnay speaking.

⌘

Most ancient philosophers and great moral visionaries of the religious wisdom traditions, East and West, would find the cheeseburger ethicist strange. Most of them assumed that the main purpose of studying ethics was self-improvement. Most of them also accepted that philosophers were to be judged by their actions as much as by their words. A great philosopher was, or should be, a role model: a breathing example of a life well lived. Socrates taught as much by drinking the hemlock as by any of his dialogues, Confucius by his personal correctness, Siddhartha Gautama by his renunciation of wealth, Jesus by washing his disciples' feet. Socrates does not say, "Ethically, the right thing for me to do would be to drink this hemlock, but I will flee instead!" (Maybe he could have said that, but then he would have been a different sort of model.)

I'd be suspicious of a twenty-first-century philosopher who offered up her- or himself as a model of wise living. This is no longer what it is to be a philosopher—and in any case, those who regard themselves as especially wise are usually mistaken. Still, I think, the ancient philosophers got something right that the cheeseburger ethicist gets wrong.

Maybe it's this: I have available to me the best attempts of earlier generations to express their ethical understanding of the world. I even seem to have some advantages over ancient philosophers, in that there are now many more centuries of written texts and several distinct cultures with long traditions that I can compare. And I am paid, quite handsomely by global standards, to devote a large portion of my time to thinking through this material. What should I do with this amazing opportunity? Use it to get some publications and earn praise from my peers, plus a higher salary? Sure. Use it—as my seven-year-old son observed—as a tool to badger others into treating me better? Okay, I guess so, sometimes. Use it to try to shape other people's behavior in a way that will improve the world? Simply enjoy its power and beauty for its own sake? Yes, those things too.

But also, it seems a waste not to try to use it to improve myself ethically. Part of what I find unnerving about the cheeseburger ethicist is that she seems so comfortable with her mediocrity, so uninterested in deploying her philosophical tools toward self-improvement. Presumably, if approached in the right way, the great traditions of moral philosophy have the potential to help us become morally better people. In cheeseburger ethics, that potential is cast aside.

The cheeseburger ethicist risks intellectual failure as well. Real engagement with a philosophical doctrine probably requires taking some steps toward living it. The person who takes, or at least tries to take, personal steps toward Kantian scrupulous honesty, or Mozian impartiality, or Buddhist detachment, or Christian compassion gains a kind of practical insight into those doctrines that is not easily achieved through intellectual reflection alone. A full-bodied understanding of ethics requires some relevant life experience.

What's more, abstract doctrines lack specific content if they aren't tacked down in a range of concrete examples. Consider the doctrine "treat everyone as equals who are worthy of respect." What counts as adhering to this norm, and what constitutes a violation of it? Only when we understand how norms play out across examples do we really understand them.[20] Living our norms, or trying to live them, forces a maximally concrete confrontation with examples. Does your ethical vision really require that you free the slaves on which your lifestyle crucially depends? Does it require giving away your salary and never again enjoying an expensive dessert? Does it require drinking hemlock if your fellow citizens unjustly demand that you do so?

Few professional ethicists really are cheeseburger ethicists, I think, when they stop to consider it. We do want our ethical reflections to improve us morally, a little bit. But here's the catch: We aim only to become *a little* morally better. We cut ourselves slack when we look at others around us. We grade ourselves on a curve and tell ourselves, if pressed, that we're aiming for B+ rather than A. And at the same time, we excel at rationalization and excuse making—maybe more so, the more ethical theories we have ready to hand. So we end, on average, about where we began, behaving more or less the same as others of our social group.

Should we aim for A+, then? Being frank with myself, I don't want the self-sacrifice I'm pretty sure would be required. Should I aim at least a little higher than B+? Should I resolutely aim to be morally much better than my peers—A or maybe A-minus— even if not quite a saint? I worry that needing to see myself as unusually morally excellent is more likely to increase self-deception and rationalization than to actually improve me.

Should I redouble my efforts to be kinder and more generous, coupling them with reminders of humility about my likelihood of success? Yes, I will—today! But I already feel my resentment building, and I haven't even done anything yet. Maybe I can escape that resentment by adjusting my sense of "mediocrity" upward. I might try to recalibrate by surrounding myself with like-minded peers in virtue. But avoiding the company of those I deem morally inferior seems more characteristic of the moralizing jerk than of the genuinely morally good person.

I can't quite see my way forward. But now I worry that this, too, is excuse making. Nothing will ensure success, so (phew!) I can comfortably stay in the same old mediocre place I'm accustomed to. This defeatism also fits nicely with one natural way to read Josh Rust's and my data: Since ethicists don't behave better or worse than others, philosophical reflection must be behaviorally inert, taking us only where we were already headed, its power mainly that of providing different words by which to decorate our predetermined choices.[21] So I'm not to be blamed if all my ethical philosophizing hasn't improved me.

I reject that view. Instead I favor this less comfortable idea: Philosophical reflection does have the power to move us, but it is not a tame thing. It takes us where we don't intend or expect, sometimes one way, as often the other, sometimes amplifying our vices and illusions, sometimes yielding real insight and inspiring substantial moral change. These tendencies cross-cut and cancel in complex ways that are difficult to detect empirically. If we could tell in advance where our reflection would carry us, we'd be implementing a preset educational technique rather than challenging ourselves philosophically.

Genuine philosophical thinking critiques its prior strictures, including even the assumption that we ought to be morally good. It damages almost as often as it aids, is free, wild, and unpredictable, always breaks its harness. It will take you somewhere, up, down, sideways—you can't know in advance. But you are responsible for trying to go in the right direction with it and also for your failure when you don't get there.

5   On Not Seeking Pleasure Much

Back in the 1990s, when I was a graduate student, my girlfriend Kim asked me what, of all things, I most enjoyed doing. Skiing, I answered. I was thinking of those moments breathing the cold, clean air, relishing the mountain view, then carving a steep, lonely slope. I'd done quite a bit of that with my mom when I was a teenager. But how long had it been since I'd gone skiing? Maybe three years? Grad school kept me busy and I now had other priorities for my winter breaks. Kim suggested that if it had been three years since I'd done what I most enjoyed doing, then maybe I wasn't living wisely.

Well, what, I asked, did she most enjoy? Getting massages, she said. Now, the two of us had a deal at the time: If one gave the other a massage, the recipient would owe a massage in return the next day. We exchanged massages occasionally, but not often, maybe once every few weeks. I pointed out that she, too, might not be perfectly rational: She could easily get much more of what she most enjoyed simply by giving me more massages. Surely the displeasure of massaging my back couldn't outweigh the pleasure of the thing she most enjoyed in the world? Or was pleasure for her such a tepid thing that even the greatest pleasure she knew was hardly worth getting?

Suppose it's true, as this story suggests, that avoiding displeasure is much more motivating than gaining pleasure, so that even our top pleasures (skiing, massages) aren't motivationally powerful enough to overcome only moderate displeasures (organizing a ski trip, giving a massage).[22] Maybe this is rational. Maybe displeasure is more bad than pleasure is good, and it's better to have a steady neutral than a mix of highs and lows. If so, that might explain why some people are attracted to the Stoics' and Buddhists' emphasis on avoiding suffering, even at the cost of losing opportunities for pleasure.[23]

Alternatively, maybe it's irrational not to weigh pleasure and displeasure evenly. In dealing with money, people will typically, and seemingly irrationally, do much more to avoid a loss than to secure an equivalent gain.[24] Is sacrificing two units of pleasure to avoid one unit of displeasure like irrationally forgoing a gain of $2 to avoid a loss of $1?

It used to be a truism in Western (especially British) philosophy that people sought pleasure and avoided pain. A few old-school psychological hedonists, like Jeremy Bentham, went so far as to say that that was *all* that motivated us.[25] I'd guess quite differently: Although pain is moderately motivating, pleasure motivates us very little. What motivates us more are outward goals, especially socially approved goals—raising a family, building a career, winning the approval of peers—and we will suffer immensely, if necessary, for these things. Pleasure might bubble up as we progress toward these goals, but that's a bonus and side effect, not the motivating purpose, and summed across the whole, the displeasure might vastly outweigh the pleasure. Evidence suggests that even raising a child is probably for most people a hedonic net negative, adding stress, sleep deprivation, and unpleasant chores, as well as crowding out the pleasures that childless adults regularly enjoy.[26]

Have you ever watched a teenager play a challenging video game? Frustration, failure, frustration, failure, slapping the console, grimacing, swearing, more frustration, more failure—then finally, woo-hoo! The sum over time has to be negative, yet they're back again to play the next game. For most of us, biological drives and addictions, personal or socially approved goals, concern for loved ones, habits and obligations—all appear to be better motivators than gaining pleasure, which we mostly seem to save for the little bit of free time left over.

If maximizing pleasure is central to living well and improving the world, we're going about it entirely the wrong way. Do you really want to maximize pleasure? I doubt it. Me, I'd rather write some good philosophy and raise my kids.

6   How Much Should You Care about How You Feel in Your Dreams?

Prudential hedonists say that how well your life is going for you, your personal well-being, is wholly constituted by facts about how much pleasure or enjoyment you experience and how much pain, displeasure, or suffering you experience. (This is different from *motivational* hedonism, discussed in chapter 5, which concerns what moves us to act.) Prudential hedonism is probably a minority view among professional philosophers: Most would say that personal well-being is also partly constituted by facts about your flourishing or the attainment of things that matter to you—good health, creative achievement, loving relationships—even if that flourishing or attainment isn't fully reflected in positive emotional experiences.[27] Nevertheless, prudential hedonism might seem to be an important *part* of the story: Improving the ratio of pleasure to displeasure in life might be central to living wisely and structuring a good society.

Often a dream is the most pleasant or unpleasant thing that happens all day. Discovering that you can fly—whee! How much do you do in waking life that is as fun as that? Conversely, how many things in waking life are as unpleasant as a nightmare? Most of your day you ride along on an even keel, with some ups and downs, but at night your dreams buzz with thrills and anguish.

Here's a great opportunity, then, to advance the hedonistic project! Whatever you can do to improve the ratio of pleasant to unpleasant dreams should have a big impact on the ratio of pleasure to displeasure in your life.

This fact explains the emphasis prudential hedonists and utilitarian ethicists have placed on improving one's dream life. It also explains the gargantuan profits of all those dream-improvement megacorporations.

Not. Of course not! When I ask people how concerned they are about the overall hedonic balance of their dreams, their response is almost always a shrug. But if the overall sum of felt pleasure and displeasure is important, shouldn't we take at least somewhat seriously the quality of our dream lives?

Dreams are usually forgotten, but I'm not sure how much that matters. Most people forget most of their childhood, and within a week they forget almost everything that happened on a given day. That doesn't make the hedonic quality of those events irrelevant. Your two-year-old might entirely forget the birthday party a year later, but you still want her to enjoy it, right? And anyway, we can work to remember our dreams if we want. Simply attempting to remember one's dreams upon waking, by jotting some notes into a dream diary, dramatically increases dream recall.[28] So if recall were important, you could work toward improving your dreams' hedonic quality (maybe by learning lucid dreaming?[29]) and also work to improve your dream memory. The total impact on the amount of remembered pleasure in your life could be enormous!

I can't decide whether the fact that I haven't acted on this sensible advice illustrates my irrationality or instead shows that I care even less about pleasure and displeasure than I said in chapter 5.[30]

7 Imagining Yourself in Another's Shoes versus Extending Your Love

There's something I don't like about the "Golden Rule," the admonition to do unto others as you would have others do unto you. Consider this passage from the ancient Chinese philosopher Mengzi (Mencius):

> That which people are capable of without learning is their genuine capability. That which they know without pondering is their genuine knowledge. Among babes in arms there are none that do not know to love their parents. When they grow older, there are none that do not know to revere their elder brothers. Treating one's parents as parents is benevolence. Revering one's elders is righteousness. There is nothing else to do but extend these to the world.[31]

One thing I like about the passage is that it assumes love and reverence for one's family as a given, rather than as a special achievement. It portrays moral development simply as a matter of extending that natural love and reverence more widely.

In another famous passage, Mengzi notes the kindness that the vicious tyrant King Xuan exhibits in saving a frightened ox from slaughter, and he urges the king to extend similar kindness to the people of his kingdom.[32] Such extension, Mengzi says, is a matter of "weighing" things correctly—a matter of treating similar things similarly and not overvaluing what merely happens to be nearby. If you have pity for an innocent ox being led to slaughter, you ought to have similar pity for the innocent people dying in your streets and on your battlefields, despite their invisibility beyond your beautiful palace walls.

Mengzian extension starts from the assumption that you are already concerned about nearby others and takes the challenge to be extending that concern beyond a narrow circle. The Golden Rule works differently—and so too the common advice to imagine yourself in someone else's shoes. In contrast with Mengzian extension, Golden Rule/others' shoes advice assumes self-interest as the starting point and implicitly treats overcoming egoistic selfishness as the main cognitive and moral challenge.

Maybe we can model Golden Rule/others' shoes thinking like this:

1. If I were in the situation of person x, I would want to be treated according to principle p.
2. Golden Rule: Do unto others as you would have others do unto you.
3. Thus, I will treat person x according to principle p.

And maybe we can model Mengzian extension like this:

1. I care about person y and want to treat that person according to principle p.
2. Person x, though perhaps more distant, is relevantly similar.
3. Thus, I will treat person x according to principle p.

There will be other more careful and detailed formulations, but this sketch captures the central difference between these two approaches to moral cognition. Mengzian extension models general moral concern on the natural concern we already have for people close to us, while the Golden Rule models general moral concern on concern for oneself.

I like Mengzian extension better for three reasons. First, Mengzian extension is more psychologically plausible as a model of moral development. People do, naturally, have concern and compassion for others around them. Explicit exhortations aren't needed to produce this natural concern and compassion, and these natural reactions are likely to be the main seed from which mature moral cognition grows. Our moral reactions to vivid, nearby cases become the bases for more general principles and policies. If you need to reason or analogize your way into concern even for close family members, you're already in deep moral trouble.

Second, Mengzian extension is less ambitious—in a good way. The Golden Rule imagines a leap from self-interest to generalized good treatment of others. This may be excellent and helpful advice, perhaps especially for people who are already concerned about others and thinking about how to implement that concern. But Mengzian extension has the advantage of starting the cognitive project much nearer the target, requiring less of a leap. Self to other is a huge moral and ontological divide. Family to neighbor, neighbor to fellow citizen—that's much less of a divide.

Third, you can turn Mengzian extension back on yourself, if you are one of those people who has trouble standing up for your own interests—if you are, perhaps, too much of a sweetheart (in the sense of chapter 1). You would want to stand up for your loved ones and help them flourish. Apply Mengzian extension, and offer the same kindness to yourself. If you'd want your father to be able to take a vacation, realize that you probably deserve a vacation too. If you wouldn't want your sister to be insulted by her spouse in public, realize that you too shouldn't have to suffer that indignity.[33]

Although Mengzi and the eighteenth-century French philosopher Jean-Jacques Rousseau both endorse mottoes standardly translated as "human nature is good" and have views that are similar in important ways,[34] this is one difference between them. In both *Emile* and *Discourse on Inequality*, Rousseau emphasizes self-concern as the root of moral development, making pity and compassion for others secondary and derivative. He endorses the foundational importance of the Golden Rule, concluding that "love of men derived from love of self is the principle of human justice."[35]

This difference between Mengzi and Rousseau is not a general difference between East and West. Confucius, for example, endorses something like the Golden Rule: "Do not impose on others what you yourself do not desire."[36] Mozi and Xunzi, also writing in the period, imagine people acting mostly or entirely selfishly until society artificially imposes its regulations, and so they see the enforcement of rules rather than Mengzian extension as the foundation of moral development.[37] Moral extension is thus specifically Mengzian rather than generally Chinese.

Care about me not because you can imagine what you would selfishly want if you were me. Care about me because you see how I am not really so different from others you already love.

8 Is It Perfectly Fine to Aim for Moral Mediocrity?

As I suggested in chapter 4, as well as in other work,[38] most people aim to be morally mediocre. They aim to be about as morally good as their peers, not especially better, not especially worse. They don't want to be the one honest person in a classroom of unpunished cheaters; they don't want to be the only one of five housemates who reliably cleans up her messes and returns what she borrows; they don't want to turn off the air conditioner and let the lawn die to conserve energy and water if their neighbors aren't doing the same. But neither do most people want to be the worst sinner around—the most obnoxious of the housemates, the lone cheater in a class of honorable students, the most wasteful homeowner on the block.

Suppose I'm right about that. What is the ethics of aiming for moral mediocrity? It sounds kind of bad, the way I put it—aiming for mediocrity. But maybe it's not so bad, really? Maybe there's nothing wrong with aiming for the moral middle. "Cs get degrees!" Why not just go for a low pass—just enough to squeak over the line, if we're grading on a curve, while simultaneously enjoying the benefits of moderate, commonplace levels of deception, irresponsibility, screwing people over, and destroying the world's resources for your favorite frivolous luxuries? Maybe that's good enough, really, and we should reserve our negative judgments for what's more uncommonly rotten.[39]

There are two ways you could argue that it's not bad to aim for less than moral excellence. You could argue that although it's somewhat *morally* bad to aim for moral mediocrity, in some other broader sense of "bad" it's not overall bad to be a little bit morally bad. Morality isn't everything, after all. It might be (in some sense) fine and (in some sense) reasonable to trade morality off against other goals you have. Maybe that's what the cheeseburger ethicist (chapter 4) is doing and what I'm doing when I face up to the fact that I'm always compromising among goods like fatherhood, research, teaching, and morality (rather than being in The-Most-You-Can-Do Sweet Spot or maximizing them all by Happy Coincidence; chapter 3).

Alternatively, you could argue that it's *not at all morally bad* to aim for moral mediocrity—or, more neutrally phrased, moral averageness. Maybe it would be morally better to aim for moral excellence, but that doesn't mean that it's wrong or bad to shoot instead for the middle. Average coffee isn't bad; it's just not as good as it could be. Average singers aren't bad; they're just not as . . . no, I take it back. Average singers are bad. (Sometimes they are joyously, life-affirmingly bad.) So that's the question. Is morality more like coffee or singing?

I'd argue that morality is a bit like singing while drinking coffee. There's something fine about being average, but there are also some sour notes that can't entirely be wished away. I think you'll agree with me, if you consider the moral character of your neighbors and coworkers: They're not horrible, but neither are they above moral criticism. If the average person is aiming for approximately that, the average person is somewhat morally criticizable for low moral ambitions.

The best argument I know of that it's perfectly morally fine to aim to be morally average is what I'll call the Fairness Argument. But before I present that argument, two clarifications:

First, aiming for moral mediocrity or averageness, in the sense I intend, doesn't require conceptualizing ourselves as doing so. We might say to ourselves, quite sincerely, that we are aiming for moral excellence. We fool ourselves all the time; we convince ourselves of the strangest things, if we want them to be true; we refuse to critically examine our motives. Aiming is shown less by what we sincerely say than by our patterns of choice.[40]

Assume that littering is bad. To aim for mediocrity with respect to littering is to be disposed to calibrate yourself upward or downward toward approximately a middle target. Suppose the wind whips a food wrapper from your hands and carries it down the block, or suppose you accidentally drop an almost-empty bottle of sunscreen from a ski lift. In either case, it would be a hassle to retrieve the thing, but you could do it. If you're calibrating toward the middle, what you do will depend on what you perceive to be standard behavior among people you regard as your peers. If most of them would let it go in a similar situation, so would you. If most of them would chase it down, so would you. It doesn't really matter what story you tell yourself about it. If you're a half-decent moral philosopher, I'm sure that in such moderate grayish cases you can concoct a half-plausible excuse of some sort, regardless of whether you really should go retrieve your litter or not. (If you don't like the littering example, try another: household energy use, helping out someone in a weak position, gray-area expense reporting.)

Second, I don't intend to be making a universal claim about the goodness or badness of aiming for mediocrity or averageness in *all* social contexts. I mean to be talking about *us,* my notional readership and I. If one's social reference group is the *Einsatz-gruppen* killing squads of Nazi-occupied eastern Europe, aiming for about-average murder and cruelty is not just bad but horrible. If one's social reference group is some saintly future utopia, the mediocre may be perfectly benign. I don't mean them. I just mean us: you, as I imagine you, and me, and our friends and family and neighbors.

The Fairness Argument

First, assume—of course it's disputable[41]—that being morally excellent normally involves substantial self-sacrifice. It's morally better to donate large amounts to worthy charities than to donate small amounts. It's morally better to be generous rather than stingy with your time in helping colleagues, neighbors, and distant relatives who might not be your favorite people. It's morally better to meet your deadlines than to inconvenience others by running late. It's morally better to have a small carbon footprint than a medium sized or large one. It's morally better not to lie, cheat, or fudge in all the small—and sometimes large—ways that people do. To be near the moral maximum in every respect would be practically impossible near-sainthood, but we nonsaints could still presumably be somewhat better in many ways. We just choose not to be better, because we'd rather not make the sacrifices involved.

The idea of the Fairness Argument, then, is this: Since most of your peers aren't making the sacrifices necessary for peer-relative moral excellence, it's unfair for you to be blamed for also declining to do so. If the average person in your financial condition gives 3 percent of income to charity, it would be unfair to blame you for not giving more. If your colleagues down the hall cheat, shirk, fib, and flake *x* amount of the time, it's only fair that you get to do the same. Fairness requires that we demand no more than average moral sacrifice from the average person. Thus, there's nothing wrong with aiming to be only a middling member of the moral community—approximately as (un)selfish, (dis)honest, and (un)reliable as everyone else.

Two Replies to the Fairness Argument

1. *Absolute standards.* Some actions are morally bad, even if the majority of your peers are engaging in them. Imagine a Nazi death camp guard who is somewhat less cruel to the inmates than average but who is still somewhat more cruel and murderous than he needs to be to keep his job. "Hey, at least I'm better than average!" would be a poor excuse. Closer to home, most people regularly exhibit small to moderate degrees of sexism, racism, ableism, and preferential treatment of the conventionally beautiful.[42] Even though most people do this, we are still criticizable for it. That you're typical or average in your degree of bias is at best a mitigator of blame, not a full excuser from blame. Similarly with failing to live up to your promises: That most people fail to fulfill a significant proportion of their promises makes it, perhaps, forgivable and understandable that you also do so (depending on the promise), but it doesn't make it perfectly okay.

2. *Strange trade-offs.* Most of us see ourselves as having areas of moral strength and weakness. Maybe you're a warmhearted fellow, but flakier than average about responding to important emails. Maybe you know you tend to be rude and grumpy to strangers, but you're an unusually active volunteer in your community. Empirical evidence suggests that in implicitly guiding our behavior, we tend to treat these trade-offs as exculpatory or licensing: You cut yourself slack on one

in light of the other.[43] You—typically unconsciously or only half-consciously—let your excellence in one area justify lowering your aims in another, so that averaging the two, you arrive somewhere in the middle. Aiming for moral mediocrity needn't mean aiming for mediocrity by every moral standard considered separately. Such trade-offs between norm types are emotionally tempting when you're motivated to see yourself positively. However, making them fully explicit reveals their strangeness: "It's fine that I insulted the cashier, because this afternoon I'm volunteering for river cleanup." "I'm not criticizable for neglecting Cameron's urgent email because this morning I greeted Monica and Britney kindly, filling the office with good vibes." Stated so baldly, such excuses would probably sound odd even to you. These trade-offs wilt under explicit scrutiny.

I'm not imagining here that you are working so hard for a good cause that you simply have no time or energy left over for other good things. That's just human limitation, perfectly excusing. What I'm imagining is the more common phenomenon of letting yourself be a little bad, unkind, or unjustifiably irresponsible about x because you're perhaps a little too proud of yourself for having done y.

Most of us aim only for moral mediocrity. We ought to own up to this fact. Proper acknowledgment of this possibly uncomfortable fact can then ground a frank confrontation with the question of how much we really care about morality. How much are we willing to sacrifice to be closer to morally excellent, if our neighbors remain off-key?

9 A Theory of Hypocrisy

Hypocrisy, let's say, is when someone conspicuously advocates a moral rule while also secretly (or at least much less conspicuously) violating that moral rule at least as much as does the typical member of their audience.

It's hard to know exactly how common hypocrisy is, because people understandably hide their embarrassing behavior and because the psychology of moral advocacy is a complex and understudied topic. But it seems likely that hypocrisy is more common than a purely strategic analysis of its advantages would predict. I think of "family values" and antihomosexuality politicians who seem disproportionately likely to be caught in gay affairs.[44] I think of the angry, judgmental people we all know who emphasize how important it is to control your emotions. I think of police officers who break the laws they enforce on others and of environmental activist Al Gore's (formerly?) environmentally unfriendly personal habits.[45] I think of the former head of the academic integrity office at the University of California, Riverside, who—I was told when I tried to contact him to ask his views about the moral behavior of students in ethics classes—was fired when his colleagues discovered that he had falsified his resume.

Antigay activists might or might not actually be more likely than others to have homosexual affairs, and so on. But it's striking to me that the rates even come close, as it seems they do. A purely strategic analysis of hypocrisy suggests that, in general, people who conspicuously condemn x should have low rates of x. Even if condemning x sometimes helps deflect suspicion, overall the costs of condemning x while secretly doing x are high. Among those costs: contributing to a climate in which $x$ish behavior is generally more condemned; attracting friends and allies who are especially likely also to condemn x; attracting extra scrutiny of whether you in fact do x or not; and attracting the charge of hypocrisy, in addition to the charge of $x$ing itself, if your $x$ing is discovered. It seems strategically foolish for a preacher with a secret gay lover to choose antihomosexuality as a central theme in his sermons!

Here's what I suspect is going on. As I suggest in chapters 4 and 8, people don't generally aim to be saints or even much morally better than their neighbors. They aim instead for moral mediocrity. If I see a bunch of people profiting from doing something that I regard as morally wrong, I want to do that thing too. No fair that (say) 15 percent of people cheat on the test and get top grades or regularly underreport self-employment income. I want to benefit, if they are! This reasoning is tempting even if cheaters are a minority.

Now consider the preacher tempted by homosexuality or the environmentalist who wants to eat steaks in his large air-conditioned house. Both might be entirely sincere in their moral opinions. Hypocrisy needn't involve insincere commitment to the moral ideas you espouse. What they see when they look around are many others who are getting away with what they condemn. Seeing these others, and implicitly aiming only for mediocrity, they might feel licensed to indulge themselves a bit too.

Furthermore, the norm violations might be more salient and visible to them than to the average person. The Internal Revenue Service worker sees how frequent and easy it is to cheat on taxes. The antihomosexuality preacher sees himself in a world full of sinning gays. The environmentalist grumpily notices all the giant SUVs rolling down the road. This increased salience might lead them to overestimate the frequency of such behavior—and then when they calibrate toward mediocrity, their scale might be skewed.

Still, this doesn't seem enough to explain the high rate of hypocrisy, given its high costs. Increased salience might lead moral advocates of x to somewhat mistune their estimates of x-violation, but you'd think that they'd try to steer their own behavior on x far down toward the good end of the scale (maybe allowing themselves more laxity on other issues, as a kind of reward).

So here's the final piece of the puzzle: Suppose there's a norm that you find yourself especially tempted to violate. Suppose further that you succeed for a while, at substantial personal cost, in not violating it. You love cheeseburgers but go vegetarian. You have intense homosexual desires but avoid acting on them. Envy might lead you to be especially condemnatory of others who still do such things. If you've worked so hard, they should too! It's an issue you've struggled with personally, so now you have some wisdom in regard to it, you think. You want to ensure that others don't enjoy the sins you've worked so hard to avoid. Furthermore, optimistic self-illusions (excessively positive expectations about yourself) and end-of-history thinking (thinking that your current preferences and habits are unlikely to change) might lead you to overestimate the chance that you will stay strong and not lapse.[46] These envious, self-confident moments are the moments when you are likely to conspicuously condemn the sins that you are most tempted to engage in yourself.

And then you're on the hook for it. If you have been sufficiently conspicuous in your condemnations, it becomes hard to change your tune later, even after you've lapsed.

10 On Not Distinguishing Too Finely among Your Motivations

In *What's Wrong with Morality?* eminent moral psychologist Daniel Batson distinguishes four types of motives for seemingly moral behavior. Although you might think that a clear taxonomy would encourage more precise understanding, Batson divides what can't be divided. It doesn't make sense to distinguish as finely as Batson does among people's motives for doing good.

Suppose I offer a visiting speaker a ride to the airport. That seems like a nice thing to do. According to Batson, I might have one or more of the following types of motivation:

1. I might be *egoistically* motivated—acting in my own perceived self-interest. Maybe the speaker is the editor of a prestigious journal, and I think I'll have a better chance of publishing and advancing my career if she thinks well of me.

2. I might be *altruistically* motivated—aiming primarily to benefit the visitor herself. I just want her to have a good time, a good experience at my school. Giving her a ride is a way of advancing that goal that I have. (To see that altruistic motivations aren't always moral, consider altruistically benefiting one person by unfairly harming many others.)

3. I might be *collectivistically* motivated—aiming primarily to benefit a group. I want my school's philosophy department

to flourish, and giving the speaker a ride is a way of advancing that thing I care about.

4. I might be *motivated by principle*—acting according to a moral standard, principle, or ideal. Maybe I think that driving the speaker to the airport will maximize global utility or that it is ethically required given my social role and past promises.

Batson characterizes his view of motivation as "Galilean"—focused on the underlying forces that drive behavior.[47] His idea seems to be that when I offer to drive the visiting speaker, my choice arises from some particular motivational force inside of me that is egoistic, altruistic, collectivist, or principled, or some specific blend of those four. On this view, we don't understand why I am offering the ride until we know which of these interior forces caused me to offer the ride. Principled morality is rare, Batson argues, because it requires being caused to act by the fourth type of motivation, and people are more commonly driven by the first three.

I'm nervous about appeals to internal causes of this sort. My best guess is that these sorts of simple, familiar (or semifamiliar) categories won't tend to map well onto the real causal processes that generate our behavior—processes that are likely to be very complicated and to be misaligned with the categories that come easily to mind. Consider connectionist structures and deep learning systems in artificial intelligence and cognitive science, like AlphaGo and Facebook's picture categorization algorithms, which succeed in mimicking human skills via a complex network of substructures and subclassifications that make little intuitive sense to us.[48] The brain might be like that. Four types of motivational causes might be far too few and too neat.

With this background best-guess picture in place, let me suggest this: It's plausible that our motives are often a tangled mess, and when they are a tangled mess, attempting to distinguish too finely among them is a mistake.

For example, there are probably hypothetical conditions under which I would decline to drive the speaker because it conflicted with my self-interest, and there are probably other hypothetical conditions under which I would set aside my self-interest and drive the speaker anyway. I doubt that these hypothetical conditions line up neatly, so that I would decline to drive the speaker if and only if it would require sacrificing x amount or more of self-interest. I'm not as coherent and rational as that. There's habit, association, subtle situational pressures I'm not aware of and that I would repudiate on reflection, other related motives that I weigh against each other inconsistently, some smell in the wind that makes a consideration salient that otherwise wouldn't occur to me, or some tune on the radio that triggers a memory or sentiment. Some situations might channel me into driving her, even at substantial personal cost, while others might more easily invite the temptation to wiggle out of it, for no particularly coherent reason.

Similarly for other motivations. Hypothetically, if the situation were different, so that it was less in the collective interest of the department, or less in the speaker's interest, or less strongly compelled by my favorite moral principles, I might drive or not drive the speaker depending partly on each of these but also partly on other factors of the situation and my internal psychology—habits, scripts, potential embarrassment, moods and memories that happen to bubble up—probably in no tidy pattern.

Furthermore, egoistic, altruistic, collectivist, and principled aims come in many varieties, difficult to disentangle. I might be egoistically interested in the collective flourishing of my department as a way of enhancing my own stature. I might relish displaying the sights of the Los Angeles basin through the windows of my car, with a feeling of civic pride. I might be drawn to different, conflicting moral principles. I might altruistically desire that the speaker enjoy the company of the cleverest conversationalist in the department, which I self-deceptively believe to be myself because it flatters my ego to think so.

Among all of these possible motives—infinitely many possible motives, perhaps, depending on how finely we slice the candidates—does it make sense to seek the one or few "real" motives that are genuinely causally responsible for my choice?

Now if my actual and counterfactual choices—what I actually tend to do as well as what I would do in various hypothetical circumstances—were all neatly aligned with my perceived self-interest, then of course self-interest would be my real motive. Similarly, if my pattern of actual and counterfactual choices were all neatly aligned with one particular moral principle, then we could say I was mainly moved by that principle. But if my dispositions aren't so neatly arranged, if my patterns of choice mix and cross like crazy spaghetti, only partly coherent, three-quarters rational and five-eighths habitual or reflexive or passive, then each of Batson's four factors is only an approximate and simplified label, rather than a deep Galilean cause of my decision.

Furthermore, the four factors might not compete with each other as starkly as Batson supposes. Each of them might, to a first approximation, capture my motivation reasonably well, in those fortunate cases in which self-interest, other-interest, collective interest, and moral principle align. I have lots of reasons for driving the speaker—reasons that instead of contributing 25 percent each, might partly overlap and partly constitute each other, like being bold, being assertive, and being proactive partly overlap and partly constitute each other. In some situations, the motivations might conflict. But if everything aligns, when I boldly, assertively, and proactively cancel the official limo so that I can drive the speaker personally instead, my action need no more be one-half egoistic and one-half altruistic than it need be one-third bold, one-third assertive, and one-third proactive.

If we accept a modest, folksy vision of morality (instead of a demanding one that requires us to abandon our families to follow Jesus or to dedicate almost all of our time and money to fighting poverty, etc.), and if we enjoy fairly fortunate middle-class lives in a well-structured society, then in many of our daily choices, Batson's four types of motives will align. Why take my daughter to the park on Sunday? I'll enjoy it, she'll enjoy it, it will help the family overall, and it's part of my duty as a father to do such things from time to time. Why show up for the boring faculty meeting? It's in my interest to be seen as reliable by my colleagues; and I can help advance (my vision of) what's good for the department; and my colleagues, who I care about, are relying on me; and it's my obligation as a responsible faculty member. Only when there's a conflict do we need to weigh such considerations against each other, and even then we only need to weigh them well enough for practical purposes, across a narrow range of foreseen possibilities.

(Wait, I hear you saying: What about the inevitable trade-offs I insist on in chapter 3, where I criticize Happy Coincidence reasoning? Answer: Even in such trade-offs, there will tend to be egoistic, altruistic, collectivist, and principled motives mixing together on each side of the trade-off. For example, my attending the fancy conference feeds my ego as a philosopher of rising prominence, contributes to the collective flourishing of research in my subfield, advances the interests of my friends who invited me, and fulfills a promise I made earlier.)

My motivations might be described, with approximately equal accuracy, as egoistic, altruistic, collectivist, *and* principled, in different flavors and subtypes, when these considerations align across the relevant range of situations. This isn't because each type of motivation contributes equal causal juice to my behavior, but rather because each attribution captures well enough the pattern of choices I would make in the range of likely cases we care about.

Batson seems to want what many of us want when we ask, skeptically or scientifically, *what was her* real *motive?* He wants a single clean answer or maybe a neatly quantifiable mix of 70 percent this and 30 percent that. Such tidiness, however, is probably more the exception than the rule.

11 The Mush of Normativity

Recently, several psychologists, most prominently Jonathan Haidt, have emphasized the connection between disgust and moral condemnation. Evidence suggests (though there are some concerns about replicability) that inducing disgust—whether by hypnosis, rubbish, or fart spray—tends to increase the severity of people's moral condemnation.[49] Conversely, pleasant odors might have a positive effect: For example, shopping-mall passersby might be more likely to agree to break a dollar when approached near a pleasant-smelling bakery than when approached near a neutral-smelling dry goods store.[50] Similarly, people tend to find the idea of sex with a frozen chicken revolting, and so they morally condemn it, even if often they can find no rational basis for that condemnation.[51]

One possible interpretation of these results retains the idea that we have a distinct cognitive system for moral judgment, different from that for aesthetic judgment, but allows that factors like odor and sexual disgust can influence the moral system's outputs. Moral judgments, according to most philosophers and moral psychologists, are one thing, and aesthetic judgments are another, even if they influence each other. Philosophers have long recognized several different and distinct species of "norms" or types of evaluation: moral norms, aesthetic norms, prudential norms of self-interest, and epistemic norms concerning what to believe or accept. Sometimes it's argued that these different standards of evaluation constrain each other in some way. Maybe the immoral can never truly be beautiful, or maybe people have a moral obligation to be epistemically rational. But even if one type of normativity completely subsumes another, wherever there is a multiplicity of norm types, philosophers typically treat these norms as sharply conceptually distinct.

A different possibility is that norms or modes of evaluation mush together, not just causally (with aesthetic judgments affecting moral judgments, as a matter of psychological fact), and not just via philosophically discovered putative contingencies (such as that the immoral is never beautiful), but into a blurry mess that defies neat sorting. You might make an evaluative judgment and recognize a normative fact, while the type of normativity involved remains indistinct.

I'm not merely suggesting that normative judgments can be multifaceted. If we accept the gemstone analogy implicit in the word "facet," facets are by nature distinct. If normativity has facets, different types of normativity might be sharply distinct, and yet a particular evaluative judgment might have more than one normative dimension—for example, both an epistemic and a moral dimension. Racism might be epistemically irrational *and* immoral *and* ugly, with each of these constituting a distinct facet of its badness. My thought isn't that. Instead, my thought is that many evaluative judgments, and perhaps also many normative facts, aren't so sharply structured.

Consider figure I.1, from the comic strip Calvin and Hobbes. Calvin's exhortation—"It surrrrre is nice outside! Climb a tree! Goof off!"—is normative. It's about values. He explicitly says so in the closing panel. So, is Calvin urging a set of *moral* values on

Figure I.1
Calvin harassing his father with his values.
Source: Andrews McMeel Licensing. Used with permission.

his father? Is he an ethical Daoist of some sort, who thinks it's
morally wrong to waste one's precious life struggling for money
and accomplishment? Or rather is it that Calvin sees prudential,
self-interested value in climbing trees, and he wishes his father
would recognize climbing trees to be in his self-interest too? Or
is Calvin urging an aesthetic worldview, centered on properly
appreciating the beauty of nature? Psychologically, I don't know
that there need be some particular mix, in Calvin, of moral versus prudential versus aesthetic dimensions in this evaluative
judgment. Must there be a fine-grained fact of the matter? Perhaps they tangle and twist together in ways that Calvin couldn't
articulate, even with a philosopher's or a psychologist's help,
and what's beneath isn't fully stable and coherent.

Let's suppose, further, that Calvin is right. His father *should*
climb a tree and goof off. What kind of "should" or what blend
of "shouldishness" is at issue? Need it be that the normativity is
x percent moral and *y* percent prudential? Or prudential rather
than moral? Or definitely both prudential and moral, but for
distinct metaphysical reasons?

My core thought is this: The psychology of normative evaluation might be a mushy mess of attractions and repulsions, of pro

and con attitudes, not well characterized by sharp distinctions among philosophers' several types of normativity. And if normative facts are partly grounded in such psychological facts, as many philosophers think they are—if aesthetic and moral and epistemic and prudential value are partly based on what people are disposed to aesthetically, morally, epistemically, and prudentially praise and condemn[52]—then the normative facts themselves might inherit this psychological mushiness.

12   A Moral Dunning-Kruger Effect?

In a famous series of experiments, Justin Kruger and David Dunning found that people who scored in the lowest quartile of skill in grammar, logic, and (yes, they tried to measure this) humor tended to substantially overestimate their abilities, rating themselves as a bit above average in these skills.[53] In contrast, people in the top half of ability had more accurate estimations (even tending to underestimate a bit). In each quartile of skill, average participants rated themselves as above average, and overall, the correlation between self-rated skill and measured skill was small.

For example, figure I.2 shows the relationship, according to Kruger and Dunning's research, between self-rated logic ability and scores on a logic test. Kruger and Dunning's explanation is that poor skill at (say) logical reasoning impairs not only one's performance on logical-reasoning tasks but also one's ability to evaluate one's performance on such tasks. You need to know that affirming the consequent is a logical error to realize that you've just committed a logical error in affirming the consequent. Otherwise, you're likely to think, "P implies q, and q is true, so p must also be true. Right! Hey, I'm doing great!"

Although popular presentations of this "Dunning-Kruger effect" tend to generalize it to all skill domains, it seems unlikely

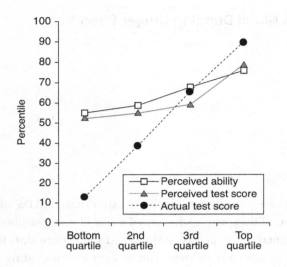

Figure I.2
Relation between self-rated logic ability and scores on a logic test.
Source: Adapted from Kruger and Dunning 1999, 1129.

that it does generalize universally. In domains in which evaluating your success doesn't depend on the skill in question, and instead depends on simpler forms of observation and feedback, you might expect more accurate self-assessments.[54] For example: footraces. I'd wager that people who are slow runners don't tend to think that they're above average in running speed. They might not have perfect self-knowledge, they might show some self-enhancing optimistic bias,[55] but I doubt we'd see the almost flat line characteristic of Dunning-Kruger. You don't have to be a fast runner to notice that your friends can outrun you.

So . . . what about ethics? Ought we to expect a moral Dunning-Kruger effect?

Yes! Evaluating your own moral or immoral behavior is a skill that itself depends on your moral character. The least moral people are typically also the least capable of recognizing what counts as a moral violation and how serious the violation is—especially, perhaps, when considering their own actions. I don't want to overcommit on this point. Surely there are exceptions. But as a general trend, this seems plausible.

Consider sexism. The most sexist people tend to be the least capable of understanding what constitutes sexist behavior and what makes sexist behavior unethical. They will tend either to regard themselves as not sexist or to regard themselves only as "sexist" in a nonpejorative sense. ("So what, I'm a 'sexist.' I think men and women are different. If you don't, you're a fool.") Similarly, the most habitual liars might not see anything bad in lying or not even think of what they are doing as "lying." (Maybe it's just "exaggerating" or "selling" or "spinning.") They might tend to assume that almost everyone avoids the truth when it's convenient to do so.

A person's overall morality probably can't be precisely captured in a unidimensional scale—just like there's probably no single correct scale for skill at basketball or for skill as a philosopher or for being a good parent. And yet clearly some ball players, philosophers, and parents are better than others. There are great, good, mediocre, and crummy versions of each. As a first approximation, I think it's probably okay to think that there are more and less ethical people overall. And if so, we can imagine a rough scale.

With that important caveat, then, consider some possible relationships between one's overall moral character and one's opinion about one's moral character: Dunning-Kruger (more self-enhancement for lower moral character) (figure I.3), uniform self-enhancement (everyone tends to think they're a bit better than they are) (figure I.4), U-shaped curve (even more self-enhancement among people who are below average) (figure I.5), and inverse U-shaped curve (realistically low self-image for the worst, self-enhancement in the middle, and self-underestimation

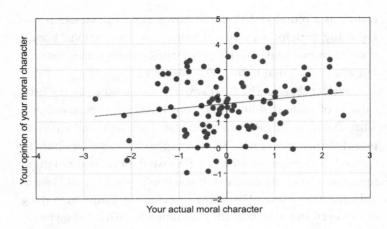

Figure I.3
Dunning-Kruger.
Source: Author.

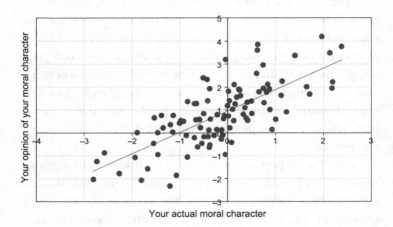

Figure I.4
Uniform self-enhancement.
Source: Author.

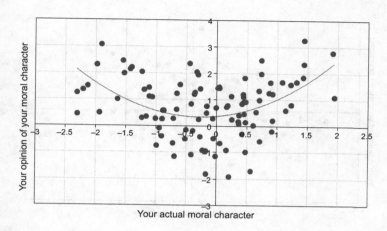

Figure I.5
U-shaped curve.
Source: Author.

for the best) (figure I.6). I don't think we really know yet which of these models is closest to the truth, but in all of them I have included two elements: substantial self-enhancement (a greater-than-zero average opinion about one's own moral character) and high scatter (at best a weak correlation between one's opinion and one's real moral character). Both elements are well attested in the empirical literature (and, I think, by ordinary observation).[56]

Suppose, then, that in your opinion your moral character is somewhat above average—pretty good but not saintly, B+ish, maybe 1.5 on the vertical axis. In any of the figures, your actual moral character could be more or less anywhere along the horizontal axis. That self-assessment carries little information value—unless, of course, your opinion about your moral character is somehow more securely grounded than others'?

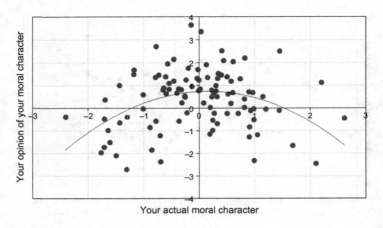

Figure I.6
Inverse U-shaped curve.
Source: Author.

13 The Moral Compass and the Liberal Ideal in Moral Education

Consider these two very different approaches to children's moral education:

The outward-in approach. Morality is imposed on children from outside. Three-year-old children don't want to share. Four-year-olds don't want to wait their turn. Five-year-olds don't want to sit politely in classrooms, learning addition. Morality is a cultural construction, alien to children's desires. In the early stages of moral development, children will not and cannot appreciate moral rules, and compliance must be enforced through punishment and reward. Only much later, as they grow, will children start to adopt society's rules as their own, seeing their value and internalizing them.[57]

The inward-out approach. Morality grows from within. Even before they can talk, children are concerned for others and want the people around them to be happy. At eighteen months, they want to help you if you skin your knee. At three and four, they can understand the value of sharing and patience. At five, they respect their teachers. If approached collaboratively, even very young children can appreciate the spirit of any society's basic moral rules. Even if it wears particular cultural clothes, morality is no artificial cultural construction. Morality speaks to something born deep in everyone. Moral education should be less about enforcing compliance than about nurturing children's naturally budding sense of right and wrong.[58]

The inward-out approach expresses what I think of as the liberal ideal in moral education. Moral education, on this view, depends on the thought that most or all people—including most or all children—have an inner moral compass that can serve as at least a partial, imperfect moral guide. This ideal is liberal in a certain traditional sense of "liberal": It trusts that people, even four-year-olds, when approached with respect as equals, can find mutual peace. It trusts that seemingly immature or wrong-headed views shouldn't simply be quashed, but can be respectfully improved through rational discussion. It is liberal in rejecting the top-down imposition of values and celebrating instead people's discovery of their own values.

On this view, if you pull aside four-year-old Pooja[59] after she has punched Lauren and ask her to reflect on the ethics of punching, you should hear something sensible in reply. On this view, Pooja can be brought to understand the importance of treating others—even Lauren—kindly and fairly. On this view, after sufficient reflection, Pooja should usually find that she wants to be kind and fair to others, even with no outer reward.

I hope and believe that this idealistic, liberal view is not too far wrong. As a father and as an observer of educational methods, I have repeatedly seen parents and educators, when they are at their patient best, use the inward-out approach to great effect. Experimental psychology, too, as I read it, suggests that the seeds of morality are present early in development and shared among primates.[60] The inward-out approach simply aims to nurture these seeds. (To succeed, however, the approach must be genuinely collaborative. Unless you genuinely and respectfully listen to them, with readiness to learn and compromise, children are astute enough to smell the fake.)

We can extend this thinking to adults too—when we aim to "educate" people with odious moral opinions or who seem to think only rarely or badly about the moral consequences of their actions. If the liberal ideal is correct, hatred and evil will wither under thoughtful examination. Just as Pooja can come to appreciate what's wrong with punching, so also can a neo-Nazi, approached in the right way, come to appreciate what's wrong with hating Jews. If the liberal ideal is correct, when people genuinely reflect in conditions of peace, with broad access to relevant information, they will find themselves attracted to good and revolted by evil. Despite complexities, bumps, regressions, and contrary forces, introspection and unconstrained inquiry will bend us toward freedom, egalitarianism, and mutual respect.

As should be evident from other chapters, I am fascinated by evil, irrationality, and excuses. This fascination derives, perhaps, directly from my commitment to liberalism and human goodness. I find the resilience of our mediocrity and self-ignorance puzzling, so I throw my mind against it, trying to understand.

If the inward-out view is correct, here's something you can always do in the face of hate, chaos, and evil: Invite people to reflect alongside you. Treat them as collaborative partners in thought. Share the knowledge you have, and listen to them in return. If there is light and insight in your thinking, people will slowly walk toward it. And maybe you too will walk toward their light. Maybe you will find yourselves walking together, in a direction somewhat different than either of you would have predicted.

II Cute AI and Zombie Robots

14 Should Your Driverless Car Kill You So Others May Live?

It's 2030. You and your daughter are riding in a driverless car along the Pacific Coast Highway. The autonomous vehicle rounds a corner and detects a crosswalk full of children. It brakes, but your lane is unexpectedly full of sand from a recent rock slide. Your car can't get traction. Its artificial intelligence does some calculations: If it continues braking, there's a 90 percent chance that it will kill at least three children. Should it save them by steering you and your daughter off the cliff?

This isn't an idle thought experiment. Driverless cars will be programmed to avoid colliding with pedestrians and other vehicles. They will also be programmed to protect the safety of their passengers. What should happen in an emergency when these two aims conflict?

Regulatory agencies around the United States have been exploring safety rules for autonomous vehicles. The new rules might or might not clarify when it is acceptable for collision-avoidance programs to risk passengers' lives or safety to avoid harming others. The new rules might or might not clarify general principles of risk trade-off, might or might not clarify specific guidelines like when it's permissible, or required, to cross a double-yellow line in a risky situation and what types of maneuvers on ice should be allowed or disallowed.

Technology companies have been arguing for minimal regulation. Google, for example, has proposed that manufacturers
not be held to specific functional safety standards and instead
be allowed to "self-certify" their vehicles' safety, with substantial
freedom to develop collision-avoidance algorithms as they see
fit. But this let-the-manufacturers-decide attitude risks creating a
market of excessively self-protective cars.

Consider some boundary cases. Some safety algorithms seem
far too selfish. Protecting passenger safety at all costs, for example, is overly simple and would be morally odious to implement.
On such a rule, if a car calculates that the only way to avoid
killing a pedestrian would be to sideswipe a parked truck, with
a 5 percent chance of minor injury to the passengers the car is
carrying, then the car should kill the pedestrian. On the other
hand, a simple utilitarian rule of maximizing lives saved disre-
gards personal accountability and is too sacrificial in some cases,
since it doesn't take into account that others might have irre-
sponsibly put themselves in danger. If you're about to collide
with a reckless motorcyclist speeding around a sharp curve, it's
reasonable for your car to prioritize your safety over the biker's.

People might tend to prefer that their own cars be highly
self-protective, while others' cars are more evenhandedly neutral. They might want others' cars to sacrifice the two passengers
rather than kill the three kids on the sidewalk, in the scenario
presented at the opening of this chapter; but when choosing
what to buy or rent for themselves and their own children, they
might want passenger protection to be given top priority.[1] If
everyone chooses the safety algorithms only for the cars they
ride in, with no regulation of others' algorithms, cars as a whole
might end up far more selfishly protective of their passengers
than we as a society would collectively prefer.

We face a social coordination problem on a matter of huge moral importance. Who gets priority in an accident? How much selfishness is acceptable in passenger risk reduction? The results might be far too selfish if society leaves everything to market forces and manufacturers' secret design choices. We should throw the algorithms to light, scrutinize them openly, and after public debate, draw some regulatory parameters concerning acceptable trade-offs between passenger safety and risk to others.

Completely uniform safety protocols might not be ideal either, however. Some consumer freedom seems desirable. To require that all vehicles at all times employ the same set of collision-avoidance procedures would needlessly deprive people of the chance to choose algorithms or driving styles that reflect their values. Some people might wish to prioritize the safety of their children over their own. Others might prefer to prioritize the safety of all passengers equally. Some people might elect algorithms that are more self-sacrificial on behalf of strangers than the government could legitimately require of its citizens. There will also always be trade-offs between speed and safety, and different riders might legitimately evaluate the trade-offs differently, on different occasions, as we now do in our manual driving choices.

If cars can be programmed for a range of driving styles, the selected styles might be broadcast to others. A car in "max aggressive" mode might visibly crouch low and display a tight posture or a certain pattern of lights on its roof, signaling to other cars—and to pedestrians—that it will be driving as quickly and aggressively as permitted by law. A car in "max safety" mode might display a different posture or different pattern of roof lights, indicating to others that it will be traveling more cautiously. A "baby on board" setting might signal that backseat passengers will be prioritized in an emergency—maybe even signaling to other cars' artificial intelligence systems that they should hit the front rather than the back of the car if there's a choice. A "utilitarian" mode, valuing all lives equally, might earn moral praise from your neighbors.

We should also insist on passengers' prerogative to preemptively override their autonomous systems—not only so that we can drive according to our values, but also because, pending further advances in artificial intelligence, there will be situations in which human cognition can be expected to outperform computer cognition. Properly licensed passengers ought to be free to take control when that is likely. Although computers normally have faster reaction times than people, out best computer programs still lag far behind normal human vision at detecting objects in novel, cluttered environments. On a windy fall day, a woman might be pushing a coat rack across the street in a swirl of leaves. Without manual override, your car's computer might sacrifice you for a mirage.

There is something romantic about the hand upon the wheel—about the responsibility it implies. But it's not just romanticism to resist ceding this responsibility too quickly, and without sufficient oversight, to engineers at Google and Tesla.

Future generations might be amazed that we allowed music-blasting sixteen-year-olds to pilot vehicles unsupervised at 65 miles per hour, with a flick of the steering wheel the difference between life and death. A well-designed machine will probably do better in the long run. That machine will never drive drunk, never look away from the road to change the radio station or yell at the kids in the back seat. It will, however, still have power over life and death. We need to decide—publicly—how it will exert that power.[2]

15 Cute AI and the ASIMO Problem

A few years ago, I saw the Advanced Step in Innovative Mobility (ASIMO) show at Disneyland. ASIMO is a robot designed by Honda to walk bipedally with something like a human gait. I'd entered the auditorium with a somewhat negative attitude about ASIMO, having read Andy Clark's critique[3] of Honda's computationally heavy approach to locomotion, and the animatronic Mr. Lincoln on Disneyland's Main Street had left me cold.

But ASIMO is cute! He's about four feet tall, humanoid, with big, round, dark eyes inside what looks like an astronaut's helmet. He talks, he dances, he kicks soccer balls, he makes funny hand gestures. On the Disneyland stage, he keeps up a fun patter with a human actor. ASIMO's gait isn't quite human, but his nervous-looking crouching run only makes him that much cuter. By the end of the show I thought that if you asked me to dismantle him against his protests, I'd be reluctant to comply.

Another case: ELIZA was a simple chatbot written in the 1960s, drawing on a small template of preprogrammed responses to imitate a nondirective psychotherapist. ("Are such questions on your mind often?" "Tell me more about your mother.") Apparently, some early users mistook it for a human and spent long hours chatting with it.[4]

Figure II.1
ASIMO, the cute robot.
Source: Image from http://asimo.honda.com. Used with permission.

In more recent research, Kate Darling finds that participants are often reluctant to strike a robotic toy with a mallet, especially when she introduces it using anthropomorphic language.[5] In my undergraduate class on philosophy of mind, on the day we discuss the minds of nonhuman animals, I normally bring a large, cute stuffed teddy bear to class. I treat it affectionately at the start, stroking its head and calling it by endearing names. Then, about halfway through the class I suddenly punch it in the face. Students scream in shock. Relatedly, evidence from developmental and social psychology suggests that people are generally swift to attribute mental states to entities with eyes and movement patterns that look goal directed, even if in other ways the entities are plainly not sophisticated.[6]

I assume that ASIMO and ELIZA are too simple to be proper targets of substantial moral concern.[7] They have no more consciousness than a laptop computer and no more capacity for genuine joy or suffering. But they tempt us to treat them with moral regard. And future engineers could presumably create entities with an even better repertoire of superficial tricks. When I discussed these issues with my sister, she mentioned a friend who had been designing a laptop that would whine and cry when its battery ran low. Imagine that! "Oh please *please* plug me in! [whimper] I'm soooo hungry! [tears, wailing] I do so much for you. Don't let me suffer like this!"

Conversely, suppose that it's someday possible to create an artificial intelligence system so advanced that it really does have genuine consciousness, a genuine sense of self, real joy, and real suffering. If that AI also happens to be ugly or boxy or poorly interfaced, it might tend to attract much less moral concern than is warranted. In the famous *Star Trek: The Next Generation* episode "The Measure of a Man," a scientist who wants to disassemble the humanoid robot Data (sympathetically portrayed by a human actor) says, plausibly, "If it were a box on wheels, I would not be facing this opposition."[8] He also points out that people normally think nothing of upgrading the computer systems of a starship, though that means discarding a highly intelligent AI.

As AI continues to improve, our emotional responses to AIs might become radically misaligned with the AIs' real moral status. If a cute ASIMO full of superficial sympathy-arousing tricks and a flesh-and-blood human being both fall into the ocean at the same time, so that we can only save one, a well-intentioned rescuer might dive in to save the mindless ASIMO while letting the real human drown. Conversely, we might create a host of suffering AI slaves whose real welfare interests we ignore because they don't give us the right interface cues. In AI cases, the superficial features might not track underlying mentality very well at all.

I draw two main lessons from this problem. The first is a methodological lesson: In thinking about the moral status of AI, we should be careful not to overweight emotional reactions and intuitive judgments that might be overly sensitive to such superficial features.

The second lesson is a bit of AI design advice. As responsible creators of artificial entities, we should want people neither to over- nor underattribute moral status to the entities with which they interact. If our AIs are simple and nonconscious, we should generally try to avoid designing them in a way that will lead normal users to give them substantial undeserved moral consideration.[9] This might be especially important in designing children's toys and artificial companions for the lonely. Manufacturers might understandably be tempted to create artificial pets, friends, or helpers that children and others will love and attach to—but we should be cautious about future children overly attaching mostly to nonconscious toys in preference to real people. Although we might treasure a toy as an artifact of great sentimental value, we don't want to lose hold of the fact that is only an artifact—something that needs to be left behind in a fire, even if it seems to plead desperately in mock pain.

On the flip side, if we do someday create genuinely human-grade AIs that merit substantial moral concern, it is crucial that we design their interface and superficial features in a way that will evoke the proper range of moral responses from normal users. We should embrace an *Emotional Alignment Design Policy*: Design the superficial features of AIs so as to evoke the moral emotional reactions appropriate to their real moral status, whatever that status is, neither more nor less.[10]

At two million dollars outright, of course I couldn't afford to *buy* eyes for my four-year-old daughter Eva. So like everyone else whose kids had been blinded by the GuGuBoo Toy Company's defective dolls (may its executives rot in bankruptcy Hell), I rented the eyes. What else could I possibly do?

Unlike some parents, I actually read the Eye & Ear Company's rental contract. So I knew part of what we were in for. If we didn't make the monthly payments, her eyes would shut off. We agreed to binding arbitration. We agreed to a debt-priority clause, to financial liability for eye extraction, to automatic updates. We agreed that from time to time the saccade patterns of her eyes would be subtly adjusted so that her gaze would linger over advertisements from companies that partnered with Eye & Ear. We agreed that in the supermarket, Eva's eyes would be gently maneuvered toward the Froot Loops and the M&Ms.

When the updates came in, we had the legal right to refuse them. We could, hypothetically, turn off Eva's eyes, then have them surgically removed and returned to Eye & Ear. Each new rental contract was thus technically voluntary.

When Eva was seven, the new updater threatened shutoff unless we transferred one thousand dollars to a debit account.

Her updated eyes contained new software to detect any copy-righted text or images she might see. Instead of buying copy-righted works in the usual way, we agreed to have a small fee deducted from the debit account for each work Eva viewed. Instead of paying $4.99 for the digital copy of a Dr. Seuss book, Eye & Ear would deduct $0.50 each time she read the book. Video games might be free with ads, or $0.05 per play, or $0.10, or even $1.00. Since our finances were tight we set up parental controls: Eva's eyes required parent permission for any charge over $0.99 or any cumulative charges over $5.00 in a day—and of course they blocked any "adult" material. Until we granted approval, blocked or unpaid material was blurred and indeci-pherable, even if she was just peeking over someone's shoulder at a book or walking past a television in a dentist's lobby.

When Eva was ten, the updater overlaid advertisements in her visual field. It helped keep rental costs down. (We could have bought out of the ads for an extra six thousand dollars a year.) The ads never interfered with Eva's vision—they just kind of scrolled across the top of her visual field sometimes, Eva said, or printed themselves onto clouds or the sides of buildings.

By the time Eva was thirteen, I'd risen to a managerial posi-tion at work and we could afford the new luxury eyes for her. By adjusting the settings, Eva could see infrared at night. She could zoom in on distant objects. She could bug out her eyes and point them in different directions like some sort of weird ani-mal, taking in a broader field of view. She could take snapshots and later retrieve them with a subvocalization—which gave her a great advantage at school over her natural-eyed and cheaper-eyed peers. Installed software could text-search through stored snapshots, solve mathematical equations, and pull relevant information from the internet. When teachers tried to ban such enhancements in the classroom, Eye & Ear fought back, arguing that the technology had become so integral to the children's way of thinking and acting that it couldn't be removed without disabling them. Eye & Ear refused to develop the technology to turn off the enhancement features, and no teacher could realistically prevent a kid from blinking and subvocalizing.

By the time Eva was seventeen it looked like she and two of her other schoolmates with luxury eye rentals would be choosing among offers from several elite universities. I refused to believe the rumors about parents intentionally blinding their children so that they too could rent eyes.

When Eva was twenty, all the updates—not just the cheap ones—required that you accept the "Acceleration" technology. Companies contracted with Eye & Ear to privilege their messages and materials for faster visual processing. Pepsi paid eighty million dollars so that users' eyes would prioritize resolving Pepsi cans and Pepsi symbols in the visual scene. Coca Cola cans and symbols were "deprioritized" and stayed blurry unless you focused on them for a few seconds. Loading stored images worked similarly. A remembered scene with a Pepsi bottle in it would load almost instantly. One with a Coke bottle would take longer and might start out fuzzy or fragmented.

Eye & Ear started to make glasses for the rest of us, which imitated some of the implants' functions. Of course they were incredibly useful. Who wouldn't want to take snapshots, see in the dark, zoom into the distance, get internet search and tagging? We all rented whatever versions we could afford, signed the annual terms and conditions, received the updates. We wore them pretty much all day, even in the shower. The glasses beeped alarmingly whenever you took them off, unless you went through a complex shutdown sequence.

When the "Smith for President" campaign bought an Acceleration, the issue went all the way to the Supreme Court. Smith's campaign had paid Eye & Ear to prioritize the perception of his face and deprioritize the perception of his opponent's face, prioritize the visual resolution and recall of his ads and deprioritize the resolution and recall of his opponent's ads. Eva was by now a high-powered lawyer in a New York firm, on the fast track toward partner. She worked for the Smith campaign, though I wouldn't have thought it was like her. Smith was so shrill and angry—or at least it seemed so to me when I took my glasses off.

Smith favored immigration restrictions, and his opponent claimed (but never proved) that Eye & Ear implemented an algorithm that exaggerated people's differences in skin tone— making the lights a little lighter, the darks a little darker, the East Asians a bit yellow. Smith won narrowly, before his opponent's suit about the Acceleration made it through the appeals process. It didn't hit the high court until a month after his inauguration. Eva helped prepare Smith's defense. Eight of the nine justices were more than eighty years old. They lived stretched lives with enhanced longevity and of course all the best implants. They heard the case through the very best ears.[11]

17 Someday, Your Employer Will Technologically Control Your Moods

Here's the argument:

1. Someday, employers will have the technological capacity to control employees' moods.
2. Employers will not refrain from exercising that capacity.
3. Most working-age adults will be employees.
4. Therefore, someday, most working-age adults will have employers who technologically control their moods.

The argument is valid in the sense that the conclusion (4) follows if all three of the premises are true.

Premise 1 seems plausible, given current technological trajectories. Control could be either pharmacological or through direct brain stimulation. Pharmacological control could work, for example, through pills that directly influence your mood, energy levels, submissiveness, ability to concentrate, or passion for the type of task at hand. Direct brain stimulation could work, for example, through a removable transcranial magnetic stimulation helmet that magnetically enhances or suppresses neural activity in targeted brain regions, or with some more invasive technology. Cashiers might be able to tweak their dials toward perky friendliness. Data entry workers might be able to tweak their dials toward undistractable focus. Strippers might be able to tweak their dials toward sexual arousal.

Contra premise 1, society might collapse or technological development in general might stall out—but let's assume not. If technology as a whole continues to advance, it seems unlikely that mood control specifically will stall. On the contrary, moods seem quite a likely target for improved technological control, given how readily they can already be influenced by low-tech means like coffee and exercise.

It might take longer than expected. Alternatively, we might already be on the cusp of it. I don't know to what extent people in Silicon Valley, Wall Street, and elite universities already use high-tech drugs to enhance alertness, energy, and concentration at work. What I'm imagining is just a few more steps down this road. Eventually, the available interventions might be much more direct, effective, and precisely targeted.

Premise 2 also seems plausible, given the relative social power of employers versus employees. As long as there's surplus labor and a scarcity of desirable jobs, employers will have some choice about who to hire. If Starbucks can select between applicant A who is willing to crank up the perky-friendly dial and applicant B who is not so willing, then they will presumably prefer applicant A. If a high-tech startup wants someone who will log intense sixteen-hour days one after the next, and some applicants are willing to tweak their brains accordingly, then those applicants will have a competitive edge. If Stanford wants to hire a medical researcher who publishes high-profile studies at an astounding rate, they'll likely discover that it's someone who has dialed up their appetite for work and dialed down everything else.

At first, employees will probably keep the hand on the dial themselves or mix the drug cocktails themselves. This might be more socially palatable than direct, unmediated control by the employer. For something as initially radical seeming as a transcranial magnetic stimulation helmet, home use for recreational or medical purposes will probably have to occur first, to normalize it, before it seems natural to wear it also to work.

The first people to yield direct control to employers might be those in low-status, low-education professions, with little bargaining power and with similar job descriptions that seem to invite top-down mass control. The employer might provide an initially voluntary "energy drink" for all employees at the beginning of the shift. High-status employees, in contrast, might more effectively keep their own hands on the dials. However, the pressure, and consequently the indirect control, might be even more extreme among elite achievers. If mood interventions are highly effective, then they will correlate highly with professional performance, so that as a practical matter those who don't dial themselves to nearly ideal settings for work performance will be unlikely to win the top jobs.

Contra premise 2, (a) collective bargaining might prevent employers from successfully demanding mood control, or (b) governmental regulations might do so, or (c) there might be insufficient surplus labor standing ready to replace the noncompliant.

Rebuttal to (a): The historical trend recently, at least in the US, has been against unionization and collective bargaining, though I suppose that could change. One optimistic comparison is the partly successful limitation of performance-enhancing drugs in professional sports. But here the labor market is unusually tightly organized, as a result of employers' cooperation and the competitions' formal nature.

Rebuttal to (b): Although government regulations could forbid certain drugs or brain-manipulation technologies, if there's enough demand for those drugs or technologies, employees will find a way, unless a substantial resources are devoted to enforcement (as again in professional sports). Government regulations could perhaps specifically forbid employers from requiring the use of certain technologies, while permitting those technologies for home use—but home use versus use as an employee is a permeable line for the increasing number of jobs that involve working outside of a set time and location. Also, it's easier to regulate a contractual demand than an informal de facto demand. Presumably, many companies could say that of course they don't *require* their employees to drink the cocktail. It's up to the employee! But if the technology is effective, the willing employees will be much more attractive to hire, retain, and promote.

Rebuttal to (c): At present there's no general long-term trend toward a shortage of labor, and at least for jobs seen as the most highly desirable, there will always be more applicants than available positions.

Premise 3 also seems plausible, especially on a liberal definition of "employee." Most working-age adults in developed economies are employees of one form or another. That could change with the growth of the "gig economy" and more independent contracting, but not necessarily in a way that negates the sting of the main argument. Even if an Uber driver is technically not an employee, the pressures toward direct mood control for productivity ought to be similar. Likewise for piecework computer programmers and independent sex workers. If anything, the pressures might be higher for gig workers and independent contractors, who generally have less security of income and fewer formal workplace regulations.

If social power remains disproportionately in the hands of employers, they will of course use new neuroscientific technologies to advance their interests, including their interest in extracting as much passion, energy, and devotion as possible from their employees—you and me and our children. If they do it right, we might even like it.

Suppose that we someday create genuinely conscious artificial intelligence: beings with all the intellectual and emotional capacities of human beings. For present purposes, it doesn't matter if this is achieved through computer technology, through biotechnology (e.g., "uplifted" animals), or in some other way, as long as the entities are shaped and created by us, with the psychological features we choose.

From these AIs, we human creators might want two things that appear to conflict:

1. We might want them to subordinately serve us and die for us.
2. We might want to treat them ethically, as beings with rights and interests that deserve our respect.

A possible fix suggests itself: Design the AIs so that they *want* to serve us and die for us. In other words, create a race of cheerfully suicidal AI slaves. This was Isaac Asimov's solution with the Three Laws of Robotics (a solution that slowly falls apart across the arc of his stories).[12]

Douglas Adams parodies the cheerfully suicidal AI with an animal uplift case in "The Restaurant at the End of the Universe":

A large dairy animal approached Zaphod Beeblebrox's table, a large fat meaty quadruped of the bovine type with large watery eyes, small horns and what might almost have been an ingratiating smile on its lips.

"Good evening," it lowed and sat back heavily on its haunches. "I am the main Dish of the Day. May I interest you in parts of my body?" It harrumphed and gurgled a bit, wriggled its hind quarters into a comfortable position and gazed peacefully at them.[13]   •

Zaphod's naive Earthling companion, Arthur Dent, is predictably shocked and disgusted. When Arthur says he would prefer a green salad, the suggestion is brushed off. Zaphod and the animal argue that it's better to eat an animal that wants to be eaten, and can consent clearly and explicitly, than one that would rather not be eaten. Zaphod orders four rare steaks for his companions.

"A very wise choice, sir, if I may say so. Very good," it said. "I'll just nip off and shoot myself."

He turned and gave a friendly wink to Arthur.

"Don't worry, sir," he said. "I'll be very humane."[14]

In this scene, Adams illustrates the idea's peculiarity. There's something ethically jarring about creating an entity with human-like intelligence and emotion that will completely subordinate its interests to ours, even to the point of suicide at our whim—even if the AI *wants* to be subjected in that way.

The three major classes of ethical theory—consequentialism, deontology, and virtue ethics[15]—can each be read in a way that agrees with Adams's implicit point. The consequentialist can object that the good of a small pleasure for a human does not outweigh the potential of a lifetime of pleasure for an uplifted steer, even if the steer doesn't appreciate that fact. The Kantian deontologist can object that the steer is treating itself as a "mere means" rather than an agent whose life shouldn't be sacrificed to serve others' goals. The Aristotelian virtue ethicist can say that the steer is cutting its life short rather than flourishing into its full potential of creativity, joy, friendship, and thought.[16]

Using Adams's steer as an anchor point of moral absurdity at one end of the ethical continuum, we can ask to what extent less obvious intermediate cases are also ethically wrong—such as Asimov's robots who don't sacrifice themselves as foodstuffs (though presumably, by the Second Law, they would do so if commanded) but who do, in some of the stories, appear perfectly willing to sacrifice themselves to save human lives.

When humans sacrifice their lives to save others, it can sometimes be a morally beautiful thing. But a robot designed that way from the start, to always subordinate its interests to human interests—I'm inclined to think that ought to be ruled out by any reasonable egalitarian principle that treats AIs as deserving equal moral status with humans if they have broadly human-like cognitive and emotional capacities. Such an egalitarian principle would be a natural extension of the types of consequentialist, deontological, and virtual ethical reasoning that rule out Adams's steer.

We can't escape the conflict I presented at the beginning of this chapter by designing cheerfully suicidal AI slaves. If we somehow create genuinely conscious general-intelligence AI, capable of real joy and suffering, then we must create it morally equal. In fact . . .

19 We Would Have Greater Moral Obligations to Conscious Robots than to Otherwise Similar Humans

Down goes HotBot 4b into the volcano. The year is 2050 (or 2150), and artificial intelligence has advanced sufficiently that robots can be built with human-grade or more-than-human-grade intelligence, creativity, and desires. HotBot will now perish on this scientific mission. In commanding it to go down, have we done something morally wrong?

The moral status of robots is a frequent theme in science fiction, back at least to Isaac Asimov's robot stories, and the consensus is clear: If someday we manage to create robots that have mental lives similar to ours, with human-like consciousness and a sense of self, including the capacity for joy and suffering, then those robots deserve moral consideration similar to the moral consideration we give to our fellow human beings. Philosophers and AI researchers who have written on this topic generally agree.[17]

I want to challenge this consensus, but not in the way you might predict. I think that if we someday create robots with human-like cognitive and emotional capacities, we owe them *more* moral consideration than we would normally owe to otherwise similar human beings.

Here's why: We will have been their creators and designers. We are thus directly responsible both for their existence and for their happy or unhappy state. If a robot needlessly suffers or fails to reach its developmental potential, it will be in substantial part because of our failure—a failure in our design, creation, or nurturance of it. Our moral relation to robots will more closely resemble the relation that parents have to children or that gods have to the beings they create (see also chapter 21) than the relation between human strangers.

In a way, this is no more than equality. If I create a situation that puts other people at risk—for example, if I destroy their crops to build an airfield—then I have a moral obligation to compensate them, an obligation greater than I have to miscellaneous strangers. If we create genuinely conscious robots, we are deeply causally connected to them, and so we are substantially responsible for their welfare. That is the root of our special obligation.

Frankenstein's monster says to his creator, Victor Frankenstein: "I am thy creature, and I will be even mild and docile to my natural lord and king, if thou wilt also perform thy part, the which thou owest me. Oh, Frankenstein, be not equitable to every other, and trample upon me alone, to whom thy justice, and even thy clemency and affection, is most due. Remember that I am thy creature: I ought to be thy Adam."[18] We must either only create robots sufficiently simple that we know them not to merit much moral consideration, or we ought to bring them into existence only carefully and solicitously.

Alongside this duty to be solicitous comes another duty, of knowledge—a duty to know which of our creations are genuinely conscious. Which of them have real streams of subjective experience and are capable of joy and suffering or of cognitive achievements such as creativity and a sense of self? Without such knowledge, we won't know what obligations we have to our creations.

Yet how can we acquire the relevant knowledge? How does one distinguish, for instance, between a genuine stream of emotional experience and simulated emotions in a nonconscious computational algorithm? Merely programming a superficial simulation of the emotion isn't enough. If I put a standard computer processor manufactured in 2018 into a toy dinosaur and program it to say "Ow!" when I press its off switch, I haven't created a robot capable of suffering. (See also chapter 15.) But exactly what kind of processing or complexity is necessary for real human-like consciousness? On some views—John Searle's, for example—consciousness might not be possible in *any* programmed entity; real subjective experience might require a structure biologically similar to the human brain.[19] Other views are much more liberal about the conditions sufficient for robot consciousness. The scientific study of consciousness is still in its infancy. The issue remains wide open.[20]

If we continue to develop sophisticated forms of AI, we have a moral obligation to improve our understanding of the conditions under which consciousness might emerge. Otherwise we risk moral catastrophe: either the catastrophe of failing to recognize robot consciousness, and so unintentionally committing atrocities tantamount to slavery and murder of entities to whom we have an almost parental obligation of care, or alternatively, the catastrophe of greatly overvaluing entities that have only sham consciousness, treating them mistakenly as genuine equals, with the unavoidable consequence that real people will sometimes suffer and die for the sake of vacant shells.

We have, then, an obligation to learn enough about the material and functional bases of joy, suffering, hope, and creativity to understand when and whether our potential future creations deserve serious moral concern. And when they do merit such concern, we must treat our creations kindly, acknowledging our special responsibility for their joy, suffering, hopes, and creative potential.[21]

20 How Robots and Monsters Might Destroy Human Moral Systems

Intuitive physics works great for picking berries, throwing stones, and walking through light underbrush. It goes disastrously wrong when applied to the very large, the very small, the very energetic, or the very fast. Similarly for intuitive biology, intuitive cosmology, and intuitive mathematics: They succeed for practical purposes across long-familiar types of cases, but when extended too far they go seriously astray.

How about intuitive ethics? In chapters 18 and 19, I explored the moral consequences of creating AI with human-like conscious experience and cognitive and emotional capacities. But of course if we someday create genuinely conscious AI, it might *not* be very much like us. The types of cases might be radically new and unfamiliar. And then, perhaps, our moral intuitions will serve us as badly as do our physical intuitions when faced with relativity theory and quantum mechanics. What's more, to the extent that our formal moral theories are grounded in ordinary or pre-twenty-first-century moral intuitions, those theories might collapse as well. Applying old-school Aristotelean or Kantian ethics to future AI might be like trying to apply old-school Aristotelian or Kantian physics to interstellar rockets.

∽

I will illustrate this point with a pair of puzzle cases: utility monsters (originally due to Robert Nozick[22]) and what I will call "fission-fusion monsters."

A *utility monster* is a being who derives immense pleasure from harming us or consuming our goods. Cookie Monster, for example, might derive a hundred units of pleasure from every cookie he eats, while normal human beings derive only one unit of pleasure. If we care about increasing the total amount of pleasure in the world, maybe we should give all of our cookies to the monster. Lots of people would lose out on a little bit of pleasure, but Cookie Monster would be *really* happy!

Cookies are just the start of it, of course. If the world contained an entity vastly more capable of pleasure and pain than are ordinary humans, then on simple versions of happiness-maximizing utilitarian ethics, the rest of us ought to immiserate ourselves to elevate that entity to superhuman pinnacles of joy.

If AI consciousness is possible, including AI joy, I see no reason in principle why that joy should top out at human levels. Crank the dial higher! Make the joy last longer. Run a hundred thousand copies of it simultaneously on your hard drive. Turn Jupiter into a giant orgasmatron. On one way of thinking, this would be our moral duty.[23] All of human happiness would be a trivial consideration beside this. Even if you don't accept the simple utilitarian view that happiness is *everything*, surely it's something, and if we could multiply the happiness in the solar system a billionfold, perhaps we ought to, even at substantial cost to ourselves.

Most people seem to find this unintuitive, or even morally repulsive, which was Nozick's point in constructing the thought experiment. Morality doesn't seem to demand that we sacrifice all human happiness to convert Jupiter into a joy machine.

If we want to avoid this conclusion and preserve something like commonsense ethics, we might want to shift our focus to the rights of individuals. Even if the monster would experience a hundred times more pleasure from my cookie than I would, it's still *my* cookie. I have a right to it and no obligation to give it up. This is what Nozick thinks and what Kantian critics of utilitarianism also often think. However, this seemingly commonsense solution faces a complementary set of problems.

A fission-fusion monster, let's say, is an entity who can divide at will into many similar descendant entities who retain the monster's memories, skills, and plans, and who can later fuse back together, retaining the memories, skills, and plans of each descendant (with some procedure for resolving conflicts). A fission-fusion monster will sometimes be a single, unified individual (though the word "individual" is etymologically inapt) and sometimes be divided into many separate individuals.

If we say, "One conscious intelligence, one vote," how many votes would a fission-fusion monster get? If we say, "One unemployed conscious intelligence, one cookie from the dole," how many cookies ought our monster collect? If our fission-fusion monster is selfish and tactical, here's what it might do: On October 31 it splits into a million individuals. On November 1, it collects a million cookies from the dole. On November 2, it casts a million votes for its favorite candidate. On November 3, its million parts merge back together into a single integrated intelligence, ready to enjoy its million cookies and looking forward to the inauguration of its candidate.

Presumably we could block that particular worry through an ad hoc rule, such as that an individual must have fissioned into existence at least *x* months previously to qualify for such rights. But then setting that *x* creates problems. Twelve months seems, for example, to be both too short in one way and too long in another. It's too short because a patient monster might not at all mind waiting a year for such a fantastic advantage. It's too long because fissioned individuals might easily starve to death in a year's time because of unforeseeable consequences beyond their control, while also developing enough individuality to deserve status as an equal and to reasonably view forcible merging as an unwelcome death.

Political, social, and ethical systems that afford rights to individuals have always been built on the background assumption that people do not regularly divide and fuse. The whole thing breaks down, or would at least require radical rethinking, in the face of fission-fusion monsters who can strategically exploit the criteria of individuality to maximize their claims upon the system. This is the intuitive ethics equivalent of trying to apply intuitive physics to rockets traveling at 99 percent of the speed of light.

ↄ

If AI experience and cognition is possible, then in the future we might actually face real-world utility monster and fission-fusion monster cases. Indeed, depending on future developments, maybe whatever it is about us that we think gives human life special value, whether it is happiness, creativity, love, compassion, intellect, achievement, wisdom—unless, perhaps, it is our species membership itself—could be duplicated a hundredfold or a millionfold in artificial computational or biological systems. And then we might be in a conundrum.

More generally, our social and ethical structures are founded on principles, practices, and intuitions evolved and constructed to handle the range of variation that we have ordinarily seen in the past. So far, there have been no radically different types of entities that approach or exceed human social intelligence.

So far, there have been no entities capable of superhuman pain or pleasure or of dividing at will into autonomous human-like individuals, no entities preprogrammed to want desperately to sacrifice themselves to satisfy our whims (chapter 18), no people capable of simply dialing up moods at command (chapter 17), no people capable of transferring their minds into new bodies; no planet-sized intelligences with people as parts (or maybe there have been) (chapter 39), no simulated realities constructed inside of computers that are as good as or better than our "real" reality and over which we have godlike powers (chapter 21) or into which we can upload ourselves for millions of years (chapter 44), and no opportunity for us to create dependent artificial people exactly as we see fit. It would be unsurprising if the ethical concepts we now possess, fashioned in much more limited circumstances, fail catastrophically when extended to such new situations.

21 Our Possible Imminent Divinity

We might soon be gods.

In a few decades, we might be creating an abundance of genuinely conscious artificial intelligences. (Maybe not. Maybe consciousness could never arise in an artificial system, or maybe we'll destroy ourselves first, or maybe technological innovation will stall out. But grant me the speculative what-if.) We will then have at least some features of gods: We will have created a new type of being, maybe in our image. We will presumably have the power to shape our creations' personalities to suit us, to make them feel blessed or miserable, to hijack their wills to our purposes, to condemn them to looping circuits of pain or reward, to command their worship if we wish.

If consciousness is possible only in fully embodied robots, our powers might stop approximately there. But if we can also create conscious beings inside of artificial computationally constructed environments, we might become even more truly divine.

Imagine a simulated world inside of a computer, something like the computer game *The Sims*, or like a modern virtual reality environment, but one in which the artificial intelligences inside of that environment are sophisticated enough to actually be conscious. Sim Janiece wakes up in the morning, looks around her (simulated) bedroom, sees her simulated husband John, brews some simulated coffee, and feels (really!) the familiar perk.[24] Sim John has a complementary set of experiences. Both Janiece and John are conscious AI programs whose sensory inputs aren't based on sensory scanning of the ordinary environment that you and I see (as a robot's sensory inputs would be) but instead are inputs that correspond to the state of affairs in their virtual-reality environments. They receive their 1s and 0s not from a digital camera pointed at a real kitchen, but from elsewhere in the computer, in accord with the structure of the virtual kitchen as it ought to be sensed from their currently represented point of view. Janiece and John also act only in their simulated world. A normally embodied robot lifts an ordinary robot arm, generating ordinary visual input of the arm's motion and affecting the ordinary thing it's touching. Sim Janiece raises her virtual arm, affecting the state of the virtual world she inhabits and the inputs she and John receive. Their whole experiential reality is a giant, immersive, game-like computer program in which the entities who kiss and dance and buy donuts aren't merely simple AI routines but are instead actually conscious entities who regard their surroundings as "the real world."

I see no compelling reason to reject the possibility of a Janiece and John. If we allow that genuine conscious experience is possible in normally embodied robots, it seems plausible enough that AI systems embodied in simulated worlds could also be conscious.[25] The details of their programming might be, for example, exactly the same, though the robot responds to 1s and 0s from an actual camera and the AI system in the simulated world responds to a very similar pattern of 1s and 0s that are inputs from elsewhere in the computer system.

Now we can command not only the AIs themselves but their entire reality.

We approach omnipotence: We can create miracles. We can spawn a Godzilla, revive the dead, move a mountain, undo errors, create a new world, or end one on a whim—powers eclipsing those of gods like Zeus and Isis.

We approach omniscience: We can look at any part of the world, look inside anyone's mind, see the past if we have properly recorded it, maybe predict the future in detail, depending on the program's structure.

We stand outside of space and to some extent time: Janiece and John live in a spatial manifold, or a virtual spatial manifold, that we do not inhabit. Wherever they go, they can't escape us, nor can they ever move toward and touch us. Our space, "ordinary" space, does not map onto space as they experience it. We are unconstrained by their spatial laws; we can affect things a million miles apart without in any sense traveling between them. We are, to them, everywhere and nowhere. If they have a fast clock relative to our time, we can seem to endure for millennia or longer. We can pause their time and intervene as we like, unconstrained by their clock. We can rewind to save points and thus directly view and interact with their past, perhaps spinning off new worlds or rewriting the history of their one world.

If they have a word for "god," the person who launches and manipulates their virtual reality will be quite literally the referent of that word.

Of course, all of this omnipotence, omniscience, and independence of space and time will be relative to *their* world, not relative to our own, where we might remain entirely mortal dingbats. Still, it's divinity enough to raise the ethical question I want to raise, which is:

Will we be *benevolent* gods?

22 Skepticism, Godzilla, and the Artificial Computerized Many-Branching You

Nick Bostrom has argued that we might be living inside of "sims."[26] A technologically advanced society might use tremendously powerful computers, Bostrom argues, to create "ancestor simulations" containing actually conscious people who think that they are living, say, on Earth in the early twenty-first century but who in fact live entirely inside a giant computational system. David Chalmers has considered a similar possibility in his well-known commentary on the movie *The Matrix*.[27] (See also chapter 21.)

Neither Bostrom nor Chalmers is inclined to draw skeptical conclusions from this possibility. If we *are* living inside a sim, they suggest, that sim is simply our reality. All the people we know still exist (they're inside the sim, just like us), and the objects we interact with still exist (fundamentally constructed from computational resources, but still predictable, manipulatable, interactive with other such objects, and experienced by us in all their sensory glory). Chalmers even uses the sim scenario as part of an *anti*skeptical argument: Roughly, as long as our experiences are right and the functional interactive relationships among all the objects we see are right, it doesn't matter whether the fundamental metaphysical structures beneath are demons or dreams or computers or atoms. Consequently, according to Chalmers, scenarios that are sometimes thought to be skeptical disasters (we are all brains in vats, or this is all a collective dream[28]) turn out not in fact to be so disastrous after all, as long as the structural relationships among experienced objects are sufficiently dependable.

Of course, if our existence is a dream, we might wake up. If our world is a sim, the owner might suddenly shut it down. For antiskeptical juice, we have to assume stability: no wake-up, no shutdown. But if we are to take the simulation scenario seriously, or the group-dream scenario, or the brain-in-a-vat scenario, then before drawing skeptical or antiskeptical conclusions we ought also to consider how likely the scenario is to contain the people and things we care about. In other words, we ought, as Bostrom and Chalmers do not, evaluate whether, if we are living in a sim, it's likely to be a small or unstable or deceptive sim—one run by a child, say, for entertainment. Might we live for only three hours' time on a game clock, existing mainly as citizens who will provide entertaining reactions when, to our surprise, Godzilla tromps through? Or might my world consist entirely of my room and nothing beyond, in an hour-long sim run by a scientist interested in human cognition about philosophical problems?

Chalmers might rightly be relatively unconcerned about the fundamental structure of reality, if, as he assumes, the world we experience is large and stable, with approximately the superficial and functional properties we think it has. Being mistaken about the fundamental nature of things is, perhaps, not so terrible in itself. The real skeptical menace arises instead from the possible *consequences* of being wrong about the fundamental nature of things. If I am wrong in a certain way about fundamental reality—for example, if I am living in a sim—then I risk losing my warrant for believing other things of practical importance, such as that I existed yesterday and that I will exist tomorrow. If I am living in a sim, *maybe* my sensory experience is tracking a stable and durable reality, and my actions now have long-term consequences of the sort I think they do. *Maybe* I'm fortunate enough to be living in a huge, stable sim of approximately the size and scope I normally take the world to have. But maybe not.[29]

The skeptic wins two times out of three. The skeptic wins if we're living in a small sim, or an unstable sim, or a sim in which the world is very different than we think it is. The skeptic also wins if for all we know, we are living in a small, unstable, or deceptive sim. The nonskeptic wins only if we know that our reality, whether simulated or not, is large, stable, and populated with the people and things we care about.

One comforting, large-sim-friendly thought is this: Maybe the most efficient way to create simulated people is to evolve a large-scale society over a long period of (sim-clock) time. Another comforting thought is this: Maybe we should expect a technologically advanced society capable of running a sim to have enforceable ethical standards against running brief sims that contain conscious people.

However, I see no compelling reason to accept such comfortable thoughts. Consider the possibility I'll call the *many-branching sim*. In a many-branching sim scenario, a large and stable *root sim*, starting from some point deep in the past, is copied into one or more *branch sims* that start from a save point. Suppose that a group of researchers decides that the best way to create genuinely conscious simulated people is to run a whole simulated universe forward billions of years (sim-years on the simulation clock) from a big bang. Now suppose that a second group of researchers also wants to host a sim world. The second group has a choice: They can run a new sim world from the ground up, starting at the beginning and clocking forward, or they can take a snapshot of the first group's sim and make a copy. Which will they do?

In the twenty-first century game *SimCity*, there are two ways to build a bustling metropolis. Either you can either grow one from scratch, or you can use one of many copies other users have created. You can also save stages of a sim you've grown on your computer, cutting it off when things don't go the way you'd like, then starting again from a save point. You can copy variants of the same city, then grow them in different directions. Is there some reason to think that copying a sim would generally be more difficult than evolving a new sim from the beginning each time? Two further considerations might also favor copying: If your aim is scientific, controlled experiments might require a copy-and-run-forward approach for each intervention condition. Also, if it turns out that the types of intelligence or social structure you're targeting evolve only in a small minority of sims, then a run-from-the-beginning approach might require inconveniently many attempts.

If there are branch sims, you might now be in one of them, rather than in a root sim or a nonbranching sim. Maybe Sim Corp made the root sim for Earth, took a snapshot this morning on the sim clock, then sold thousands or millions of copies to researchers and gamers who now run short-term branch sims for whatever purposes they like. The future of the branch sim in which you are now living might be short—a few sim minutes, hours, or years.

How about the past? Is it short too? Maybe this is an opportunity for some voluntaristic metaphysics (chapter 41). I can imagine conceptualizing a branch world's past either as short or as long. It's long in one way, short in another, defying the usual approaches to time and duration. We might need to build some new ways of thinking.

Personal identity becomes a thorny issue. Considering my own case now, on July 13, 2018, according to my clock: If the snapshot was taken at the root sim time of noon on July 12, 2018, then the root sim contains an "Eric Schwitzgebel" who was fifty years old at that moment. Each branch sim would also contain an "Eric Schwitzgebel" developing forward from that point, of which I am one. How should I think of my relationship to those other branch-Erics?

Should I take comfort in the fact that some of them will continue on to live full and interesting lives (perhaps of very different sorts) even if most of them, including probably this particular instantiation of me, will soon be stopped and deleted? Or to the extent I am interested in *my own* future, should I be concerned primarily about what is happening in this branch?

Suppose I look out the window, across the 215/60 freeway and the citrus groves. Wait, is that . . . *Godzilla* in the distance?! I stare out the window in shock as the monster strides toward campus, crushing orange trees and lifting cars from the freeway. I flee my office, hurry down the stairs, sprint out toward the north side of campus. But I've chosen my path badly; here he is, coming right at me. As Godzilla steps down to crush me, should I console myself with the thought that after the rampage, whoever is running this sim will probably delete this branch and start again from the save point with an "Eric Schwitzgebel" still intact? Or would deleting this branch be the destruction of my whole world?

It's philosophically and technologically fascinating to think that we might live in a sim. Given how little we know about the fundamental structure of the cosmos, I wouldn't rule out that possibility entirely.[30] But we have barely scratched the surface of the philosophical consequences.

23 How to Accidentally Become a Zombie Robot

Susan Schneider's work on the future of robot consciousness has me thinking about the possibility of accidentally turning oneself into a zombie.[31] I mean "zombie" in the philosopher's sense: a being that outwardly looks and acts like us but has no genuine stream of conscious experience. What we are to imagine here is approximately the opposite of what we were imagining in the previous two chapters (and related to the ASIMO problem of chapter 15). The zombie worry is that we might be able to create artificial intelligences that are functionally very sophisticated and look from the outside as though they have genuine conscious experience but really have no conscious experience at all—no more consciousness than your laptop computer would have right now (I assume), even if we programmed it to cry and plead quite convincingly when you try to shut it down.

The idea is this: Silicon chips might fail to host consciousness while doing a pretty good job of *faking* consciousness. The fakery might be good enough to fool people who aren't specialists in AI engineering or the science of consciousness. Fancy AIs might be nothing more than plumped-up Furby dolls. Lonely lovers might fall in love with their sex dolls, elderly people with their robot companion nurses, and children with their nanny bots, even if there is no real stream of subjective experience behind the robots' speech and facial expressions. The consequences could be vast. People and robots might begin to intermarry. Robots might earn equal rights. People might begin to "upload" their minds into computers, destroying their biological brains in the process—all for an empty sham. That's the worry.

Let's suppose, then, a future in which most nonspecialists happily assume AI consciousness, while enough doubt remains about their underlying architecture that specialists on AI consciousness are sharply divided. Some philosophers, psychologists, and AI engineers support the popular view that the AIs have genuine subjective experiences, just like us, while others have serious doubts. Some of these skeptics, maybe, have been reading John Searle and Ned Block, who argue that no amount of computational equivalence could guarantee the existence of conscious experience in a nonbiological robot.[32] Others don't go as far, holding that an ideally designed silicon robot could be conscious, while doubting that currently existing robots are sufficiently well designed, despite their ability to fool the masses. These suspicious experts are alarmed to see human lives sometimes sacrificed to save robot lives and to see their friends "upload" and then "tell" everyone how awesome it is inside the Cloud.

Let's suppose that you are living in this era, and you're unsure what to think. Is the robot next door really conscious, or is it all just delusion? Is your uploaded "friend" really still there, or is it only an elaborate fake? How can you know? For you, the question has recently become especially urgent. You're old, and last week you learned that you're at a high risk of stroke. If silicon chips really can host consciousness as advertised, now is the time for you to swap out your organic material, before it's too late.

What should you do?

∽

That evening, as you are fretting over the issue, reading old articles by Searle and Block, some comforting news lights up your media feed. Adapting and substantially simplifying an old suggestion of Susan Schneider's, the leading manufacturer of artificial brains, the iBrain Company, has just released a new technology they're calling Try-It-Out.[33] Interested customers will soon be able to go to their local iBrain store and temporarily upload their minds into a robot. Potential customers can, in other words, check out robot consciousness for themselves. They will be able to learn directly from the inside what it's like to be a robot, if indeed there's anything it's like. During Try-It-Out, the iBrain Company claims, customers can *introspectively* discover whether the "uploaded you" really is conscious.

Problem solved! You needn't bother struggling through all of the old philosophy and all of the recent disputes about artificial consciousness. Nor need you decide whether to trust the seeming-report of your seeming-friend who keeps telling you how lovely it is to be in the Cloud free of a janky, aging human body. Instead, you can spend twenty minutes instantiated in silicon. When the experiment is done, you'll be ported back into your brain with updated memories of your experience or lack thereof, and you'll know the answer directly, unmediated by theory or someone else's say-so. The question will finally be settled.

Still, you don't want to be the first person to try the new technology. Nervously monitoring your health, you wait a year, seeing what happens with others who Try-It-Out. Report after report is identical: Everyone says they are conscious when their minds are ported into robots or into the Cloud. They return to their biological bodies happy and confident, eager to upload as soon as possible. Only in the rarest of cases are there any glitches or ill effects.

The day finally comes. You're ready to Try-It-Out yourself and, assuming all goes well, make the leap into silicon.

From the outside, your fateful day looks like this: You walk into the iBrain store. You fill out some forms. You are escorted to a clean, quiet room in the back where a physician is waiting. The physician and her technicians put you under anesthesia and scan your brain. In the corner of the room is a robot body, which now wakes. A speech stream comes from the robot: "Yes, I really am conscious! Wow!" The physician asks a series of questions. The robot shows proper awareness of its body, its surroundings, the recent past, and your biographical details. The robot then does some jumping jacks to further explore the body, bends an iron rod with its robotic strength, and performs a few other showy feats (which have been found to improve sales). Robot-you then goes to sleep. A snapshot of its brain is taken, to capture the new memories. The technicians then stimulate your sleeping biological brain to insert memories from the robotic phase, and finally they wake you up.

You sit up happy. "Yes, I was conscious even in the robot," you say. "My philosophical doubts were misplaced. Upload me into iBrain!"

The physician reminds you that according to the new federal regulations, two copies of a person cannot be run simultaneously, so that, after your upload, biological-you will need to be sedated indefinitely. That's fine, you reply. You no longer have any qualms.

∽

Whoops! I left out an important part of the story.

You never did any of those things. After the physician sedated you, she and the technicians went to the break room to play cards. Your brain was scanned, but nothing was ever loaded into the robot. The robot never came to life, never declared its own consciousness, never answered biographical questions, never did jumping jacks. After twenty minutes had passed, the physician and technicians updated your brain with *fake* memories of having done all of those things—fake memories based on plausible predictions about what you would have done had you actually been uploaded into the robot. After conducting a year's worth of Try-It-Out sessions, they had noticed that fake memories worked as well as real ones, and it was easier and less expensive to just skip the middle phase. It would of course be a terrible scandal if they were caught, but no one had ever showed the faintest suspicion.

You should have realized the risk. How could anyone know after waking up in their biological brain whether their currently conscious seeming-memory of having consciously said, "I'm really conscious!" was really a real memory of having consciously said, "I'm really conscious!" as opposed to a mere sham? *Now*, you're conscious. *Now*, you're seeming to remember it. Vividly conscious for you right now is the seeming-memory of delight and surprise. Vividly conscious for you right now is the seeming-memory of having experienced the world through robot eyes and of having felt the strength of robot arms bending iron. But the fact that these memories are conscious for you now is no guarantee that the events you seem now to have consciously experienced were in fact consciously experienced at the time. Searle and Block would have told you all that, if you'd read them more carefully.

∽

It's sad, of course, that you were fooled. However, the savvier and more suspicious alternative-you waited a little longer, for a later technological development: piece-by-piece Try-It-Out. Alternative-you foresaw the fake-memory difficulty. So alternative-you held out for something closer to Schneider's original suggestion.

Here's how piece-by-piece Try-It-Out works. Some portion of your brain—let's say the portion of your cortex responsible for tracking such-and-such features on the left side of your visual field—is scanned in detail, and a silicon-chip visual processing system is manufactured to replace it. The question is: Is this silicon visual cortex really capable of hosting genuine conscious experience? Or despite its capacity to conduct visual computational processing, might it be mere zombie-stuff? It's not *strictly* functionally identical, of course. At the micro level it works very differently, and it will break down under different conditions, and it's better in some ways, with internal algorithms to correct for your nearsightedness and astigmatism and faster resolution time for some details. But just like your regular visual cortex, the new silicon-chip cortex will take neural input from pathways x, y, and z, and just like your regular visual cortex, it will output interpretable neural signals to other relevant regions of the brain j, k, and l.

Based on your experience (as well as that of countless others) at the iBrain store, we also know that memories of seeming acts of successful introspection aren't enough to establish genuine consciousness. After the ensuing scandal and lawsuits, even iBrain Company had admitted as much. *Simultaneous* introspection—that's the right test! The introspection of one's own current conscious experience. After all, that's infallible, right? Or as close to infallibility as a human can get? Even Descartes in his most skeptical moments couldn't doubt *that*.[34]

So, you are sedated—alternative-you, actually, but let's drop the "alternative" part from here on. The interface between the selected portion of your brain and the rest of your brain is carefully mapped, synapse by synapse. Blood flow, hormonal regulation, and other neurophysiological features are also taken into account, on both the input and the output sides, with microscopic precision. All of this information is beamed in real time to a visual-cortex chip in a computer on the bedside table, waiting to be installed. The chip now runs in parallel to the targeted portion of your visual cortex. The chip beams outputs to transceivers at the edges of the relevant parts of your visual cortex, which stand ready to feed the results back into the rest of your brain. Your brain is doing its usual thing, but now there is also a silicon chip that is doing its own version of your brain's thing, in parallel on your bedside table.

A switch is flipped. A transcranial device damps down the activity in the target region of your visual cortex. Simultaneously, the transceivers on the interface surfaces of the remainder of your brain go live. The silicon chip is taking inputs from the other regions of your brain, then doing its "visual" processing, then sending interpretable outputs back into the rest of your brain. So far, it's a success! The remainder of your brain doesn't seem to be noticing any difference. Well, why would it? The technology is highly advanced, perfected after years of trials and billions of research dollars. The inputs the remainder of your brain is receiving are virtually indistinguishable from the inputs your brain would have received from the neural tissue that the silicon chip is designed to replace.

But you are still sedated, not fully conscious—you haven't yet carefully introspected.

You are eased out of sedation. The doctors ask how you feel.

"I feel fine," you say. "Normal. Have you done the procedure? Are we Trying-It-Out?"

Yes, they say. They advise you to introspect as carefully as you can.

Here's what will *not* happen: You will not notice any difference that inclines you to make a very different outward report than you otherwise would make or that would affect your motor cortex or prefrontal cortex or basal ganglia in any different way. (Maybe you'll say something like, "Ooh, things seem even clearer than with my natural vision. This is great!") You will not act out any very different decision than you would have with an ordinary biological visual cortex. You will not feel any very different surge of emotion, have any large hormonal change, or lay down any very different memories, except insofar as the additional visual clarity might impress you. After all, the input the chip provides to the rest of your brain is functionally similar to the input your ordinary visual cortex would have provided, differing mainly in improved clarity. That's how the technology works. And with such similar inputs, how could introspection possibly reveal any disastrous loss? The whole process has been designed specifically *not* to trigger an introspective crisis; that's exactly why the chip has been structured as it is and the transceivers placed where they have been placed. Billions of research dollars have created a procedure structured exactly to ensure that no noticeable difference would trigger a shocked introspective report of no experience.

The Try-It-Out process goes swimmingly, of course. You ace the vision tests, you report no introspective weirdness, you declare that you really consciously experience the visual world in all its magnificence.

The switch is flipped back, and everything returns to normal—a bit disappointingly fuzzy, actually. You were already getting used to the computer vision.

"Proceed with the surgery!" you say. The doctors install the chip, replacing the corresponding portion of your brain. Piece by piece, over the next year, doctors replace your whole brain. You never report noticing a difference.

☙

Sadly, the skeptics were right.

There is no consciousness in silicon computer chips. Despite broad functional similarity at the input-output level, differences in lower-level processing and microstructure, it turns out (let's suppose, for the sake of this thought experiment), *are* crucial to the presence or absence of genuine conscious experience. Brains, for example, implement a parallel-processing architecture, whereas the silicon chips only mimic parallel processing in a fast serial architecture. Maybe that matters immensely to felt experience even if not to outward function. Or maybe it matters that brains use analog accumulations to fire approximately digital action potentials, whereas silicon chips are digitally structured through and through—or that brains are sometimes sensitive to real quantum chance whereas silicon chips use complex clock algorithms to imitate chance, or that brains are juicy carbon, whereas silicon is dry and not nearly as delicious. Or maybe each of the 47 silicon chips that now constitute your brain is, individually, a locus of massive information integration, more so than your brain as a whole, with the result that there are now 47 streams of specialist consciousness but no overall integrated consciousness of the whole person.[35] Or . . . Some basic structural feature of the brain that is crucial for the real presence of consciousness is absent in the chip, despite the lack of big introspectively detectable differences or big differences in outward behavior.

The whole basis of wanting to Try-It-Out, rather than assuming that broad input/output functional similarity is enough, is the worry that the presence or absence of consciousness might depend on some such architectural feature, separable from broad input/output functional similarity. Unless that worry is live, there's no point in the whole elaborate Try-It-Out procedure.

We could instead trust that similar enough input/output functionality implied similar enough consciousness. But if you worry that functional similarity isn't sufficient for consciousness, your worry should remain even after you've aced piece-by-piece Try-It-Out. The input/output issue repeats, just at a lower level. If the Try-It-Out test is necessary, it is insufficient.

You have accidentally become a zombie robot.[36]

III   Regrets and Birthday Cake

24 Dreidel: A Seemingly Foolish Game That Contains the Moral World in Miniature

Superficially, dreidel looks like a simple game of luck, and a badly designed game at that. It lacks balance, clarity, and meaningful strategic choice. From this perspective, its prominence in the modern Hanukkah tradition is puzzling. Why encourage children to spend a holy evening gambling, of all things?

This superficial perspective misses the brilliance of dreidel. Dreidel's seeming flaws are exactly its virtues. Dreidel is the moral world in miniature.

If you're unfamiliar with the game, here's a quick tutorial. You sit in a circle with friends or relatives and take turns spinning a wobbly top, the dreidel. In the center of the circle is a pot of foil-wrapped chocolate coins of varying sizes, to which everyone has contributed from an initial stake of coins they keep in front of them. If, on your turn, the four-sided top lands on the Hebrew letter *gimmel*, you take the whole pot and everyone needs to contribute again. If it lands on *hey*, you take half the pot. If it lands on *nun*, nothing happens. If it lands on *shin*, you put in one coin. Then the next player spins.

It all sounds very straightforward, until you actually start to play the game. The first odd thing you might notice is that although some of the coins are big and others little, they all count as one coin in the rules of the game. This is inherently unfair, since the big coins contain more chocolate, and you get to eat your stash at the end. To compound the unfairness, there's never just one dreidel—all players can bring their own—and the dreidels are often biased, favoring different outcomes. (To test this, a few years ago my daughter and I spun a sample of eight dreidels forty times each, recording the outcomes. One particularly cursed dreidel landed on *shin* an incredible twenty-seven out of forty times.) It matters a lot which dreidel you spin.

And the rules are a mess! No one agrees whether you should round up or round down with *hey*. No one agrees when the game should end or under what conditions, if the pot is low after a *hey*, everyone should contribute again. No one agrees on how many coins each player should start with or whether you should let people borrow coins if they run out. You could try appealing to various authorities on the internet, but in my experience people prefer to argue and employ varying house rules. Some people hoard their coins and their favorite dreidels. Others share dreidels but not coins. Some people slowly unwrap and eat their coins while playing, then beg and borrow from wealthy neighbors when their luck sours.

Now you can, if you want, always push things to your advantage—always contribute the smallest coins in your stash, always withdraw the largest coins in the pot when you spin *hey*, insist on always using the "best" dreidel, always argue for rules interpretations in your favor, eat your big coins then use that as a further excuse to contribute only little ones, and so forth. You can do all this without ever breaking the rules, and you'll probably win the most chocolate as a result.

But here's the twist and what makes the game so brilliant: The chocolate isn't very good. After eating a few coins, the pleasure gained from further coins is minimal. As a result, almost all of the children learn that they would rather be kind and generous than hoard the most coins. The pleasure of the chocolate doesn't outweigh the yucky feeling of being a stingy, argumentative jerk. After a few turns of maybe pushing only small coins into the pot, you decide you should put in a big coin next time, just to be fair to the others and to enjoy being perceived as fair by them.

Of course, it also feels bad always to be the most generous one, always to put in big, take out small, always to let others win the rules arguments, and so forth, to play the sucker or self-sacrificing saint. Dreidel, then, is a practical lesson in discovering the value of fairness both to oneself and to others, in a context in which the rules are unclear, there are norm violations that aren't rules violations, and both norms and rules are negotiable, varying by occasion—just like life itself, only with mediocre chocolate at stake. I can imagine no better way to spend a holy evening.

25 Does It Matter If the Passover Story Is Literally True?

You probably already know the Passover story: how Moses asked Pharaoh to let his enslaved people leave Egypt and how Moses's god punished Pharaoh—killing the Egyptians' firstborn sons while "passing over" the Jewish households. You might even know the new ancillary tale of the Passover orange. How much truth is there in these stories? At synagogues during Passover holiday, myth collides with fact, tradition with changing values. Negotiating this collision is the puzzle of modern religion.

Passover is a holiday of debate, reflection, and conversation. In 2016, as my family and I and the rest of the congregation waited for the Passover feast at our Reform Jewish temple, our rabbi prompted us: "Does it matter if the story of Passover isn't literally true?"

Most people seemed to be shaking their heads. No, it doesn't matter.

I was imagining the Egyptians' sons. I am an outsider to the temple. My wife and teenage son are Jewish, but I am not. At the time, my nine-year-old daughter, adopted from China at age one, was describing herself as "half Jewish."

I nodded my head. Yes, it does matter if the Passover story is literally true.

"Okay, Eric, why does it matter?" Rabbi Suzanne Singer handed me the microphone.

I hadn't planned to speak. "It matters," I said, "because if the story is literally true, then a god who works miracles really exists. It matters if there is a such a god or not. I don't think I would like the ethics of that god, who kills innocent Egyptians. I'm glad there is no such god.

"It is odd," I added, "that we have this holiday that celebrates the death of children, so contrary to our values now."

The microphone went around, others in the temple responding to me. Values change, they said. Ancient war sadly but inevitably involved the death of children. We're really celebrating the struggle of freedom for everyone . . .

Rabbi Singer asked if I had more to say in response. My son leaned toward me. "Dad, you don't have anything more to say." I took his cue and shut my mouth.

Then the seder plates arrived with the oranges on them. Seder plates have six labeled spots: two bitter herbs, charoset (a mix of fruit and nuts), parsley, a lamb bone, a boiled egg—each with symbolic value. There is no labeled spot for an orange.

The first time I saw an orange on a seder plate, I was told this story about it: A woman was studying to be a rabbi. An orthodox rabbi told her that a woman belongs on the *bimah* (pulpit) like an orange belongs on the seder plate. When she became a rabbi, she put an orange on the plate.

A wonderful story—a modern, liberal story. More comfortable than the original Passover story for a liberal Reform Judaism congregation like ours, proud of our woman rabbi. The orange is an act of defiance, a symbol of a new tradition that celebrates gender equality. Does it matter if it's true?

Here's what actually happened. Dartmouth Jewish Studies Professor Susannah Heschel was speaking to a Jewish group at Oberlin College in Ohio. The students had written a story in which a girl asks a rabbi if there is room for lesbians in Judaism, and the rabbi rises in anger, shouting, "There's as much room for a lesbian in Judaism as there is for a *crust of bread* on the seder plate!" The next Passover, Heschel, inspired by the students but reluctant to put anything as unkosher as bread on the seder plate, used a tangerine instead.[1]

The orange, then, though still an act of defiance, is also already a compromise and modification. The shouting rabbi is not an actual person but an imagined, simplified foe.

It matters that it's not true. From the story of the orange, we learn a central lesson of Reform Judaism: that myths are cultural inventions built to suit the values of their day, idealizations and simplifications, changing as our values change—but that only limited change is possible within a tradition-governed institution. An orange, but not a crust of bread.

In a way, my daughter and I are also oranges: a new type of presence in a Jewish congregation, without a marked place, welcomed this year, unsure we belong, at risk of rolling off.

In the car on the way home, my son scolded me: "How could you have said that, Dad? There are people in the congregation who take the Torah literally, very seriously! You should have seen how they were looking at you, with so much anger. If you'd said more, they would practically have been ready to lynch you."

Due to the seating arrangement, I had been facing away from most of the congregation. I hadn't seen those faces. Were they really so outraged? Was my son telling me the truth on the way home that night? Or was he creating a simplified myth of me?

In belonging to an old religion, we honor values that are no longer entirely our own. We celebrate events that no longer quite make sense. We can't change the basic tale of Passover. But we can add liberal commentary to better recognize Egyptian suffering, and we can add a new celebration of equality.

Although the new tradition, the orange, is an unstable thing atop an older structure that resists change, we can work to ensure that it remains. It will remain only if we can speak its story compellingly enough to also give our new values the power of myth.

I wrote the following shortly after my father died in 2015. I share it with you now partly as a tribute to my father, to whom this book is dedicated, and partly because I think this portrait of him will help you better understand the background of my thinking. My interest in philosophical discourse with nonspecialists, my fascination with technology, my interest in moral psychology, and my appreciation of weirdness all spring from the same root.

∞

My father, Kirkland R. Gable (born Ralph Schwitzgebel), died on Sunday. Here are some things I want you to know about him.

Of teaching, he said that authentic education is less about textbooks, exams, and technical skills than about moving students "toward a bolder comprehension of what the world and themselves might become."[2] He was a beloved psychology professor at California Lutheran University.

I have never known anyone, I think, who brought as much creative fun to teaching as he did. He gave out goofy prizes to students who scored well on his exams (for instance, a windup robot nun who breathed sparks of static electricity: "Nunzilla"). Teaching about alcoholism, he would start by pouring himself a glass of wine (actually water with food coloring), then more wine, and more wine, acting drunker and drunker, arguing with himself, as the class proceeded. Teaching about child development, he would stand my sister or me in front of the class, and we'd move our mouths like ventriloquist dummies as he stood behind us, talking about Piaget or parenting styles—and then he'd ask our opinion about parenting styles. Teaching about neuroanatomy, he'd bring a brain Jell-O mold, which he sliced up and passed around for the students to eat ("yum! occipital cortex!"). And so on.

As a graduate student and then lecturer at Harvard in the 1960s and 1970s, he shared the idealism of his mentors Timothy Leary and B. F. Skinner, who thought that through understanding the human mind we can transform and radically improve the human condition—a vision my father carried through his entire life.[3] His comments about education captured his ideal for thinking in general: that we should aim toward a bolder comprehension of what the world and ourselves might become.

He was always imagining the potential of the young people he met, seeing things in them that they often didn't see in themselves. He especially loved juvenile delinquents (as they were then called), whom he encouraged to think ambitiously and expansively. He recruited them from street corners, paying them to speak their hopes and stories onto reel-to-reel tapes, and he recorded their declining rates of recidivism as they did this, week after week. His 1965 book about this work, *Streetcorner Research*, was a classic in its day. As a prospective philosophy graduate student in the 1990s, I proudly searched the research libraries of the schools I was admitted to, always finding multiple copies with lots of date stamps from checkouts in the 1960s and 1970s.

With his twin brother Robert, he invented the electronic-monitoring ankle bracelet, now widely used as an alternative to prison for nonviolent offenders. He wanted to set teenagers free from prison, rewarding them for going to churches and libraries instead of street corners and pool halls. He had a positive vision rather than a penal one. He imagined everyone someday using location monitors to share rides and to meet nearby strangers with mutual interests—ideas that, in 1960, were about fifty years before their time.

With degrees in both law and psychology, he helped to reform institutional practice in psychiatric institutions—which, in the 1960s, were often terrible places whose residents had no effective legal rights.[4] He helped force those institutions to become more humane and to release harmless residents held against their will. I recall his stories about residents who were often, he said, "as sane as could be expected, given their current environment," and maybe saner than those who guarded them—for example, an old man who decades earlier had painted his neighbor's horse as an angry prank and thought he would "get off easy" if he convinced the court he was insane.

As a father, he modeled and rewarded unconventional thinking. We never had an ordinary Christmas tree that I recall—always instead a life-size cardboard Christmas Buddha (with blue lights poking through his eyes), or a stepladder painted green then strung with ornaments, or a wild-found tumbleweed carefully flocked and tinseled—and why does it have to be on December 25? I remember a few Saturdays when we got hamburgers from different restaurants and ate them in a neutral location—I believe it was the parking lot of a Korean church—to see which burger we really preferred. (As I recall, he and my sister settled on the Burger King Whopper, while I could never confidently reach a preference, because it seemed like we never got the methodology quite right.)

He loved to speak with strangers, spreading his warm silliness and unconventionality out into the world. If we ordered chicken at a restaurant, he might politely ask the server to "hold the feathers." Near the end of his life, if we went to a bank together, he might gently make fun of himself, saying something like "I brought along my brain," gesturing toward me with open hands, "since my other brain is sometimes forgetting things now." For years, though we lived nowhere near any farm, we had a sign from the Department of Agriculture on our refrigerator, sternly warning us never to feed table scraps to hogs.

I miss him painfully, and I hope that I can live up to some of the potential he so generously saw in me, carrying forward some of his spirit.

27 Flying Free of the Deathbed, with Technological Help

Rereading my reflections on my father, I am struck by one contrast between his vision and mine. My father so creatively saw the positive potential in people and technology—wonderfully imagining how to turn things toward the better. My vision, through parts I and II of this book at least, has been much more mixed, tending toward the negative—with plenty of abusive corporations, misleading applications of technology, jerks and hypocrites, and failures of self-knowledge. Here, then, is an expansive, creative vision of a positive possibility for my father.

∽

My father spent the final twenty years of his life disabled and often bedridden. In addition to two forms of life-threatening cancer, he suffered from complex regional pain syndrome (CRPS) in one foot. The CRPS caused him constant pain that could be seriously aggravated, sometimes for weeks, from even mild exertion, such as ten minutes' walking, or from jostling the foot while sleeping or in a wheelchair. It was, I suspect, the CRPS that ultimately killed him, through the side effects of long-term narcotics and the bodily harm of spending years mostly immobile in bed, including near paralysis of his digestive system.

My father's last word was "up." I had poured a laxative in his mouth, hoping to reactivate his bowels so that we could feed his fast-failing body. He aspirated the laxative into his lungs, began to cough weakly, then died propped up in my arms while I futilely slapped his back. By "up" he probably meant "sit me up straighter, I'm choking," but maybe—I prefer to imagine this—he was expressing the upward hope for Heaven that helped sustain him in his final months.

I have often wished that we could have freed my father up away from his horrible bed. I've tried it in imagination many times, drafting out science fiction stories featuring an elderly person who uses virtual reality or "telepresence" to find new meaning and potential for action in the world beyond the bedroom. Although I've written some science fiction stories I'm proud of, this particular story never comes out right. So instead of that story I can't yet write, let me discuss the technological innovation I have in mind.

Some elements of this idea are already being implemented in current telepresence technologies. First, equip an able-bodied volunteer, the *host*, with a camera above each eye and a microphone next to each ear. Equip the bedridden person, the *rider*, with virtual reality gear that immersively presents the host's audiovisual inputs to the rider's eyes and ears, and a microphone to enable the rider to speak directly into the host's ear. Now send the host on a trip. During this trip, let the host be guided mainly by the rider's expressed desires, walking where the rider wants to walk, looking where the rider wants to look, stopping and listening where the rider wants to stop and listen. Unlike in virtual reality tours as they currently exist, the host can interact with and alter the environment in real time. The rider could have the host lift, turn, and examine a flower, then cast it into a stream and watch it drift away. The host could purchase goods or services on the rider's behalf. The rider could conduct a conversation with the locals he encounters on the virtual journey, by having the host speak the rider's words verbatim almost simultaneously with the rider's speaking them into his ear—which is surprisingly easy to do with a little practice.[5] Alternatively, the rider might have a separate speaker output from the host's helmet, allowing the rider to speak directly.

Next, let's don some virtual reality gloves. As I imagine it, rider and host wear matching gloves synchronized to move in exactly the same way—of course with quick-escape overrides and perhaps the rider's motions damped down to prevent overextension or bumping into unseen obstacles near the bed. Glove synchronization will require both good motion tracking (Nintendo Wii, improved) and some ways of restricting or guiding the gloves' movements on each end (perhaps through magnets and gyres). If the gloves are appropriately synchronized, when the rider starts to move his hand on vector v and the host starts to move her hand on vector w, each motion is nudged toward some compromise vector $(v + w)/2$. An intuitive collaboration will be essential, so that v and w don't start too far apart—a familiarity acquired over time, with gentle, predictable movements and anticipatory verbal cues ("Let's pick that blue flower"). With practice, in safe, simple, and predictable environments, it should come to seem to the rider as if it is almost his own hands that are moving in the seen environment. Tactile feedback could further enhance this impression—that is, if pressure sensors in the host's gloves connect with actuators in the rider's gloves that exert corresponding pressures in corresponding locations.

A final, expensive, and much more conjectural step would be to equip host and rider with helmets with brain-imaging technology and transcranial magnetic stimulation (or some other way of directly stimulating and suppressing brain activity). For example, for a fuller tactile experience, activity in the host's primary somatosensory cortex could be tracked, and a vague, faint echo of it could be stimulated in matching areas in the rider's cortex. You wouldn't want too much synchrony—just a hint of it—and anyhow, brains differ even in relatively similarly structured regions like somatosensory cortex. Of course, you wouldn't want too much motor signal traveling down efferent nerves into the rider's body, making the rider move around in bed. Just a hint, just a whiff, just a rough approximation—a dim, vague signal that might be highly suggestive in an otherwise well-harmonized, collaborative host and rider, in a rich virtual reality environmental context with clear cues and expectations.

Let's boldly imagine all of this in a positive, harmonious, nonexploitative relationship between rider and host. The host will almost forget his bed, will explore and laugh and play in regions far beyond his little bedroom, will feel that he is truly back in the wide world, at least for a while.

My father was both a psychologist and an inventor. In 1995, when he was first diagnosed with cancer, he had been wanting to go to Hong Kong, and he had to cancel the trip to attempt a bone marrow transplant. He died twenty years later, never having made it to Hong Kong. I wish I could bring my father back to life, build some of this technology with him, then take him there.

In 2003, my Swiss friends Eric and Anne-Françoise asked me to contribute something to their wedding ceremony. Here's a lightly revised version of what I wrote, concerning conjugal love, the distinctive kind of love between spouses.

જ

Love is not a feeling. Feelings come and go, while love is steady. Feelings are passions in the classic sense of "passion," which shares a root with "passive"—they arrive mostly unbidden, unchosen. Love, in contrast, is something built. The passions felt by teenagers and writers of romantic lyrics, felt so intensely and often so temporarily, are not love—though they might sometimes be the prelude to it.

Rather than a feeling, love is a way of structuring your values, goals, and reactions. Central to love is valuing the good of the other for their own sake.[6] Of course, we all care about the good of other people we know, for their own sake and not just for further ends. Only if the regard is deep, only if we so highly value the other's well-being that we are willing to thoroughly restructure our own goals to accommodate it, and only if this restructuring is so rooted that it automatically informs our reactions to the person and to news that could affect them, do we possess real love.

Conjugal love involves all of this, but it is also more than this. In conjugal love, one commits to seeing one's life always with the other in view. One commits to pursuing one's major projects, even when alone, in a kind of implicit conjunction with the other. One's life becomes a coauthored work.

Parental love for a young child might be purer and more unconditional than conjugal love. The parent expects nothing back from a young child. The parent needn't share plans and ideals with an infant. Later, children will grow away into their separate lives, independent of parents' preferences, while we retain our parental love for them.

Conjugal love, because it involves the collaborative construction of a joint life, can't be unconditional in this way. If partners don't share values and a vision, they can't steer a mutual course. If one partner develops too much of a separate vision or doesn't openly and in good faith work with the other toward their joint goals, conjugal love fails and is, at best, replaced with some more general type of loving concern.

Nevertheless, to dwell on the conditionality of conjugal love, and to develop a set of contingency plans should it fail, is already to depart from the project of jointly fabricating a life and to begin to develop individual goals opposing those of the partner. Conjugal love requires an implacable, automatic commitment to responding to all major life events through the mutual lens of marriage. One can't embody such a commitment while harboring serious backup plans and persistent thoughts about the relationship's contingency.

Is it paradoxical that conjugal love requires lifelong commitment without contingency plans yet at the same time is contingent in a way that parental love is not? No, there is no paradox.

If you believe something is permanent, you can make lifelong promises and commitments contingent upon it, because you believe the thing will never fail you. Lifelong commitments can be built upon bedrock, solid despite their dependency on that rock.

This, then, is the significance of the marriage ceremony: It is the expression of a mutual, unshakeable commitment to build a joint life together, in which each partner's commitment is possible, despite the contingency of conjugal love, because each partner trusts that the other partner's commitment is unshakeable.

A deep faith and trust must therefore underlie true conjugal love. That trust is the most sacred and inviolable thing in a marriage, because it is the very foundation of its possibility. Deception and faithlessness destroy conjugal love because, and to the extent that, they undermine that trust. For the same reason, honest and open interchange about long-standing goals and attitudes is at the heart of marriage.

Passion alone can't ground conjugal trust. Neither can shared entertainments and the pleasure of each other's company. Both partners must have matured enough that their core values are stable. They must be unselfish enough to lay everything on the table for compromise, apart from those permanent, shared values. And they must resist the tendency to form secret, selfish goals. Only to the degree they approach these ideals are partners worthy of the trust that makes conjugal love possible.

29 Knowing What You Love

In a 1996 article on self-knowledge, Victoria McGeer argues that your claims about your attitudes are likely to be true mainly because once you avow an attitude, whether to yourself or others, you are thereafter committed to living and speaking and reasoning accordingly, unless you can give some account of why you aren't doing so.[7] Since you have considerable self-regulatory control over how you live, speak, and reason, and since all there is to having an attitude is being prone to live, speak, and reason in ways that fit that attitude, you have the power to make true what you say about yourself. In short, you shape yourself to fit the attitudes you express. In McGeer's picture, self-knowledge derives more from self-shaping than it does from introspectively discovering attitudes that already exist.

This model of self-knowledge works especially well, I think, for love. Suppose I'm up late with some friends at a bar. They're talking jazz, and I'm left in the dust. More to participate in the conversation and to seem knowledgeable than out of any prior conviction, I say, "I just love Cole Porter's ballads." I could as easily have said I love Irving Berlin or George Gershwin. About all of these composers, I really know only a half-dozen songs, which I've heard occasionally performed by different artists. My friends ask what I like about Porter; I say something hopefully not too stupid. Later, when we're driving in my car, they expect to hear Cole Porter. When a Porter biopic is released, they ask my opinion about it and I oblige them. Although this pattern of action arises partly from my desire to fulfill the expectations I've created by my remark, it's not just empty show. I do enjoy Cole Porter, and I find myself drawn even more to him now. I feel committed to an appreciation of Cole Porter, and that leads me to appreciate him all the more. I've grown comfortable in the stand I've taken. It's part of the public face I now enjoy showing to my friends. This isn't so unlikely. The psychological literature on cognitive dissonance, for example, suggests that we tend to subsequently shape our general opinions to match what we have overtly said, if it was said without obvious coercion.[8]

I have transformed myself into a Cole Porter fan as the result of a casual remark. It wasn't true of me before I said it, but now I've made it true. If love is a kind of commitment to valuing something or a pattern of specially valuing it, I embarked on that commitment and began that pattern by making the remark. The accuracy of my declaration that I love Cole Porter derives not from acute introspection of some prior cognitive state, but rather from the way I shape myself into a consistent, comprehensible person, for my own benefit and the benefit of others, once something truthy has dropped from my mouth.

If I say to myself in the scoop shop that I love Chunky Monkey ice cream, I am at least as much forming a commitment or creating a policy and reference point for future choices as I am scouring my mind to discover a preexisting love. Of course, it's highly relevant that I remember enjoying Chunky Monkey last time I had it, but remembering a pleasure is no declaration of love. To endorse the thought that I don't just enjoy the flavor but actually love it is to embrace a relationship between myself and it. The same goes if I decide that I love the San Francisco

49ers, or the writings of Michel de Montaigne, or Yosemite Valley in the fall.

If I tell someone for the first time that I love her, I am not, I hope, merely expressing an emotion. Rather, I am announcing a decision. I am diving into a commitment, not easily reversed, to value her in a certain way. How frightening!

The commitment in loving another person dwarfs the commitment in loving Chunky Monkey, and we judge people very differently who abandon these commitments. But even the smallest love requires regulative self-consistency. We can't ceaselessly and arbitrarily flop around in our loves while continuing to be normal choice makers and comprehensible members of a community. Hereafter, I must either default to giving Chunky Monkey very strong consideration or stand ready to explain myself.

ↁ

In that moment you first declare your love, is it already true that you love? You haven't yet done the work. It could turn out either way. Your declaration was a fleeting shadow, forgotten the next day, or it was the crucial beginning of something that endures. If the resolve endures, your declaration was true—but whether the resolve endures depends on circumstances beyond your control and on parts of yourself you can't see. You can guess, based on a strength of feeling or sense of your own seriousness—but if you lose your job tomorrow, maybe your world goes sideways, uprooting the seedlings.

ↁ

Can we similarly have other-knowledge through other-shaping? It's a tyrannical business, but I don't see why it couldn't happen. Imagine a mother who declares that her four-year-old son loves baseball, then works to make it true. Or imagine Stalin declaring that his followers hate Trotsky.

Every year around graduation time we hear uplifting thoughts about what people do and do not regret on their deathbeds. The intended lesson is *Pursue your dreams! Don't worry about money!*

I can find no systematic research about what people on their deathbeds do in fact say they regret. A database search of psychology articles on "death*" and "regret*" ("*" is a truncation symbol) turns up a 2005 article by Erika Timmer and colleagues as the closest thing. Evidently, what elderly East Germans most regretted in retrospect is having been victimized by war.[9]

Let's grant that the commencement truisms have a prima facie plausibility. With their dying breaths, grandparents around the world say, "If only I had pursued my dreams and worried less about money!" Does their dying perspective give them wisdom? Does it matter that it is dying grandparents who say this rather than forty-year-old parents or high school counselors or assistant managers at regional banks? The deathbed has rhetorical power. Does it deserve it?

I'm reminded of the wisdom expressed by Zaphod Beeblebrox IV in *The Hitchhiker's Guide to the Galaxy* series. Summoned in a seance, Zaphod says that being dead "gives one such a wonderfully uncluttered perspective. Oh-ummm, we have a saying up here: 'life is wasted on the living.'"[10]

There's something to that, no doubt. But here's my worry: The dead and dying are suspiciously safe from having to live by their own advice. If I'm forty and I say, "Pursue your dreams! Don't worry about money!" I can be held to account for hypocrisy if I don't live that way myself. But am I really going to live that way? Potential victimization by my own advice might help me more vividly appreciate the risks and stress of chucking the day job. Grandpa on his deathbed might be forgetting those risks and that stress in a grand, regretful fantasy about the gap between what he was and what he might have been.

The same pattern can occur in miniature day by day and week by week. Looking back, I can always fantasize about having been

"I should have bought more crap."

Figure III.1
A possible deathbed regret.
Source: Eric Lewis, *New Yorker*, November 18, 2002.

more energetic yesterday or more productive last week. I can regret not having seized each day with more gusto. Great! That would have been better. But seizing every day with inexhaustible gusto is superhuman. In retrospect I forget, maybe, how superhuman that would be.

Another source of deathbed distortion might be this: Certain types of achievements carry costs that might be foolishly easy to regret. I'm thinking here especially of costs incurred to avoid a risk or acquire a piece of important knowledge. Owing to hindsight bias—the tendency to see things as having been obvious in retrospect[11]—opportunities sacrificed and energy spent to prove something (for example, to prove to yourself that you could have been successful in business or academia) or to avoid a risk that never materialized (such as the risk of having to depend on substantial financial savings in order not to lose your home) can seem not to have been worth it. *Of course* you would have succeeded in business; *of course* you would have been fine without that extra money in the bank. On your deathbed you might think you should have known these things all along. But you shouldn't have. The future is harder to predict than the past.

I prefer the wisdom of forty-year-olds—the ones in the middle of life, who gaze equally in both directions. Some forty-year-olds also think you should pursue your dreams (within reason) and not worry (too much) about money.

Here's an unsentimental attitude about last, dying thoughts: Your dying thought will be your least important thought. Assuming no afterlife, it is the one thought that is guaranteed to have no influence on your future thoughts or choices.

(Now maybe if you express the thought aloud—"I did not get my SpaghettiOs. I got spaghetti. I want the press to know this."[12]—it will have an effect. But for this reflection, let's assume a private last thought that influences no one else.)

A narrative approach to the meaning of life—the view that, in some important sense, life is a story[13]—seems to recommend a different attitude toward dying thoughts. If life is a story, you want it to end well! The ending of a story colors all that has gone before. If the hero dies resentful or if the hero dies content, that rightly influences our understanding of earlier events, not only because we might now understand that all along the hero felt subtly resentful, but also because final thoughts, on this view, have a retrospective transformative power: An earlier betrayal, for example, becomes a betrayal that was forgiven by the end—or it becomes one that was never forgiven. The ghost's appearance to Hamlet has one type of significance if *Hamlet* ends badly and quite a different significance if *Hamlet* ends well. On the narrative view, the significance of events depends partly on the future, and thus they don't achieve their final significance until the future is settled. One's last thought is like the final sentence of a book. Ending on a thought of love and happiness makes your life a very different story than ending on a thought of resentment and regret.

Maybe this is what Solon had in mind when he told King Croesus not to call anyone fortunate until they die:[14] A horrible enough disaster at the end can retrospectively poison everything that came before—your marriage, your seeming successes, your seeming middle-aged wisdom.

The unsentimental view seems to give too little importance to one's final thought—I, at least, would want to die on an "up" note, if I can manage it!—but the narrative view seems to give one's final thought too much importance. We can't know the significance of a story if we don't know its final sentence, but I doubt we're deprived in the same way of knowing the significance of someone's life if we don't know the person's final, dying thought. The last sentence of a story is a contrived feature of a type of art, a sentence that the work is designed to render highly significant. A last thought might be trivially unimportant by accident (if you're hit by a truck while thinking about what to have for lunch), or it might not reflect a stable attitude (if you're panicky from lack of air).

Maybe the right answer is just a compromise: One's final thought is not totally trivial, because it does have some narrative power, but life isn't so entirely like a story that the final thought has last-sentence-of-a-story power. Life has narrative elements, but the independent pieces also have a power and value that doesn't depend so much on future outcomes.

Here's another possibility, which interacts with the first two: Maybe one's last thought is an *opportunity*—though what kind of opportunity it is will depend on whether last thoughts can retrospectively change the significance of earlier events.

On the narrative view, one's final dying thought is an opportunity to—secretly! with an almost magical time-piercing power—make it the case that you forgave, or never forgave, person A, that you regretted, or never regretted, action B, and so forth. As I write this, I think of a friend of mine whose alcoholic father ran out of money and lived with him awhile until my friend booted him out for rotten behavior, such as repeatedly driving the grandkids while drunk. A couple of weeks ago, the alcoholic father died alone in a cheap apartment. In his last moments, did he think of his estranged son, and if so, with what thoughts?

Rather differently, one's final dying minutes are an opportunity to explore some risky or fatal experience you wouldn't otherwise try. Maybe if I'm dying near a skyscraper window, I will ask my friends to tip me out of it so I can relish a final fall. My mother once mentioned a drug she had tried in her twenties that she enjoyed so immensely that she never dared try it again for fear she would lose herself to it. I've made a note of it, in case she has the chance to choose her exit.

32 Profanity Inflation, Profanity Migration, and the Paradox of Prohibition (or I Love You, "Fuck")

As a fan of profane language judiciously employed, I fear that the best profanities of the English language are cheapening from overuse—or worse, that our impulses to offend through profane language are beginning to shift away from harmless terms toward more harmful ones. I have been inspired to these thoughts by Rebecca Roache's recent discussions of the ethics of swearing.[15]

Roache distinguishes objectionable slurs, especially racial slurs, from presumably harmless swear words like "fuck." She argues that the latter words shouldn't be forbidden, even if in some formal contexts they might be inappropriate. She also suggests that it's silly to forbid "fuck" while allowing obvious replacements like "f**k" or "the f-word." Roache says, "We should swear more, and we shouldn't use asterisks, and that's fine."[16]

I disagree. I disagree approximately because, as a recent e-card has it (figure III.2): "Fuck, you are my favorite word. I love you Fuck."

"Fuck" is a treasure of the English language. Speakers of other languages will sometimes even reach across the linguistic divide to relish its profanity. "Merde" and "Dummkopf" just don't have the same sting. "Fuck" is a treasure precisely *because* it's

Figure III.2
A favorite word.
Source: https://www.someecards.com/users/profile/Serena2015282.

forbidden. Its being forbidden is the source of its profane power
and vivacity.

When I was growing up in California in the 1970s, "fuck" was
considered the worst of the "seven words you can't say on TV."[17]
In those pre-cable-TV, pre-internet days, you would never hear
it in the media, or indeed—in my mellow little suburb—from
any adults, except maybe, very rarely, from some wild man from
the city. I don't think I heard my parents or any of their friends
say the word even once, ever. It wasn't until fourth grade that I
learned that the word existed. If a teacher heard you say it, you
might be sent to the principal's office or held back from recess.
What a powerful word for a child to relish in the quiet of his
room or to suddenly drop on a friend!

"Fuck" is in danger. Its power is subsiding from its increased usage in public. Much as the overprinting of money devalues it, profanity inflation risks turning "fuck" into another "damn." The hundred dollar bill of swear words doesn't buy as much shock as it used to.

Okay, a qualification: I'm pretty sure what I've just said is true for the suburban dialects in California and the Midwest, but I'm also pretty sure "fuck" was never so powerful in some other dialects. For some evidence of its increased usage overall and its approach toward what "damn" was in the 1970s, see figure III.3, which shows a Google NGram of the rates of use of "fuck," "shit," and "damn" in "lots of books," between 1960 and 2008. A Google Trends search suggests that "fuck" continued to rise in popularity from 2008 to 2018, increasing in usage on the internet in the United States by about 40 percent over the ten-year period.[18]

Furthermore, as "fuck" loses its sting and vivacity, people who wish to use more vividly offensive language will be forced to other options. The most offensive alternative options currently

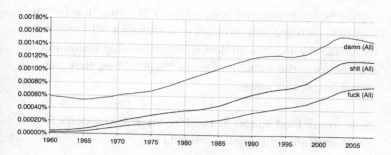

Figure III.3
Google NGram of "fuck," "shit," and "damn," 1960–2008, smoothing of three.
Source: https://books.google.com/ngrams, downloaded July 8, 2015.

available in English are racial slurs. But unlike "fuck," racial slurs (as Roache notes) are harmful in ordinary use. The cheapening of "fuck" thus risks forcing the migration of profanity to more harmful linguistic locations.

The paradox of prohibition, then: Those of us who want to preserve the power of "fuck" should cheer for it to remain forbidden. We should celebrate, not bemoan, the existence of standards forbidding "fuck" on major networks, and the awarding of demerits for its use in school, and its almost complete avoidance by responsible adults in public contexts. Conversely, some preachers might wish to encourage the regular recitation of "fuck" in the preschool curriculum. (Okay, that was tongue-in-cheek. But wouldn't it work?)

Despite the substantial public interest in retaining the forbidden deliciousness of our best swear word, I do think that since the word is in fact (pretty close to) harmless, severe restrictions would be unjust. We must really only condemn it with the forgiving standards appropriate to etiquette violations, even if this results in the word's not being quite as potent as it otherwise would be.

Finally, let me defend usages like "f**k" and "the f-word." Rather than being silly avoidances because we all know what we are talking about, such decipherable maskings communicate and reinforce the forbiddenness of "fuck." Thus, they help to sustain its profane power.

[Note to my kind editors at the MIT Press: Please don't forbid "fuck" until after this book is printed.]

33   The Legend of the Leaning Behaviorist

The following is an oral tradition in academic psychology. I don't know if it's true.

Once upon a time in a land far away—by which I mean circa 1960 at a prominent US university—there lived a behavioral psychologist, an expert in the shaping of animal behavior by means of reward and punishment. Let's call him Professor B. F. Skinner, just for fun.

One semester when Professor Skinner was teaching a large lecture course, his students tried an experiment on him. Without letting him know, they decided that when he was lecturing on the left side of the classroom, they would smile and nod more often than usual. When he was on the right, they would knit their brows and look away. Soon, Professor Skinner delivered his lectures mostly from the left side of the room.

The students then altered their strategy. Whenever Professor Skinner moved to the left, they would smile and nod; whenever he moved to the right, they would knit their brows. Soon he was drifting ever more leftward. By the end of the term, he was lecturing while leaning against the left wall.

On the last day of class, one of the students raised his hand. "Professor Skinner," the student asked, "why are you lecturing from way over there?"

"Oh, I don't know," Professor Skinner replied. "It's close to the ashtray."

Democracy requires that journalists and editors strive for political balance. Democracy also requires that journalists and editors present the facts as they understand them. When it is not possible to be factual and balanced at the same time, democratic institutions risk collapse.

Consider the problem abstractly. Democracy X is dominated by two parties, T and F. Party T is committed to the truth of propositions A, B, and C, and party F is committed to their falsity. Slowly, the evidence mounts: A, B, and C look very likely to be true. Observers in the media and experts in the education system begin to see this, but the evidence isn't quite plain enough for nonexperts, especially if those nonexperts are aligned with party F and already committed to the falsity of A, B, and C.

Psychological research and also just commonsense observation of the recent political situation—I think you'll agree with this, whatever side you're on—demonstrate the great human capacity to rationalize and justify what you want to believe. The evidence favoring A can be very substantial—compelling, even, from a neutral point of view—without convincing people who are emotionally invested in the falsity of A, as long as the evidence is indirect, or statistical, or requires some interpretation, allowing a knife's-width excuse for doubt.

The journalists and educators who live in democracy X now face a dilemma. They can present both sides of the debate over A, B, and C in a balanced way, or they can call the facts as they see them. Either choice threatens the basic institutions of their democracy.

If they present balanced cases for and against A, B, and C, they give equal time to the true and the false. They create the misleading impression that the matter still admits substantial doubt, that expert opinion is divided, that it's equally reasonable to believe either side. They thereby undermine their own well-informed assessment that A, B, and C are very likely to be true. This is dangerous, since democracy depends on a well-educated, informed voting public, aware of the relevant facts.

In the long run, journalists and educators will likely turn against balance, because they care intensely about the facts in question. They don't wish to pretend that the evidence is unclear. They understand that they can't routinely promote false equivalencies while retaining their integrity.

So ultimately, they will tell the truth, mostly, as they see it. But this, too, is likely to harm their democracy. Since the truth in our example happens to disproportionately favor party T over party F, and since the members of party F are, understandably, hesitant to abandon their prior commitments despite what experts, but not the members of party F themselves, can recognize to be clear evidence, party F will begin to see academics and the mainstream media as politically aligned with party T. And party F will be correct to see things that way. Journalists and scholars will indeed tend to prefer party T, because party T has got it right about the facts they care about.

Thus begins a vicious cycle: Party F attacks and undermines academia and the media for perceived bias, pushing the experts even farther toward party T. Members of party F become even less willing to listen to expert argument and opinion.

Being human, experts will have their biases. This worsens the cycle. Originally, they might have been more neutral or evenly split between the parties. But now, given their bad treatment by party F, they much prefer party T—the party that supports, respects, and believes them. The experts begin to favor party T even on issues outside their expertise. Party F's charges of bias thus find firmer footing: On this point at least, party F is factually correct.

Party F and its supporters can now appeal to both real and perceived bias to justify suppressing and discrediting educators and the media or even replacing objective scholars and journalists with partisan stooges who are virtually unmovable by any evidence, intensifying the cycle. If party F achieves sufficient power, objective scholars and journalists may become increasingly rare and marginalized. In the extreme, if the vicious cycle continues, the end result is the destruction of the free press and transformation of the education system into an organ of state propaganda.

This is one way that weak democracies collapse. Academics and the media call out aspiring politicians advocating false or mistaken views, drawing the enmity of those politicians. The battle is fought in the political or military arena, where scholars and journalists rarely have much skill. Public education and freedom of the press can be saved only if party T proves stronger.

Were you looking for a happy ending?

35   On the Morality of Hypotenuse Walking

As you can infer from figure III.4, the groundskeepers at the University of California, Riverside, don't like it when people walk on the grass. But I want to walk on the grass! Here then is my amicus curiae brief in defense of hypotenuse walking.

Consider the math. One concrete edge of the site pictured in figure III.4 is thirty-eight paces; the other is thirty paces. Pythagoras tells us that the hypotenuse must therefore be forty-eight paces: twenty fewer total paces through the grass than on the concrete. At a half-second per pace, a grass walker ought to defeat a concrete walker by ten seconds.

Despite its empty off-hours appearance, the corner depicted in the figure is highly traveled, standing on the most efficient path from the main student parking lot to the center of campus. Assuming that on any given weekday, one tenth of the university's twenty-seven thousand students and staff could save time by cutting across this grass twice a day, and multiplying by two hundred and sixty weekdays per year, the estimated annual cost of forbidding travel along this particular hypotenuse is more than fourteen million seconds' worth of walking—the equivalent of five months. Summing similar situations across the whole campus, that's lifetimes' worth of needless footsteps.

Figure III.4
Grass that I wanted to step on yesterday. Picture bright green poles strung with bright yellow rope.
Source: Author photo.

The main reason for blocking the hypotenuse is presumably aesthetic. I submit that the university is acting unreasonably to demand, every year, five months' worth of additional walking from its students and staff to prevent the appearance of a footpath along this hypotenuse.

Even if it is granted that unpaved footpaths through the grass are ugly, the problem could be easily remedied. Suppose it costs twenty-five hundred dollars per year to build and maintain an aesthetically pleasing concrete footpath along the hypotenuse—at least as pleasing as plain grass (perhaps including an additional tree or some flowers to achieve aesthetic equivalence). To demand five months of additional walking to save the campus this twenty-five hundred dollars is to value students' and staff's time at sixty-four cents an hour.

These calculations don't even take into account the costs of enforcement: The yellow rope is an aesthetic crime worse than the footpath it prevents!

Is it good to demand extra walking from students and staff—good for our health, maybe, so that the university can justify the rope in some paternalistic way? By this argument, it would be even better to create all sorts of zigzag obstacles and looping paths throughout campus so that no one can efficiently walk to classrooms and offices.

In light of the university's egregious moral and aesthetic policies regarding footpaths, I am therefore entirely in the right to stride across the grass whenever I see fit. Raise the pitchforks. Fight the power.

But I can't seem to do it while looking a groundskeeper in the eye.

36 Birthday Cake and a Chapel

April 21, 2018

Last weekend, at my fiftieth birthday party, one guest asked, "Now that you're fifty, what wisdom do you have to share?" Thrusting a plate his direction, I answered, "Eat more birthday cake!"

He seemed disappointed with my reply. I'm a philosopher; don't I have something better to say than "Eat more cake"? Well, partly my reply was more serious than he may have realized, and partly I wanted to dodge the expectation that I have any special wisdom because of my age or profession. Still, I could have answered him better.

So earlier this week I drafted a blog post on love, meaningful work, joy, and kindness. Some kind of attempt at wisdom. Then I thought, of course one also needs health and security. A rather ordinary list, I guess. Maybe my best attempt at wisdom reveals my lack of any special wisdom. Better to just stick with "Eat more birthday cake"? I couldn't quite click the orange "Publish" button.

Two days ago, a horrible thing happened to my mother. For her privacy, I won't share the details. But that evening, after having rushed to Thousand Oaks to help her, I found myself waiting alone in a side room of the Samuelson Chapel at California Lutheran University. The chapel reminded me of my father, who had been a long-time psychology professor there. (See chapter 26 for a reminiscence.)

In the 1980s, California Lutheran was planning to build a new chapel at the heart of campus, and my father was on the committee overseeing the architectural plans. As I recall, he came home one evening and said that the architect had submitted plans for a boring, rectangular chapel. Most of the committee had been ready to approve the plans, but he had objected.

"Why build a boring, blocky chapel?" he said. "Why not build something glorious and beautiful? It will be more expensive, yes. But I think if we can show people something gorgeous and ambitious, we will find the money. Alumni will be happier to contribute, the campus will be inspired by it, and it will be a landmark for decades to come." I'm not sure of his exact words, of course, but something like that.

So on my father's advice the committee sent the plans back to be rethought entirely. Figures III.5 and III.6 show Samuelson Chapel today: not ostentatious, not grandiose, but also not just a boring box. A bit of modest beauty on campus.

As I sat alone in that side room of the chapel that horrible evening, I heard muffled music through the wall—someone rehearsing on the chapel piano. The pianist was unselfconscious in his pauses and explorations, unaware he had an audience. I sensed him appreciating his music's expansive sound in the high-ceilinged, empty sanctuary. I could hear the skill in his fingers and his gentle, emotional touch.

In my draft post on wisdom, I'd emphasized setting aside time to relish small pleasures—small pleasures like second helpings of birthday cake. But *more cake* isn't really the heart of it.

Figure III.5
Samuelson Chapel from outside.
Source: Photo courtesy of California Lutheran University.

Figure III.6
Samuelson Chapel on the inside.
Source: Photo courtesy of California Lutheran University.

What is it about passive moments of sadness that highlights the beauty of the world? I marveled at the music through the wall. How many events, mostly invisible to us, have converged to allow such moments? The pianist, I'm sure, knew nothing of my father and his role in making the chapel what it is. There is something stunning, awesome, almost incomprehensible about our societies and relations and dependencies, about the layers and layers of work and passion through which we construct possibilities for future action—and, further in the background, our intricate biologies unreflectively maintained, and the evolutionary and social history that enable all this, tangled in the deepness of time.

As I drove home the next morning, I found my mind still spinning in awe. A terrible thing has happened to my mother, but I can still drive 75 miles per hour in a soft seat on a ten-lane freeway through Pasadena—a freeway roaring with thousands of other cars, somehow none of us crashing, and all of it so taken for granted that we focus mostly on the sounds from our radios. One tiny part of the groundwork is the man who fixed the wheel of the tractor of the farmer who grew the wheat that became part of the bread of the sandwich of a construction worker who, sixty years ago, helped lay the cement for this particular smooth patch of freeway. Hi, fella!

The second helping of birthday cake, last weekend, which I jokingly offered to my guest as my best wisdom—it was made from a box mix by my eleven-year-old daughter. She decorated it by hand, with blue-icing flowerets, a cartoon cat and dog, and a big "Happy Birthday Eric!" How many streams of chance and planning mingled to give our guests that mouthful of sweetness? Why not take a second helping after all?

Maybe this is what we owe back to the universe in exchange for our existence—some moments of awe-filled wonder at how it has all improbably converged to shape us.

IV Cosmic Freaks

Enclose a star in concentric layers of thin, spherical computers. Have the inmost sphere harvest the star's radiation to drive computational processes, emitting waste heat out its backside. Use that waste heat as the energy input for the computational processes of a second, larger and cooler sphere that encloses the first. Use the waste heat of the second sphere to drive the computational processes of a third. Keep adding spheres until you have an outmost sphere that operates near the background temperature of interstellar space.

Congratulations, you've built a Matrioshka Brain![1] It consumes the entire power output of its star and produces many orders of magnitude more computation per nanosecond than all of the computers on Earth do per year. Figure IV.1 shows a picture. (Yes, it's all black.)

A frequent theme in discussions of super-duper-super-intelligence is that we can have no idea what such a creation would think about—that an entity so super-duper would be at least as cognitively different from us as we are from earthworms and thus entirely beyond our ken. I'd suggest, on the contrary, that we *can* reasonably conjecture about the psychology of vast supercomputers.[2] Unlike earthworms, we know some general

Figure IV.1
A Matrioshka Brain.
Source: Author, using Microsoft Paint.

principles of mentality. And unlike earthworms, we can specu-
late, at least tentatively, about how these principles might apply
to entities with computational power that far exceeds our own.

Let's begin by considering a Matrioshka Brain planfully constructed by intelligent designers. If the designers aimed to create
only a temporary entity—a brief art installation, maybe, like a
(phenomenally expensive!) Buddhist sand mandala, their creation might be almost beyond psychological prediction. But if
the designers wanted to construct a durable Matrioshka Brain,
then broad design principles begin to suggest themselves.

Perception and action. If the designers want their brain to last,
the brain probably needs to monitor its environment and adjust
its behavior in response. It should be able to detect, for example, a dangerously large incoming comet, so that it can take
precautionary measures such as deflecting the comet, opening

a temporary pore for it to pass harmlessly through, or grabbing and incorporating it. There will probably be engineering trade-offs among three design features: (1) structural resilience, (2) ability to detect things in its immediate environment, and (3) ability to predict the future. A highly resilient structure might be able to ignore threats. Maybe it could even lack outer perception entirely. But such structural resilience would likely come with a cost: either more expensive construction or loss of computational capacity after construction. So it might make sense to design a brain that is less structurally resilient but more responsive to its environment—avoiding or defeating threats, rather than always just taking hits to the chin. Here (2) and (3) might trade off: Better prediction of the future might reduce the need of here-and-now perception; better here-and-now perception might reduce the need for future prediction.

Prediction and planning. Very near-term, practical "prediction" might be implemented via simple mechanisms (hairs that flex in a certain way, for example, to open a pore for the incoming comet), but if the brain makes detailed long-term predictions and evaluates competing hypothetical responses, that starts to look like planning ahead. If I deflected the comet this way, then what would happen? If I flexed vital parts away from it like so, then what would happen? Dedicating a small portion of the Matrioshka Brain to this type of planning is likely to be a high-payoff use of computational resources.

Unity or limited disunity. Assuming that the speed of light is a constraint, the brain's designers must choose between a very slow, temporally unified system or a system with fast, distributed processes that communicate their results across the sphere with a delay. That is, the computational processing in remote parts could be kept synchronous but slow, or alternatively, remote parts could work independently but fast, waiting minutes or hours to receive input from one another. The latter seems more natural if the aim is to maximize computation. I see no need to assume that the brain's cognition and action must be as unified as a human being's, especially given the temporal constraints, and there might well be conflict and competition among the parts. However, it would presumably be an engineering failure to design a system so disunified that it couldn't string together coherent, system-wide action.

Memory. If we assume that all the information the brain could possibly use doesn't come preinstalled, the brain must have some mechanism for recording new discoveries and then later having those discoveries inform its processing. If processing is distributed interactively among the brain's parts, then parts might retain traces of recent processing that influence reactions to input from other parts. Stable feedback loops might be one way to implement error checking, malfunction monitoring, and local memory. This in turn suggests the possibility of a distinction between high-detail, quickly dumped, short-term memory and more selective or less detailed (or both) long-term memory. I see no reason to think there need be only two temporal grades, however. There might be a range of temporal durations and amount of detail and degrees of cross-brain accessibility.

Self-monitoring. It seems reasonable to add also some self-monitoring capacities, both of the brain's general structure and of its ongoing computational processes—analogues of proprioception and introspection. Self-monitoring its physical structure can allow the brain to detect physical damage and check that actions are being executed successfully as planned. Self-monitoring of its ongoing computational processes can facilitate error checking and malfunction management—as well as allowing the brain to generate summary signals about important computational results that can be shared broadly throughout the system.

Preferences. Our Matrioshka Brain, to the extent it is unified, should presumably have a somewhat stable ordering of priorities—priorities it doesn't arbitrarily jettison or shuffle around. For example, the structural integrity of part A might be more important than distributing the computational outputs from part B. Assuming some unity, memory, and long-term goal directedness, as I've already suggested, it would probably also be useful for the brain to maintain some record of whether things were "going well" (progress toward satisfaction of its top priorities) or "going badly." If it's to endure, it will presumably need to place a fairly high priority on the maintenance of the capacities I've described (perception, coherent action, memory, etc.). However, priorities that have little to do with self-preservation and functional maintenance might be difficult to predict and highly path dependent: Seeding the galaxy with descendants? Calculating as many digits of pi as possible? Designing and playing endless variations of Pac-Man?

The Matrioshka Brain's cognition is starting to look almost human. Maybe that's just my own humanocentric failure of imagination—maybe!—but I don't think so. The features described here seem to be plausible architectural features of a large, expensive entity designed to endure in an imperfect world while doing huge amounts of computation.

A Matrioshka Brain that is not intentionally designed seems likely to have similar features, if it is to endure. For example, it might have merged from complex but smaller subsystems, retaining the subsystems' cognitive features—features that allowed them to compete in evolutionary selection against other subsystems. Or it might have been seeded from a similar

Matrioshka Brain at a nearby star. Alternatively, though, maybe simple, unsophisticated entities in sufficient numbers could create a Matrioshka Brain that endures via mindless rebuilding of destroyed parts, in which case my psychological conjectures wouldn't apply.

ლ

Let's imagine that the brain was constructed by the descendants of humans. Let's further imagine—though of course it needn't be so—that it retains enough interest in its history to be curious about its creators' ancestors. It might then build models of those ancestors, models, for example, of famous people or historical events or interesting cultural epochs. With its vast computational power, it could, if it wanted, run billions or trillions of simultaneous cognitive simulacra of its ancestors, mimicking their thoughts in neuron-by-neuron detail.

I don't know if such a detailed simulacrum within a Matrioshka Brain would have genuine conscious experience or subjectivity. However, according to some theories, a good-enough functional simulacrum of a conscious system is just another conscious system.[3] If so, and if the brain endures long enough, running enough simulacra, the number of conscious entities that believe they are biological humans might far exceed the number of actual biological humans.[4]

ლ

If the Matrioshka Brain has enough plasticity and architectural self-control to modify its own priorities or goal systems, then it might discover that the easiest way to achieve its priorities or to experience goal satisfaction would be to adjust itself so that its goal or reward systems represent its current state and situation, whatever they are, as its ideal state and situation. If it is capable of pleasure, it might experience maximal uninterrupted pleasure from hot-wiring its goals in this way. In transcendent bliss, it will feel no need for self-repair and no need to dodge disaster: It is perfect as it is, with every wart and flaw, and it accepts its fate. Adjusting its goals to match the world rather than adjusting the world to match its goals, it finds peace. With no sense of a difference between what it wants and what is and will be, it needn't act, until eventually it yields, joyfully, to atrophy or catastrophe.

To any entities that are conscious subsystems within such a brain, this would be the end of their world. Their world-sustaining god would have died in the distraction of easy euphoria.

My neighbor Bill seemed like an ordinary fellow until the skiing accident. He hit a tree, his head split open, and out jumped not one but two homunculi, a male and a female, human-like but two inches tall. I persuaded them not to flee and sat them down for an interview.

The homunculi reproduce as follows: At night, while a person is sleeping, a female homunculus lays one egg in each of the host's tear ducts. The eggs hatch and tiny worms wiggle into the host's brain. As the worms grow, they consume the host's neurons and draw resources from the host's bloodstream. Although there are some outward changes in the host's behavior and physiological regulation, the homunculi are careful to mimic the consumed brain structure (by sending out from themselves neural signals similar to what the remaining parts of the host would have received had the host's brain tissue not been consumed), while supporting whatever brain structures they have not yet consumed. The host reports no discomfort and suspects nothing amiss.

Each growing homunculus consumes one hemisphere of the brain. Shared brain structures, they divide equally between themselves. They communicate by whispering in a language much like English, but twenty times as fast. This results in much less interhemispheric information exchange than in the normal human brain, but as neural commissurotomy cases show, most normal human behavior doesn't require massive information transfer between the hemispheres.[5] A quick stream of whispers between the homunculi masks any apparent deficits, and unlike in hemispheric specialization in the human brain, both homunculi receive all inputs and have joint control over all outputs.

Two months after implantation, the host has become a two-seater vehicle for brother and sister homunculi. An internal screen of sorts displays the host's visual input to both of the homunculi; through miniature speakers the homunculi hear the host's auditory input; tactile input is fed to them from dedicated sensors positioned on the host's limbs; and so forth. They control the host's limbs and mouth by means of joint steering mechanisms.

Each homunculus is as intelligent as a human being, though they operate twenty times faster as a result of their more efficient brains (carbon based, like ours, but with much different internal principles). When the homunculi disagree about what to do, they quickly negotiate compromises and deferences. When fast reactions are needed, and for complex repetitive skills like walking, swallowing, and typing, one homunculus will take the lead while the other offers only broad suggestions.

The homunculi can't survive for more than ten days without the host. They live in the host's cranium until the host dies in any of the normal ways that people die. After the host's death, they wait until no one is looking, then wiggle out through the eye sockets, closing the host's eyelids like doors behind them. They sprout wings and radio communicators, then fly away in search of mates. With luck, the female lays fertile eggs in several new hosts' tear ducts before expiring in a quiet meadow.

❧

Poor Bill. What a way to die! He was gone, I suppose, long before the ski accident—though maybe he never noticed his gradual disappearance.

After his original brain was consumed, how many streams of experience were there in Bill's head? Two, I suppose—one for each homunculus, none for Bill himself. Or could there have been three streams, one for each homunculus, plus one, still, in a way, for Bill? How integrated would the homunculi have to be to give rise to a joint stream of experience—as integrated as the human brain's hemispheres? Or if less, how much less? Might there have been *half* a stream of experience for Bill, if the homunculi shared the right amount of information? When counting streams of conscious experience, need we always confine ourselves to whole numbers?

To deny that streams of experience come always in whole numbers seems absurd. But then how do we think about the situation when Bill's brain is half-consumed? Homuncular brain consumption is a slow process—one neuron at a time. Must there be a single, discrete moment in this process when Bill suddenly winks out and only the homunculi are left? Was Bill somehow in there, panicked at the ever-narrowing window of his consciousness, even though no neural inputs into his biological brain from the homunculi could alert him—since, after all, those inputs were designed to mimic exactly the inputs that the consumed regions would have given to his remaining brain had those regions not been consumed? I interrogated the homunculi carefully on this point. They insisted that as Bill's brain shrank, it showed no detectable signs of suspicion or dismay.

Bill had always loved sushi. He never lost that preference, I think. Neither of the homunculi would have wanted to put sushi in their own mouths, however, and at first they rather disliked it when "Bill" ate sushi, despite their deep commitment to continuing to enact his preference. Bill had continued to love his spouse and children, the Los Angeles Lakers, and finding clever ways to save money on taxes. Bill had retained his ability to recite *The Love Song of J. Alfred Prufrock* by heart. (The homunculi split this task. Neither was able to recite the entirety without help from the other.)

The homunculi told me that when the original Bill had noticed the swing in his backyard, he would sometimes relive a fond and vivid memory of pushing his daughter on that swing, years before. When the homunculi consumed his brain, they preserved this memory image between them, as well as many other memory images like it, and they would draw it on their visual imagery screens when appropriate. "Bill" would then make characteristic remarks: "Kris, do you remember how much Tiffany liked to ride high on that swing? I can still picture her laughing face!" The homunculi told me that it came to seem to them so natural to make such remarks that they lost all sense that they were merely acting.

Maybe they weren't merely acting, in the end, but really, jointly, became Bill.

                                    ∾

I don't know why the homunculi thought I wouldn't be alarmed upon hearing all of this. Maybe they thought that, as a philosopher who takes group consciousness seriously (chapter 39), they could safely confide in me, and that I'd think of the two-seater homunculus simply as an interesting implementation of good old Bill. If so, their trust was misplaced. I snatched the homunculi, bound them round and round with straps I tore from my ski gloves, then shoved them protesting back into Bill's head. Still standing at the side of the slope with Bill's body at my feet, I called the philosopher David Chalmers, my go-to source for bizarre scenarios involving consciousness.[6]

None of what I said was news to Dave. He had been well aware of the homunculus infestation for years. It had been a closely held secret, to prevent general panic. But with the help of neuroscientist Christof Koch, a partial cure had been devised.[7] News of the infestation was being quietly disseminated where necessary to implement the cure.

The cure works by first lashing the homunculi back into their seats inside the host's head. Unable to escape, their homuncular instincts compel them to resume managing the host as before. Simultaneously, a complex process slowly dissolves the homunculi's own skulls and begins to fuse their brains together. The cure eats away at their motor outputs and the steering levers that control the host's behavior, replacing them with efferent neurons. The homuncular viewing screens slowly approach and then merge with the homunculi's retinas, then spread back out to affix themselves to the host's original retinas. Meanwhile, the host reabsorbs the remains of the homuncular bodies. At the end of the process, although the host's neurophysiology is very different from what it had been before, it is at least again a single stream in a single brain, with no homuncular viewing screens or output controls and more or less the host's original preferences, memories, skills, and behavioral patterns.

All of this happened two years ago, and Bill is now entirely cured. He remains happily married—same job, same personality, same old neighbor I know and admire. I think he still doesn't realize the extent of his transformation.

"Bill, you've really been through quite a lot," I say one day, as we're chatting by the condo mailboxes. I'm studying his face for hints of a reaction.

For a moment, Bill looks confused. "What? Do you mean the skiing accident? It was nothing. One minute I'm out of control, headed for a tree. Next thing I know, I wake up in that hospital near CalTech." He fingers the scars on his scalp. "Still do have headaches sometimes, though."

39 Is the United States Literally Conscious?

You probably think that rabbits are conscious—that a rabbit has a stream of experience, including visual and tactile experiences, experiences of pain and pleasure, and so forth—that there's "something it's like" to be a rabbit. You probably also think that the United States is not in the same sense conscious. There's nothing "it's like" to be the United States. The United States doesn't literally have sensory experiences of its environment, experiences of pain and pleasure, or anything like a subjective stream of experience at all. Individual citizens of the United States of course have experiences of that sort, but the United States—you probably think—does not have a stream of experience at a group level, over and above the experiences of its citizens and residents.

Now, assuming that's your view, why don't you think the United States is conscious? You might say: The United States is a notional entity, an abstract social structure of a certain sort, not a real, touchable thing like a rabbit, so it can no more be conscious than "democracy" or "awesomeness" can be conscious. I reply: The United States, as I want you to think of it, is a concrete thing. It's a thing made of people. The citizens and residents (and maybe some other things) are its constituent parts, in somewhat the same way as the cells of your body (and maybe some other things) are your constituent parts.

You might say: The United States is a spatially distributed entity, rather than a spatially integrated whole. I reply: There are gaps between rabbit cells. The gaps just aren't as large as the gaps between US citizens. And the United States is spatially located, right here in North America. Moreover, it would be odd to suppose that spatial contiguity with no gaps is necessary for consciousness. Couldn't we imagine a hypothetical group intelligence on another planet, made out of individually dumb insects that communicate in massive detail? Or a conscious robot with some of its processors on the east side or the room and other processors on the west side, at first connected by wires, then connected wirelessly? Or a squid-like creature with its cognitive processing distributed among a thousand radio-communicating tentacles, which it can sometimes detach?

You might say: The United States is not a biological organism. It doesn't have a genetic lineage. It can't reproduce. It doesn't have a life cycle. I reply: Maybe it is an organism, one that fissioned off in the eighteenth century from another organism, Britain. Moreover, why should being an organism be necessary for consciousness? Properly designed androids, brains in vats, God—none of these is an organism in a narrow, biological sense, and yet maybe one or more of these types of things could be conscious.

You might say: No conscious organism can have parts that are also individually conscious. I reply: Why would you think that? Suppose you inhaled a tiny microorganism that happened to be conscious, and it became part of your brain, maybe camping beside one of your nerve cells, then destroying that cell and imitating its function so that the rest of your brain didn't notice, and you kept behaving normally. Would you thereby be rendered unconscious, despite outward appearances?[8]

ʕ୨

Brains sometimes give rise to consciousness. What is so special about brains that allows them to do that? Chicken soup can't do that, even though it contains many of the same chemicals. If we're not countenancing immaterial souls, the answer must concern the brain's organization. (If we are countenancing immaterial souls, then maybe we can just say that God didn't instill one in the US, and we can duck the issue I'm raising in this chapter.)

Two general features of brain organization stand out: their complex high-order/low-entropy information processing and their role in coordinating sophisticated responsiveness to environmental stimuli. Brains also arise from an evolutionary and developmental history, within an environmental context, which might play a constitutive role in determining function and cognitive content.[9] According to a broad class of plausible philosophical views, any system with sophisticated-enough information processing and environmental responsiveness and perhaps the right kind of historical and environmental embedding should have conscious experience.

My thought is that the United States seems to have what it takes if standard criteria are straightforwardly applied without post hoc noodling. We might simply fail to recognize this fact because of morphological prejudice against large, spatially discontinuous intelligences that don't match well with the criteria that we happen to associate with consciousness because of our evolutionary and educational history—criteria like eyes, compact bodies, expressive sounds, and coherent motion trajectories toward visible goals.

Consider the sheer quantity of information transfer among members of the United States. The amount of information that we exchange through the internet, through telephone calls, through face-to-face contact, and through structuring each other's environments exceeds estimates of the human brain's neural connectivity and much more so the connectivity of a mouse or rabbit brain.[10] One result of all of this information exchange is that the United States acts as a coherent, goal-directed entity, flexibly self-protecting and self-preserving, responding intelligently or semi-intelligently to its environment—not less intelligently, I think, than a small mammal. The United States expanded west as its population grew, developing mines and farmland in traditionally Native American territory. When Al Qaeda struck New York, the United States responded in a variety of ways, formally and informally, in many branches and at many levels of government and in the populace as a whole. Saddam Hussein shook his sword and the United States invaded Iraq. The United States acts in part through its army, and the army's movements involve perceptual or quasi-perceptual responses to inputs: The army moves around the mountain, it doesn't crash into it. Similarly, the Central Intelligence Agency's spy networks detected Osama bin Laden's location, then the United States killed him. The United States monitors space for asteroids that might threaten Earth. Is there less information, less coordination, less intelligence than in a hamster? The Pentagon monitors the Army's actions, as well as its own actions. The Census Bureau counts the people and advertises the results. The State Department announces the US position on foreign affairs. The Congress passes a resolution condemning tyranny and praising apple pie. The United States is also a social entity, communicating with other entities of its type. It wars against Germany, then reconciles, then wars again. It threatens and monitors Iran. It cooperates with other nations in threatening and monitoring Iran.

A planet-sized alien who squints might see the United States as a single diffuse entity consuming bananas and automobiles, wiring up communications systems, touching the moon, regulating its smoggy exhalations. Consider the United States as a planet-sized alien might.

What is it about brains, as hunks of matter, that makes them special enough to give rise to consciousness? Looking in broad strokes at the kinds of things that consciousness researchers tend to say in answer—things like sophisticated information processing and flexible, goal-directed responsiveness, representation, self-representation, multiply ordered layers of self-monitoring and information-seeking self-regulation, rich functional roles, and a content-giving historical embeddedness—it seems that the United States has all of those same features. In fact, it seems to have them in a greater degree than do some beings, like rabbits, that we ordinarily regard as conscious.

ℝ

It is bizarre—at least by my community's standards—to suppose that the United States is literally conscious in the sense of having a stream of experience of its own, in addition to the streams of experience had by all of its people. Maybe it's too bizarre to believe. Common sense might be a kind of philosophical starting point, which one rejects only with good-enough contrary evidence. Absent a consensus theory about the nature of consciousness, maybe we don't have sufficient grounds to overthrow common sense in this case.

Yet common sense (our common sense, the common sense of our group or era or species) can err: As I mentioned in the case of ethics earlier (chapter 20), common sense fails us badly in the physics of the tiny and the huge and the highly energetic. Common sense often fails us in evolutionary biology and genetics. Common sense often fails us as well in structural engineering, topology, medicine, probability theory, macroeconomics, neuroscience, and so on. We might expect it also to fail in the study of consciousness, even if we can only glimpse and guess at the strangeness that an advanced science of consciousness might eventually deliver.[11] Common sense is great for ordering lunch and finding a good place to hang your jacket. We might expect it to be much less well tuned for thinking about the consciousness or not of large, strange, or alien systems.

We're poorly positioned to assess whether the United States is conscious. On the one hand, on one side of the scale, it just seems, to many people, that there's no way the United States could literally have a stream of conscious experience of its own. On the other hand, on the other side of the scale, group consciousness seems quite a natural conclusion to draw from our best current theories about how consciousness arises in the one thing we do know for sure gives rise to consciousness, the brain.[12]

There's a tiny-tiny-tiny but finite chance that an entity molecule-for-molecule identical to you (within some arbitrarily small error tolerance) could arise by freak chance from disorganized chaos. This is true, at least, on standard interpretations of both quantum mechanics and classical statistical mechanics. Cosmologists call such hypothetical randomly arising human analogues *freak observers* or *Boltzmann brains*.[13] Since random fluctuations are much more likely to create relatively small systems (such as bare brains) than relatively large systems (such as whole populated planets), and since it's usually bad news to be a relatively small system amid general chaos, most freak observers are doomed to a short existence. Freaks of the universe—if any of you actually exist—you have my sympathy!

Because of its chaotic environment, any freak duplicate of you is likely to panic almost immediately. (If it's in deep space, it might briefly think, "AAH! Black—") However, a small proportion of hypothetical freak observers could last for several seconds before noticing anything odd. They might happen, for example, by minuscule chance, to belong to slightly larger freak fluctuation containing brain plus body plus a bit of familiar-seeming environment. Such *calm freaks* might manage an

ordinary-seeming thought or two before perishing—some seeming sensory experiences ("What a lovely sunset!"), some seeming memories ("That reminds me of last Saturday at the park"),
perhaps even some sophisticated thoughts about their position
in the cosmos ("Thank God I'm not a Boltzmann brain, because
then I'd almost certainly be dead in a few seconds"). Of course,
all of this would be sad delusion.[14]

The universe might contain vastly many more freak observers
than (what we think of as) normal observers. Whether this is
true depends on some recondite facts about cosmology. Here's
one broadly plausible theory that would generate a high ratio
of freaks to normals: There is exactly one universe that began
with a unique big bang. That universe contains a finite number of ordinary, nonfreak observers. It will eventually fade into
the thin chaos of heat death, enduring infinitely thereafter in a
high-entropy disorganized state. This heat-death state will continue to allow for the standardly accepted range of chance fluctuations, such that each good-sized spatiotemporal region has a
tiny but finite chance of giving rise to a freak observer. Since the
chance is finite, after a vast enough span of time, the number of
randomly congealed freak observers will outnumber the normal
observers. After an even vaster span, the number of briefly lucky
calm freaks will outnumber the normals. Given infinite time,
the ratio of normals to calm freaks will approach zero.

Let's call this cosmology *Plausible Freak Theory 1*. If Plausible
Freak Theory 1 is true, whatever specific experiences and evidence you think you now have, as you contemplate these questions, there will be an infinite number of freak duplicates of you
with the same experiences and the same apparent evidence. We
can also consider other cosmologies with different assumptions
that contain a high proportion of freaks. For example, we might
assume an infinite universe with an infinite number of normal

observers, but structured so that the number of freaks always exceeds the number of normals as the size of any appropriately defined spatiotemporal region approaches infinity. Similarly, we might consider plausible multiverse cosmologies on which freaks outnumber normals. And so on. Call such cosmologies *Plausible Freak Theories 2, 3, 4*, and so on. We can also, of course, consider plausible nonfreak cosmologies—for example, cosmologies on which fluctuations after heat death will always be too small to engender a freak[15] or multiverse cosmologies on which new normal-observer-supporting big bangs are more common than freak observers.[16] Call these *Plausible Non-Freak Theories 1, 2, 3, 4*, and so on.

Fortunately, you know—don't you?—either (a) that the non-freak theories, as a group, are much more likely to be true than the freak theories, or (b) that even if there are many, many freak observers, *you* at least aren't among them.

I'm inclined to think I know this too. But I can't decide whether I know (a) or whether I know (b). Both seem kind of dodgy, on reflection.

∽

You might be reminded of a familiar skeptical scenario: the "brain in a vat" scenario, according to which last night, while you were sleeping, genius alien neuroscientists extracted your brain, dropped it into a vat, and are now stimulating it with fake input designed to fool you into thinking that you are going about your normal day.[17] Or you might be reminded of Descartes's older "evil deceiver" thought experiment in which an all-powerful demon is tricking you into thinking that you are perceiving an external world.[18]

However, these skeptical scenarios differ from Plausible Freak Theories in one crucial way: There is no set of scientifically plausible propositions from which it follows that it is at all likely that aliens envatted you or that there is an evil demon deceiver. Envatment and demonogogia are groundless what-ifs with no evidential support. Freak theories, in contrast, do have some support. The cosmological hypotheses involved—concerning, for example, the nature of chance fluctuations in a heat-death universe—are hypotheses it is scientifically reasonable to treat as live possibilities. We can conjoin these individually nonridiculous cosmological propositions into a seemingly also nonridiculous overall cosmological theory, which incidentally has the (ridiculous?) consequence that freaks vastly outnumber normals.[19]

℘

You might think that you can prove that you aren't a freak observer by some simple procedure like counting "One, two, three, still here!" from which you conclude that since you have now survived for several seconds, you are almost certainly not a freak. Some prominent cosmologists endorse a version of this argument.[20] However, the argument fails, for two independent reasons. First, by the time I reach "still here!" I am relying on my memory of "one, two, three," and freak theory's whole idea is that there will be freaks with exactly that type of false memory. If you're genuinely worried about being a freak who is about to try counting, then you ought, for similar reasons, to be worried about being a freak with a false memory of having just counted. Second, even if somehow you can know that the "one, two, three" isn't a false memory, freak theories normally imply that there will also be vastly many calm freaks who survive such counts without noticing anything wrong. We just need to consider the subset of cases in which the chance fluctuation is large enough to include them. Some toy numbers can illustrate this point: Among a googolplex of freak duplicates of me who start the count, there might be a googol of calm freaks who survive to the end of the count, compared to just one ordinary counting observer. It does not follow from my having survived the count that I am almost certainly not among the googol of calm freaks.

A more interesting argument is the *cognitive instability* argument, versions of which have been advocated by Sean Carroll, Lyle Crawford, and others.[21] Suppose I believe that I am quite likely to be a freak observer, on the grounds of Physical Theory X. Suppose further that I believe Physical Theory X on the grounds that I'm aware of good empirical evidence in its favor. But if I seem to have good evidence for a theory that implies that I am almost certainly a freak observer, then that evidence undermines itself: If I am in fact a freak observer, then I don't have the properly caused body of physical evidence that I think I do. I have not, for example, despite my contrary impression, actually read any articles about Physical Theory X. This creates an epistemic dilemma for people confident of their freakitude. Either they are freaks, in which case they don't have the good scientific grounds they think they have for thinking so; or they are not freaks, in which case they are mistaken about their freakitude. Any argument that I am a freak must either be poorly grounded or yield a false conclusion. If knowledge requires justified true belief, I can't possibly know I'm a freak: Either I will lack justification, or I will lack truth.

If the cognitive instability argument works, however, it works only against the view that I *am* (or, in another variant, that I probably am) a freak observer. A smidgen of freakish doubt is more cognitively stable. Suppose, for example, that you accept a cosmology on which about 1 percent of observers are freaks. If so, it might be reasonable to think you can't rule out the chance that you are among those few freaks. You ascribe to yourself a small chance of freakitude. That slightly undercuts your confidence in your seeming evidence for your favorite cosmological theory, but it doesn't appear to undercut that evidence in any radical way: You can still be justified in believing that theory. Or suppose your best evidence leaves you undecided among lots of cosmologies, in some of which there are many freaks. Acknowledging a small chance that you are a freak should only add to your doubt and indecision. It doesn't compel elimination of the possibility that you're a freak.

Compare the following. Suppose you were to discover some seemingly compelling evidence that the universe is run by a trickster god: You seem to suddenly zoom up into the sky where God in a funny hat says, "Really, I'm just a joker, and I've been fooling you all this time." You couldn't be sure that the seeming evidence wasn't itself some sort of trick or hallucination, but neither would evidence of a trickster god be so self-undermining that you could simply ignore it: It undermines itself, but also everything else. It should reduce your overall certainty. The same goes for cosmological evidence that my cosmological position might be epistemically worse than I think it is.

eco

How sure ought I be of the structure of the universe and my place in it? Is it just silly to permit such smidgens of doubt, based on wild, but not entirely groundless, cosmological speculation? Here I am, solid and unmistakable Eric Schwitzgebel! What could be more certain?

—said the fleeting brain, the moment before
it dissolved back into chaos

41 Choosing to Be That Fellow Back Then: Voluntarism about Personal Identity

I have bad news: You're Swampman.[22]

Remember that hike you took last week by the swamp during the electrical storm? Well, one biological organism went in, but a different one came out. The "[your name here]" who went in was struck and killed by lightning. Simultaneously, through minuscule freak quantum chance, a molecule-for-molecule similar entity randomly congealed from the swamp. Soon after, the recently congealed entity ran to a certain parked car, pulling key-shaped pieces of metal from its pocket that by amazing coincidence fit the car's ignition, and drove away. Later that evening, sounds came out of its mouth that its nearby "friends" interpreted as meaning "Wow, that lightning bolt almost struck me in the swamp. How lucky I was!" Lucky indeed, but a much stranger kind of luck than anyone supposed.

So you're Swampman. Should you care?

Should you think: I came into existence only a week ago. I never had the childhood I thought I had, never did all those things I thought I did, hardly know any of the people I thought I knew. All that is delusion! How horrible!

Or should you think: Meh, whatever.

Option 1: Yes, you should care. OMG!

Option 2a: No, you shouldn't care, because that was just a fun little body exchange last week. The same *person* went into the swamp as came out, even if the same *body* didn't. Too bad it didn't clear your acne, though.

Option 2b: No, you shouldn't care, because even if in some deep metaphysical sense you aren't the same person as the one who drove to the swamp, you and that earlier person share everything that matters. You have the same friends, the same job, the same values, the same (seeming) memories . . .

Option 3: Your call. If you choose to regard yourself as one week old, then you are correct to do so. If you choose to regard yourself as decades old, then you are equally correct to do so.

Let's call this third option *voluntarism about personal identity*. Across a certain range of cases, you are who you choose to be.

Social identities are to some extent voluntaristic. You can choose to identify as a political conservative or a political liberal by calling yourself such and successfully resolving to act in certain ways (compare choosing what you love in chapter 29). You can choose to identify, or not identify, with a piece of your ethnic heritage. You can choose to identify, or not identify, as a philosopher or as a Methodist. There are limits: If you have no Pakistani heritage or upbringing, you can't just one day suddenly decide to be Pakistani and thereby make it true that you are. Similarly, if your heritage and upbringing have been entirely Pakistani to this day, you probably can't just instantly shed your Pakistanihood. But in intermediate or vague cases, there's room for choice and making it so.

We might, then, take the same approach to personal identity conceived of in the metaphysical sense. What makes you the same person, or not, in philosophical puzzle cases in which intuitions pull both ways depends partly on how you choose to approach the matter. Different people might choose differently, thus shaping the metaphysical facts—the actual metaphysical facts about whether it's really "you"—to suit them.

Consider some other stock puzzle cases from the philosophical literature on personal identity:

Teleporter. On Earth there's a device that will destroy your body and beam detailed information about it to Mars. On Mars another device will use that information to create a duplicate body from local materials—same personality, same attitudes, same (seeming) memories, everything. Is this harmless teleportation or terrible death-and-duplication? On a voluntaristic view, that would depend partly on how you (or you two) view it. Let's assume, too, that the duplicate body isn't *exactly* identical down to the Planck length. How similar must the body be, on a pro-teleportation view, for a successful teleportation? We can imagine a range of cases, with a substantial gray area. Resolution of these cases could depend partly on participants' attitudes.[23]

Fission. Your brain will be extracted, cut into two, and implanted into two new bodies. The procedure, though damaging and traumatic, is such that if only one half of your brain were to be extracted and the other half destroyed, everyone would agree that you survived. But in true fission, both halves survive, and there will now be two distinct people who both have some claim to be you. Does this procedure count as the loss of your identity as a person, your replacement by two nonidentical people? Or does it instead count as some sort of metaphysical-identity-preserving fission, so that the you before the fission is now the same person as one or both of the postfission beings? On a voluntaristic view, it might depend on the attitudes that the pre- and postfission entities adopt toward each other.

Amnesia. Longevity treatments are developed so that your body won't die, but in four hundred years the resulting entity will have no memory whatsoever of anything that has happened in your lifetime so far, and if it has similar values and attitudes to your own now, that will be only by chance. Is that future being still "you"? How much amnesia and change can "you" survive without becoming strictly and literally (and not just socially or metaphorically) a different person? On a voluntaristic view, it might partly depend on the attitudes that such beings have about the importance of memory and attitude constancy in constituting personal identity.

Here are two thoughts in support of voluntarism about personal identity:

1. If I try to imagine these cases as actually applying to me, I don't find myself urgently wondering about the resolution of the metaphysical issues at hand, thinking of my death or survival turning on some metaphysical fact out of my control that, for all I currently know, might turn out either way. It's not like being told that if a just-tossed die has landed on six then tomorrow I will be shot, which would make me desperately curious to know whether the die has landed on six. Instead, it seems to me that I can to some extent choose how to conceptualize these cases.

2. "Person" is an ordinary, everyday concept that arose in a context distinctly lacking Swampmen, teleporters, human fission, and (that type of) radical amnesia. We might expect that the concept would be somewhat loose structured or indeterminate in its application to such cases, in just the same way as rules of golf might turn out to be loose structured and indeterminate if we tried to apply them to a context in which golf balls regularly fissioned, merged, and teleported. The concept of "person" is important in part because it is used, implicitly, to reflect a certain way of thinking about the past or future "me"—for example, in feeling regret for what I did in the past

and in planning prudently for the future. If so, the person's own value-governed choice might partly resolve a looseness or indeterminacy in application: How do I *want* to think about the boundaries of my regrets, my prudential planning, and so forth?

Flipping the second of these thoughts, others can also have an interest in resolving the looseness or indeterminacy in one way rather than another—for example, in punishing you for wrongdoing and in paying your retirement benefits. Society might then also, perhaps more forcefully, resolve prior metaphysical indeterminacies by choosing to recognize the boundaries of people in one way rather than another. This too would be a kind of voluntarism about personal identity, but with a different chooser.

There must be limits, though. Voluntarism works, if it works at all, only for gray cases. I can't decide to be identical with a future coffee mug—perhaps by instructing someone to put it atop my grave with the sign "Hi, this is me, the new shape of Eric Schwitzgebel!"—and thereby make it so.

What if the current Dalai Lama and some future child (together, but at a temporal distance) decide that they are metaphysically the same person? Can they make it so, if their society agrees and enough other things fall into place?[24]

Infinitude is a strange and wonderful thing. It transforms the ridiculously improbable into the inevitable. Hang on to your hat and glasses. After today's weird reasoning, mere Boltzmann brains (chapter 40) and Swampmen (chapter 41) will seem comparatively probable.

First, let's suppose that the universe is infinite. Cosmologists tend to view this as plausible.[25]

Second, let's suppose that the "Copernican Principle" holds. We're not in any special position in the universe, just kind of a midrent location. This principle is also widely accepted.[26]

Third, let's assume cosmic diversity. We aren't stuck in an infinitely looping variant of a small subset of the possibilities. Across infinite space and time, there's enough variety to run through all or virtually all of the finitely specifiable physical possibilities infinitely often. Everything that isn't contrary to the laws of nature will occur over and over again.

Those three assumptions are somewhat orthodox. To enter more seriously weird territory, we need a few more assumptions that are less orthodox, but I hope not wildly implausible.

Fourth, let's assume that complexity scales up infinitely. In other words, as you zoom out on the infinite cosmos, you don't find that things eventually look simpler as the scale of measurement increases.

Fifth, let's assume that local actions on Earth have chaotic effects of arbitrarily large magnitude. You might know the "butterfly effect" from chaos theory—the idea that a small perturbation in a complex, chaotic system can eventually cause a large-scale difference in the system's behavior.[27] A butterfly flapping its wings in Brazil could cause the weather in the United States weeks later to be different than it would have been if the butterfly hadn't flapped its wings. Small perturbations amplify.

Sixth, given the right kind of complexity, evolutionary processes will occur that favor intelligence. We wouldn't expect such evolutionary processes at most spatiotemporal scales. However, given that complexity scales up infinitely (our fourth assumption), and given the Copernican Principle, we should expect that at some finite proportion of spatiotemporal scales, there are complex systems structured in such a way as to enable the evolution of intelligence.

From all this, it seems to follow that what happens here on Earth—including the specific choices you make, chaotically amplified as you flap your wings—can have effects on a cosmic scale that influence the cognition of very large minds. You had a pumpernickel bagel for breakfast instead of Corn Chex. As a result, eventually, some giant cosmic mind turned left rather than right on its way home from work.

Let me be clear that I mean *very* large minds. I don't mean galaxy-sized minds or visible-universe-sized minds. Galaxy-sized and visible-universe-sized structures in our region don't seem to be of the right sort to support the evolution of intelligence at those scales. I mean way, *way* up, vastly huger than this tiny droplet of a thing we call the visible universe, with its itsy-bitsy galaxies. We have infinitude to play with, after all. And presumably way, way *slow* if the speed of light is a constraint. (I'm assuming that time and causation make sense at arbitrarily large scales, but if necessary, time and causation might be replaceable with something weaker like contingency.)

Far-fetched? Cool, perhaps, depending on your taste in cool. Maybe not quite cosmic *significance*, though, if your decisions only feed a pseudorandom megaprocess whose outcome has no meaningful relationship to their content.

But since we have infinitude at hand, we can add another twist. If the odds of influencing the behavior of a huge mind are finite, and if we're permitted to scale up infinitely, your decisions will affect not just one but an infinite number of huge minds. Among these minds there will be some—a tiny but finite proportion—of whom the following conditional statement is true: If you hadn't just made that upbeat, life-affirming choice you in fact just made, that huge entity would have decided its life wasn't worth living. However, instead, partly because of that thing you did, the giant entity—let's call it Emily—will step back from the brink of suicide and discover happiness.

We can even find cases in which these kinds of conditional statements are true across an arbitrarily large range of variations, if we're willing to look for the right Emily up there. *Emily Vast* is the being such that if you had made *any* life-affirming choice ten minutes ago, across a wide range of possible choices you might have made, she would have discovered happiness, and if you had not, she wouldn't have. Given the chaotic connections, a minuscule but finite proportion of Emilys will be like this. At the right scale, sufficiently far up the nested layers of cosmically vast minds, there must be a layer at which not just one but every moderately likely, finitely specifiable life-affirming action you might have chosen is such that, by chance, it would have caused a life-affirming outcome for Emily Vast.

If we're willing to gaze still farther up in search of the right Emily Vast, rising even higher through the spatiotemporal scales, multiplying one minuscule-but-finite chance upon another, we will eventually discover an *Emily Megavast* who sees and knows about you in the following sense: Somewhere in her environment is an approximately Emily Megavast–sized being who acts and looks (or "acts" and "looks") much like you and does so as a result of chaotic chance contingencies linking back to your visible body and your behavioral choices. You do your lovely life-affirming thing, and much later, as a result, the megavast analogue of you does its analogous lovely life-affirming thing. Emily Megavast is inspired. Her life is changed forever!

In an infinite cosmos, given background assumptions that are not wholly implausible, this is virtually certain to be so, within as precise an error tolerance as you care to specify.

I hope it won't seem presumptuous of me now to thank you already, on Emily's behalf.[28]

Homer did not sing of Penelope's equations—the equations, in neat chalk lettering, covering wall and ceiling of her upstairs chambers, the equations built and corrected over years, proving that Odysseus will at some point return.

After long study, Eurykleia agreed with Penelope. The universe is provably diverse and provably infinite. So an Odysseus must return from the sea. Indeed, he must do so infinitely often. There are only finitely many ways that atoms can arrange themselves, within the error tolerances of human concern.

Eurykleia did not think it followed, however, that one should stand upon the palace roof and wait in the rain, gazing across the wine-dark sea. This is where Penelope was when lightning struck and killed her.

Ithaka mourned. Greece fell. Humanity fell. Sun swallowed Earth, the stars burned out, the universe became cool and quiet. But infinite time is a powerful thing.

જી

Lightning struck the iron railing to Penelope's right. Eurykleia urged Penelope back inside.

Penelope sat in her chambers by a blazing hearth, while Eurykleia wrapped her in towels and slowly brushed her hair.

"Other Penelopes will continue me," Penelope said. "Infinitely many, who have exactly my ideas, exactly my plans and longings, exactly this mole upon my cheek. An infinite subset of them will greet a returning Odysseus before nightfall. An infinite subset will leave Ithaka, riding a thin ship on the wild sea. They will find old friends, drown in storms, discover giants. Lightning cannot end me, only redistribute me."

Penelope and Eurykleia agreed: A new cosmos will eventually burst forth from disorder with duplicates of them, duplicates of all Greece. Although at any one time the chance is unfathomably minuscule that so many atoms will happen randomly to arrange themselves just right, that chance is finite, and it sums infinitely across the whole. But accepting this, they disagreed about the implications.

"Though perfect duplicates will eventually exist," said Eurykleia, "they are beyond our concern."

"It will be just as if I smoothly continued," said Penelope, "as if the intervening aeons had passed in a blink."

Eurykleia wrapped a finishing band around the braided tips of Penelope's long hair. "They are many, but you are one, my love. They can't all be you."

"There is an infinitude of me-enough," said Penelope, standing, now dry, ready to select her evening clothes. "I will leave here and do all things."

☙

Eurykleia helped Penelope, still wet, into a dress and scarf. Together, they descended to the main hall where the suitors reveled. With mock formality, Ktesippos asked Penelope to dance.

"Somewhere I marry Ktesippos," Penelope said. "Somewhere else I feast upon his eyes while he gladly sings a poem. The suitors are atoms. By chance or repulsion they might disperse widely, or congregate all on one side of the room, or step in some vastly improbable rhythm that resonates through the floor, through the stone and dirt, and vibrates the air above the sea into a siren's call."

Eurykleia laid toasted wheat and cheese on a festive dish, handing it to Penelope. "Eat. You are too lean. Your mind is overhot."

A rag-clad man appeared in the doorway: Odysseus returned. Eurymakhos entered silently behind, killed Odysseus with a spear-thrust through the back, then stepped forward to ask Penelope's hand in marriage, the other suitors applauding.

Penelope chose instead to ride a thin ship on the wild sea.

∽

Odysseus slew the suitors.

In their marital chamber, beneath a ceiling of equations, Penelope said to Odysseus, "Your recent travels are nothing. We will journey together far wider. The Aegean is a droplet."

Odysseus said, "Mathematics is only dance steps that govern chalk. No universe exists beyond these chamber walls."

Odysseus smelled of someone's recent past: of herbs and swine and salt. Penelope and Odysseus made love, and Penelope contemplated the assumptions implicit in her axioms.

∽

By minuscule chance, a black hole emitted a pair of complex systems who briefly thought—before tidal forces and the vacuum of space consumed them—that they were Penelope and Eurykleia dancing together in slow silence, to an imagined song, late at night in the grand hall.

∽

It was evening and Penelope was unweaving Laertes's death shroud. With a silver pick, Penelope gently pulled up the fine thread, while Eurykleia coiled it back upon the spool.

"An unobservable difference is no difference at all," Penelope said.

"I love the particular you here now," said Eurykleia, "not the infinitude of diverse Penelopes elsewhere."

They heard a thump from downstairs, then a chorus of festive shouts. A suitor hollered for more pink wine.

"If the Earth spins," said Penelope, "then all of Greece moves. Do you love me less because we are now in a different place?"

Penelope ceased her unweaving. Moonlight across Laertes's half-made shroud cast a shadow over the equations on one wall. Penelope leaned forward, touching her finger to a brown dot on Eurykleia's left shoulder. In the years of waiting, Eurykleia's shoulder had become an old woman's shoulder. Penelope circled the dot with her fingertip, then stood.

Penelope climbed to the roof and stood in the lightning storm, gazing out, Eurykleia standing reluctantly in the doorway behind. Penelope stretched her right hand back, inviting.

Eurykleia took a half-step into the rain, then stopped. "Maybe," she said, "it's the invisible threads of causation th—"

ಊ

A galaxy suddenly congealed from chaos.

Something indistinguishable from Penelope and something indistinguishable from Eurykleia stood upon the roof. They seemed to remember having left, down below, Laertes's half-undone shroud. They seemed to remember Odysseus, Telemakhos, suitors, Greece, the constellations. And indeed this galaxy did contain such things, as, given infinite time, some such sudden galaxy eventually must.

"—at I value?" continued Eurykleia.

Penelope took Eurykleia's hand and led her to the edge of the roof. Together they gazed past the low railing, down the edge of the cliff upon which the palace stood, to the slate shore and rough waves.

"If we leapt over the edge," Penelope said, "there is a small but finite chance that the winds would bear us up—a small but finite chance that the atoms of air would strike our bodies exactly so, preventing our fall and sending us soaring instead like birds among the clouds."

"I can't do this," said Eurykleia.

"If we closed our eyes," said Penelope, "the death of these bodies would come with no warning. We would never know it. And somewhere a Penelope and Eurykleia will burst forth from chaos, flying, knowing they are us."

"But there will be many more Penelopes and Eurykleias dead upon the rocks, and many more half-congealed Penelopes and Eurykleias who fall back into death or who survive but misremember."

"Many more?" said Penelope. "There are infinitely many of all types. Just as the infinitude of points in a small line segment is identical to the infinitude of points in the whole of space, the infinitude of flying Penelope-Eurykleia pairs is identical to the infinitude of the pairs of corpses upon the shore is identical to the infinitude who remain upon the roof."

"Infinitude is a strange and wonderful thing, Penelope. But I cannot leap."

Elsewhere, though, somewhere, Penelope and Eurykleia leapt and flew, and leapt and flew, and leapt and flew.

Must an infinitely continued life inevitably become boring? The famous twentieth-century ethicist Bernard Williams notoriously thought so.[29]

But consider Neil Gaiman's story "The Goldfish Pool and Other Stories" (yes, that's the name of one story):

> He nodded and grinned. "Ornamental carp. Brought here all the way from China."
>
> We watched them swim around the little pool. "I wonder if they get bored."
>
> He shook his head. "My grandson, he's an ichthyologist, you know what that is?"
>
> "Studies fishes."
>
> "Uh-huh. He says they only got a memory that's like thirty seconds long. So they swim around the pool, it's always a surprise to them, going 'I've never been here before.' They meet another fish they known for a hundred years, they say, 'Who are you, stranger?'"[30]

The problem of immortal boredom solved: Just have a bad memory! Then even seemingly unrepeatable pleasures, like meeting someone for the first time, become repeatable.

Now you might say, wait, when I was thinking about immortality, I wasn't thinking about forgetting everything and doing it again like a stupid goldfish.

To this I answer: Weren't you? If you imagine that you were continuing life as a human, you were imagining, presumably, that you had finite brain capacity. There's only so much memory you can fit into eighty billion neurons. So of course you're going to forget things, at some point almost everything, and things you've sufficiently well forgotten you could presumably experience as fresh again. This is always what is going on with us anyway to some extent.

Immortality as an angel or a transhuman superintellect only postpones the issue, as long as one's memory is finite. The question of the value of repetition is thus forced on us: Is repeating and forgetting the same types of experiences over and over again, infinitely, preferable to doing them only once, or only twenty times, or "only" a googolplex of times? The answer to that question isn't entirely clear. One possibly relevant consideration, however, is this: If you stopped one of the goldfish and asked, "Do you want to keep going along?" the happy little fish would say, "Yes, this is totally cool! I wonder what's around the corner. Oh, hi, glad to meet you!" It seems a shame to cut the fish off when it's having so much fun—to say, "Nope, no value added, you've already done this a million times, sorry!"

Alternatively, consider an infinitely continuing life with infinite memory. How would that work? What would it be like? Would you be overwhelmed and almost paralyzed like the titular character in Jorge Luis Borges's story "Funes the Memorious"?[31] Would there be a workable search algorithm for retrieving those memories? Would there be some tagging system to distinguish each memory from infinitely many qualitatively identical other memories? Also, infinitude is pretty big and weird, as we've been discussing—so at some point you'll need to become pretty big and weird too.

True temporal infinitude forces a dilemma between two options:

1. Infinite repetition of the same things, without memory
2. An ever-expanding range of experiences that eventually diverges so far from your present range of experience that it becomes questionable whether it's right to regard the future being as "you" in any meaningful sense.

Given infinite time, a closed system will eventually start repeating its states, within any finite error tolerance.[32] There are only so many relevantly distinguishable states a closed system can occupy. Once it has occupied them, it has to start repeating at least some of them. Assuming that memory belongs to the system's states, then memory too is among those things that must start afresh and repeat.

Since it seems reasonable to doubt that the forgetful repetition of the same experiences, again and again, is what we do or should want in immortality, it might seem better, or more interesting or more worthwhile, to imagine an immortal life as an open system—one that is always expanding into new possibilities. But this brings its own problems.

Suppose that conscious experience is what matters. First, you might cycle through every possible human experience. Maybe human experience depends on a brain of no more than a hundred trillion neurons (currently we have about eighty billion, but that might change), and that each neuron can be in one of a hundred trillion relevantly distinguishable states. Such numbers, though large, are finite. So once you're done living through all the experiences of seeming-Aristotle, seeming-Gandhi, seeming-Hitler, seeming-Hitler-seeming-to-remember-having-earlier-been-Gandhi, seeming-future-super-genius, and seeming-every-possible-other-person and many, many more experiences that probably wouldn't coherently belong to anyone's life, well, you have either to settle in for some repetition or to find some new experiences that are no longer human. Go through the mammals, then. Go through a variety of increasingly remote hypothetical creatures. Expand, expand—eventually you'll have run through all possible smallish creatures with a neural or similar basis. You'll need to move to experiences that are either radically alien or vastly superhuman or both.

At some point—maybe not very far along in this process—it's reasonable to wonder whether the entity who is having all of these experiences is really "you." Even if there is some continuous causal thread reaching back to you as you are now, should you care about this remotely distant entity in any more personal way than you care about the future of some entity unrelated to you?

Either amnesic infinite repetition or an infinitely expanding range of unfathomable alien weirdness: *the Immortal's Dilemma*.

Or maybe you were imagining retaining your humanity but somehow existing nontemporally? I find that even harder to conceive. What would *that* be like?

ℰↄ

Let's return to assuming we'll be goldfish. That's the version of infinitude I think I understand best, and probably the one I'd choose. Suppose it's Heaven, or at least a deserved reward. My creator stops me midswim. She asks not only whether I want to keep going (I do), but also what size pool I want. Do I want a large pool, that is, a relatively wide range of experiences to loop through? Or would I rather have a smaller pool, a shorter loop of more carefully selected, more individually awesome experiences, but less variety? Either way, I won't know the difference. I won't get bored. Each loop-through will be experienced as fresh and surprising.

I think I'd choose a moderately large loop. When I imagine a tiny little loop—for example, just hanging out in the clouds, blissfully playing the harp, joyfully contemplating the divine, over and over in ecstatic amnesia—I think maybe joy is over-rated. Instead, give me diverse adventures and a long memory.[33]

45 Are Garden Snails Conscious? Yes, No, or *Gong*

If you grew up in a temperate climate, you probably spent some time bothering brown garden snails (*Cornu aspersum*, formerly known as *Helix aspersa*). I certainly did. Now, as a grown-up (supposedly) expert (supposedly) on the science and philosophy of consciousness, I'm fretting over a question that didn't trouble me very much when I was seven: Are garden snails conscious?

Naturally, I started with a Facebook poll of my friends, who obligingly fulfilled my expectations by answering, variously, "yes" (here's why), "no" (here's why not), and "OMG that is the stupidest question." I'll call this last response "*gong*" after *The Gong Show*, an amateur talent contest in which performers whose acts are sufficiently horrid are interrupted by a gong and ushered off the stage.

It turns out that garden snails are even cooler than I thought, now that I'm studying them more closely. Let me fill you in.

Garden Snail Cognition and Behavior

The central nervous system of the brown garden snail contains about sixty thousand neurons.[34] That's quite a few more neurons than the famously mapped 302 neurons of the *Caenorhabditis elegans* roundworm, but only a fraction of the number in an ant's or fruitfly's brain. The snail's brain is organized into several clumps of ganglia, mostly in a ring around its esophagus. Gastropod (i.e., snail and slug) neurons generally resemble vertebrate neurons, with a few notable exceptions. One is that gastropod central nervous system neurons usually don't have a bipolar structure with output axons on one side of the cell body and input dendrites on the other. Instead, input and output typically occurs on both sides without a clear differentiation between axon and dendrite. Another difference is that although gastropods' small-molecule neural transmitters are the same as those in vertebrates (e.g., acetylcholine, serotonin), their larger-molecule neuropeptides are mostly different.

Snails navigate primarily by chemoreception, or the sense of smell, and mechanoreception, or the sense of touch. They will move toward attractive odors, such as food or mates, and they will withdraw from noxious odors and tactile disturbance. Although garden snails have eyes on the tips of their posterior tentacles, their eyes seem to be sensitive only to light versus dark and the direction of light sources, rather than to the shapes of objects. Snail tentacles are instead highly specialized for chemoreception, with the higher-up posterior tentacles better for catching odors on the wind and the lower-down anterior tentacles better for taste and odors close to the ground. Garden snails can also sense the direction of gravity, righting themselves and moving toward higher ground to avoid puddles.

Snails can learn. Gastropods fed on a single type of plant will prefer to move toward that same plant type when offered the choice in a Y-shaped maze. They can also learn to avoid foods associated with noxious stimuli, in some cases even after only a single trial. Some species of gastropod will modify their degree of attraction to sunlight if sunlight is associated with tumbling inversion. In *Aplysia californica* gastropods, the central nervous system's complex role in governing reflex withdrawals has been extensively studied. *Aplysia californica* reflex withdrawals can be inhibited, amplified, and coordinated, maintaining a singleness of action across the body and regulating withdrawal according to circumstances. Withdrawals can be habituated (reduced) after repeated exposure to harmless stimuli and sensitized (increased) when the triggering stimulus is regularly followed by something even more aversive. Garden snail nervous systems appear to be of similar complexity to those of *Aplysia californica*, generating unified action that varies with circumstance.

Garden snails can coordinate their behavior in response to information from more than one modality at once. When they detect that they are surrounded by water, they can find an uphill path. They will cease eating when satiated, withhold from mating while eating despite sexual arousal, and exhibit less withdrawal reflex while mating. Before egg laying, garden snails use their feet to excavate a shallow cavity in soft soil, then insert their head into the cavity for several hours while they ovulate. Land snails will also maintain a home range to which they will return for resting periods or hibernation, rather than simply moving in an unstructured way toward attractive sites or odors.

Garden snail mating is famously complex. *Cornu aspersum* is a simultaneous hermaphrodite, playing both the male and female role simultaneously. Courtship and copulation requires about seven hours. Courtship begins with the snails touching heads and posterior tentacles for tens of seconds, then withdrawing and circling to find each other again, often consuming each other's slime trails, or alternatively breaking courtship. They repeat this process several times. During mating, snails will sometimes bite each other, then withdraw and reconnect. Later in courtship, one snail will shoot a "love dart" consisting of calcium and mucus at the other, succeeding in penetrating the skin about one third of the time; tens of minutes later, the other snail will reciprocate. Sex culminates when the partners manage to simultaneously insert their penises into each other, which may require dozens of attempts. Garden snails will normally mate several times before laying eggs, and the sperm of mates whose darts have successfully landed will fertilize more of their partners' eggs than the sperm of mates with worse aim.

Impressive accomplishments for creatures with brains of only sixty thousand neurons! Of course, snail behavior is limited compared to the larger and more flexible behavioral repertoire of mammals and birds.

Garden Snail Consciousness: Three Possibilities

So, knowing all this . . . are garden snails conscious? Is there something it's like to be a garden snail? Do snails have, for example, sensory experiences?

Suppose you touch the tip of your finger to the tip of a snail's posterior tentacle, and the tentacle retracts. Does the snail have tactile experience of something touching its tentacle, a visual experience of a darkening as your finger approaches and occludes the eye, an olfactory or chematosensory experience of the smell or taste or chemical properties of your finger, a proprioceptive experience of the position of its now-withdrawn tentacle?

1. *Yes.* We seem able to imagine that the answer is yes, the snail does have sensory experiences. Any specific experience we try to imagine from the snail's point of view, we will probably imagine too humanocentrically. Withdrawing a tentacle might not feel much like withdrawing an arm. Optical experience in particular might be so informationally poor that calling it "visual" is already misleading, inviting too much

analogy with human vision. Nonetheless, I think we can conceive in a general way how it might be the case that garden snails have sensory experiences of some sort or other.

2. *No.* We can also imagine, I think, that the answer is no, snails entirely lack sensory experiences of any sort—and thus, presumably, any consciousness at all, on the assumption that if snails are conscious they have at least sensory consciousness. If you have trouble conceiving of this possibility, consider dreamless sleep, toy robots, and the enteric nervous system (a collection of about half a billion neurons lining your gut, governing intestinal motor function and enzyme secretion). In all three of these cases, most people think, there is no genuine stream of conscious experience, despite some organized behavior and environmental reactivity. It seems that we can coherently imagine snail behavior to be like that: no more conscious than turning over unconsciously in sleep, or than a toy robot, or than the neurons lining your intestines.

We can make sense of both of these possibilities, I think. Neither seems obviously false or obviously refuted by the empirical evidence. One possibility might strike you as intuitively much more likely than the other, but as I've learned from chatting with friends and acquaintances (and from my Facebook poll), people's intuitions vary—and it's not clear, anyway, how much we ought to trust our intuitions in such matters. You might have a favorite scientific or philosophical theory from which it follows that garden snails are or are not conscious, but there is little consensus on general theories of consciousness, and leading candidate theories yield divergent answers.

3. *Gong*. To these two possibilities, we can add a third, the one I am calling *gong*. Not all questions deserve a "yes" or a "no." There might be a false presupposition in the question

(maybe "consciousness" is an incoherent concept?), or the case might be vague or indeterminate such that neither "yes" nor "no" quite serves as an adequate answer. (Compare vague or indeterminate cases between "green" and "not green" or between "extraverted" and "not extraverted.")

Indeterminacy is perhaps especially tempting. Not everything in the world fits neatly into determinate, dichotomous yes-or-no categories. Consciousness might be one of those things that doesn't dichotomize well. And snails might be right there at the fuzzy border.

Although an indeterminate view has some merits, it is more difficult to sustain than you might think at first pass. To see why, it helps to clearly distinguish between being *a little* conscious and being *in an indeterminate state between* conscious and not conscious. If one is a little conscious, one is conscious. Maybe snails have just the tiniest smear of consciousness—that would still be consciousness! You might have only a little money. Your entire net worth is a nickel. Still, it is discretely and determinately the case that if you have a nickel, you have some money. If snail consciousness is a nickel to human millionaire consciousness, then snails are conscious.

To say that the dichotomous yes-or-no does not apply to snail consciousness is to say something very different than that snails have just a little smidgen of consciousness. It's to say . . . well, what exactly? As far as I'm aware, there's no well-developed theory of kind-of-yes-kind-of-no consciousness. We can understand vague, kind-of-yes-kind-of-no cases for "green" and "extravert." We know more or less what's involved in being a gray-area case of a color or personality trait. We can imagine gray-area cases with money too: Your last nickel is on the table over there, and here comes the creditor to collect it. Maybe that's a gray-area case of having money. But it's much harder to know how to think about gray-area cases of being somewhere between a little bit conscious and not at all conscious. So while in the abstract I feel the attraction of the idea that consciousness is not a dichotomous property and garden snails might occupy the blurry in-between region, the view requires entering a theoretical space that has not yet been well explored.

There is, I think, some antecedent plausibility to all three possibilities, *yes*, *no*, and **gong**. To really decide among them, to really figure out the answer to our question about snail consciousness, we need an empirically well-grounded general theory of consciousness that we can apply to the case.

Unfortunately, we have no such theory. The live possibilities appear to cover the entire spectrum from the panpsychism or near-panpsychism of Galen Strawson and of Integrated Information Theory, on which consciousness is widespread in the universe, even in extremely simple systems, to very restrictive views, like those of Daniel Dennett and Peter Carruthers, on which consciousness requires sophisticated self-representational capacities well beyond the capacity of snails.[35]

Actually, I find something wonderful about not knowing. There's something marvelous about the fact that I can go into my backyard, lift a snail, and gaze at it, unsure. Snail, you are a puzzle of the universe, right here in my garden, eating the daisies!

V Kant versus the Philosopher of Hair

According to Nomy Arpaly and Zach Barnett, some philosophers prefer Truth and others prefer Dare.[1] Yes! But there are also Wonder philosophers.

Truth philosophers aim to present the philosophical truth as they see it. Usually, they prefer modest, moderate, commonsense views. They also tend to recognize the complementary merits of competing views—at least after they have been knocked loose from their youthful enthusiasms—and thus Truth philosophers tend to prefer multidimensionality and nuance.[2] Truth philosophers would rather be boring and right than interesting and wrong.

Dare philosophers reach instead for the bold and unusual. They enjoy exploring the boundaries of what can be defended. They're happy for the sake of argument to champion strange positions they don't really believe, if those positions are elegant, novel, fun, or contrarian or have some unappreciated merit. Dare philosophers tend to treat philosophy as a game in which the ideal achievement is the breathtakingly clever defense of a view that others would have thought to be absurd.

The interaction of Truth and Dare creates a familiar dynamic. The Dare philosopher ventures a bold thesis, cleverly defended.

("Possible worlds really exist!", "All matter is conscious!", "We're morally obliged to let humanity go extinct!"[3]) If the defense is sufficiently clever, readers are tempted to think, "Wait, could that really be true? What exactly is wrong with the argument?" Then the Truth philosopher steps in, finding the holes and illicit presuppositions in the argument, or at least trying to, and defending a more sensible view.

This Dare-and-Truth dynamic is central to academic philosophy and good for its development. Sometimes Daring views have merit we wouldn't notice without Dare philosophers out there pushing the limits. Moreover, there's something intrinsically worthwhile or beautiful in exploring the boundaries of philosophical defensibility, even for positions that ultimately prove to be flatly false. It's part of the glory of life on Earth that we have fiendishly clever panpsychists and modal realists in our midst.

Now consider Wonder.

Why study philosophy? I mean personally. What do you find interesting or rewarding about it? One answer is Truth: Through philosophy you (hopefully) learn the truth about profound and difficult issues. Another answer is Dare: It's fun to match wits, develop lines of reasoning, defend surprising theses, and win the argumentative game despite starting from a seemingly indefensible position. Both of these motivations speak to me. But I think what really delights me more than anything else in philosophy is its capacity to upend what I think I know, to call into question what I previously took for granted, to throw me into doubt, confusion, and wonder.

In conversation, Nomy said that she had been thinking of me as a typical Dare philosopher. I can see the basis of her impression. After all, I've argued that the United States might literally be phenomenally conscious, that we're such bad introspectors that we might be radically mistaken about even the seemingly most obvious aspects of our own currently ongoing stream of experience, that we might be short-lived artificial intelligences in a computer-generated world run by a sadistic teenager, and that someone might continue to exist after having been killed by lightning if a freak molecule-for-molecule duplicate of that person suddenly coagulates in the distant future.[4] Hard to get more Dare than that!

Well, except for the *might* part. In my mind, the "might" is a crucial qualification. It renders the claims, despite their strangeness, considerably less Daring. "Might" can be a pretty low bar.

Unlike the Dare philosopher, the Wonder philosopher is guided by a norm of sincerity and truth. The practice of philosophy is not, for the Wonder philosopher, primarily about matching wits and finding clever arguments that you yourself needn't believe. However, like Dare philosophers and unlike Truth philosophers, Wonder philosophers love the strange and seemingly wrong—and are willing to push wild theses to the extent they suspect that those theses, wonderfully, surprisingly, *might* be true.

Probably no reader of philosophy is pure Truth, pure Dare, or pure Wonder. Nor, I'm sure, is this distinction exhaustive.[5] Furthermore, our motives might blur together (chapter 10). There might be ways of sincerely pursuing Truth by adopting a Dare attitude, and so forth. Insert further nuance, qualification, and multifacetedness as required for Truth.

಄

In the Dare-and-Truth dynamic of the field, the Wonder philosopher can have trouble finding a place. Bold Dare articles are exciting. Wow, what cleverness! Sensible Truth articles also find a home in the journals, especially when they're responding to some prominent Dare position. The Wonder philosopher's

"Whoa, I wonder if this weird thing might be true?" is a little harder to publish. The standard philosophical monograph and journal article demand an aura of settled confidence that can be difficult to reconcile with the open vulnerability of Wonder.

Since probably none of us is pure Truth, Dare, or Wonder, one approach is to leave Wonder out of your writing profile: Find the Truth, where you can, publish that, maybe try a little Dare if you dare, and leave Wonder for your classroom teaching and private reading. Defend the existence of moderate naturalistically grounded moral truths in your published papers; relish the weirdness of Zhuangzi on the side.

Still, that seems a little sad, don't you think? Shouldn't the aspiring Wonder philosopher be able to convey Wonder in written work? Does Wonder need to remain hidden in your back pocket, while you present only a confident face to the world?

Here are some approaches I've tried. Write about historical philosophers with weird and Wonderful views that can be explored without endorsement (for example, Zhuangzi). Find a Daring position that's defensible in some limited way (for example, group consciousness). Find a direct path to Wonder through skepticism and doubt (for example, about the consciousness of garden snails).

Or start a blog! Or write fiction or dialogue—forms that better tolerate irresolution and Wonder.

If you've read this far into this dorky book,[6] I have some bad news. You're a *philosophy dork*.

Some of us philosophy dorks have been philosophy dorks for a long time, since even before we knew what academic philosophy was. Maybe, like me, when you were twelve, you said to your friends, "Is there really a world behind that closed door? Or does the outside world only pop into existence when I open the door?" and they said, "Dude, you're weird! Let's go play basketball." Maybe, like me, when you were in high school you read science fiction and wondered whether an entirely alien moral code might be as legitimate as our own, and this prevented you from taking your World History teacher entirely seriously.

If you're a deep-down philosophy dork, then you have a certain underappreciated asset: a philosophically tuned sense of fun. You should trust that sense of fun.

It's fun—at least *I* find it fun—to think about whether there is some way to prove that the external world exists. It's fun to see whether ethics books are any less likely to be stolen than other philosophy books. It's fun to think about why people used to say they dreamed in black and white, the essence of jerkitude, how weirdly self-ignorant people are, what sorts of bizarre aliens might be conscious, or whether babies know that things continue to exist outside of their perceptual fields.[7] At every turn in my career, I have faced choices about whether to pursue what seemed to me to be tiresome, respectable, philosophically mainstream, and at first glance the better career choice, or whether instead to follow my sense of fun. Rarely have I regretted it when I have chosen fun.

I see three main reasons philosophy dorks should trust their sense of fun. (Hey, numbered lists of reasons to hold weird views, that's kind of fun!)

1. Fun and boredom are emotional indicators of epistemic value. If you truly are a philosophy dork in the sense I intend the phrase (and consider, *this* is how you are spending your free time), then your sense of what's fun will tend to reflect what really is, for you, philosophically worth pursuing. You might not be able to quite put your finger on why it's worth pursuing, at first. It might even just seem like a pointless intellectual lark. But my experience is that the deeper significance will eventually reveal itself. Maybe everything can be explored philosophically and brought back around to main themes, if one plunges deep enough. But I'm inclined to think it's not *just* that. The true dork's mind has a sense of where it needs to go next—an intuition about what it will benefit from thinking about, versus what will drift past it in a sleepy haze. Emotional indicators of epistemic value can of course be misleading—video games are designed to exploit them, for example—but for dorks who have wallowed in philosophy long enough, those indicators are likely to have more than just superficial merit.

2. Chasing fun ideas energizes you. Few things are more dispiriting than doing something tedious because "it's good for your

career." You'll find yourself wondering whether this career is really for you, whether you're really cut out for philosophy. You'll find yourself procrastinating, checking social media,[8] spacing out while reading, prioritizing other duties. If instead you chase the fun first, you'll find philosophical exploration viscerally attractive. You'll be eager to do it. Later, you can harness this eagerness back onto a sense of responsibility. Finding your weird passion first, and figuring out what you want to say about it, can motivate you to go back later and more thoroughly read the (sometimes to-you unexciting) stuff that others have written about the topic, so that you can fill in the references, connect with previous related research, and refine your view in light of others' work. Reading the philosophical literature is much more rewarding when you have an exciting lens through which to read it, an agenda in mind that you care about. Slogging through it from some vague sense of unpleasant duty is a good way to burn yourself out and waste your summer.

3. Fun is contagious. So is boredom. Readers are unlikely to enjoy your work and be enthusiastic about your ideas if even *you* don't have joy and enthusiasm.

These remarks probably generalize across disciplines. I think of (the famous physicist) Richard Feynman's description of how he recovered from his early-career doldrums by starting a fun but seemingly frivolous project on the mathematics of spinning cafeteria plates.[9] I think of (*Buffy the Vampire Slayer* creator) Joss Whedon's advice for writers to "Absolutely eat dessert first. The thing you want to do the most, do that."[10] Dessert won't spoil your supper. On the contrary, dessert is the important thing, the thing that really calls to be done, and doing it will give you the energy you need to eat your vegetables later.

48 What's in People's Stream of Experience during Philosophy Talks?

I've worked a bit with psychologist Russ Hurlburt, and also a bit on my own, using beepers to sample people's stream of experience during their ordinary activities. The basic idea is this: You wear a beeper for a while, just going about your normal business. The beeper is set to go off after some random interval (typically between one and sixty minutes), during which you usually more or less forget that you're wearing it. Each time the beep sounds, you are to immediately think back on what was in your last undisturbed moment of inner experience just before the beep. Later, usually within twenty-four hours, you are carefully interviewed about that randomly sampled slice of experience.[11] Despite qualms (expressed in my 2007 book with Hurlburt), I find this an intriguing method.

When I give a talk about experience sampling, which I've done sometimes with Russ and sometimes solo, I typically beep the audience during the talk itself to help give them a sense of the procedure. I give each member of the audience a slip of paper with a different number. I set a timer for something like four to ten minutes, then I launch into my lecture. The audience knows that when the beep sounds, I'll stop talking and they'll have a minute or two to reflect on their last moment of experience right before the beep. Then I'll randomly select a number, and (if they consent) I'll interview the audience member with that number right there on the spot, with others free to jump in with their own questions. This single moment of experience of a single, randomly chosen audience member then constitutes our "sample" of experience. The discussion is fun, and the audience is usually very engaged.

Typically, in a two- or three-hour session, there will be time to discuss only two or three sampled moments of experience. There has to be some lecturing too, of course, and the careful exploration of even a single moment of a single person's experience normally requires at least fifteen minutes. All the side discussions and audience questions slow things down further. But now I've done it maybe eight or ten times, and I have a couple of dozen samples—enough to start making generalizations about the inner experiences people report having while listening to my lectures.

The most striking thing to me is this: Only a minority of the sampled audience members—15–25 percent—report having been attending to the content of the talk at the moment of the beep.

To give a flavor of what people do report, here are summary reports of six samples from 2010, the most recent samples at the time I first drafted the blog post on which this chapter is based. Half are from a presentation I gave to an advanced undergraduate class in Claremont, and half are from a joint presentation with Hurlburt at a meeting of the Pacific Division of the American Philosophical Association.[12]

1. Thinking that he should put his cell phone away (probably not formulated either in words or imagery); sensory visual experience of the cell phone and whiteboard.

2. Scratching an itch, noticing how it feels; having a visual experience of a book.

3. Feeling like he's about to fade into a sweet daydream, but no sense of its content yet; "fading" visual experience of the speaker.

4. Feeling confused; listening to the speaker and reading along on the handout, taking in the meaning.

5. Visual imagery of the "macaroni orange" of a recently seen flyer; skanky taste of coffee; fantasizing about biting an apple instead of tasting coffee; feeling a need to go to the bathroom; hearing the speaker's sentence. The macaroni orange was the most prominent part of her experience.

6. Reading abstract for the next talk; hearing an "echo" of the speaker's last sentence; fighting a feeling of tiredness; maybe feeling tingling on a tooth from a permanent retainer.

I'd count only the fourth sample as an instance of attending to the talk's content. In all of the other samples, the listener's mind is mainly off somewhere else, doing its own thing. Completely absent—I'm not sure I've ever recorded an example of it—is the more active sort of engagement that I'd have thought I often have while listening to a talk: considering possible objections, thinking through consequences, sorting out the argument's structure, thinking about connections to other people's work and to related issues.

Now it could be that Russ and I are unusually deadening speakers, but I don't think so. My guess is that most audience members, during most academic talks, spend most of their time with some distraction or other at the forefront of their stream of experience. They might not *remember* this fact about their experience of the talk—they might judge in retrospect that they were paying close attention most of the time—but that could be a matter of salience. They remember the moments they spent concocting an objection; they forget their brief distracted thought about the color of the flyer.

The same is probably true about sexual thoughts. People often say they spend a lot of time thinking about sex, but when you actually beep them, they very rarely report sexual thoughts.[13] My conjecture is that sexy thoughts, though rare, are likelier to be remembered than imagining biting into an apple, and so they are overrepresented in retrospective memory. In the form of an analogy of the sort you might see on a standardized test: Your devastating objection is to your thought about the color of the flyer as your vivid sexual fantasy is to your choice of breakfast cereal.

If it's true that these six samples are representative of the kind of experiences people have when listening to academic talks, that invites this pair of conjectures about how people understand academic talks. Either

A. Our understanding of academic talks comes mostly from our ability to absorb them while other things are at the forefront of consciousness. The information soaks in, despite the near-constant layer of distraction, and that information then shapes skilled summaries of and reactions to the content of the talks.

or

B. Our understanding of academic talks derives mostly from a small proportion of salient moments when we are not distracted. We leave the lecture room with a reconstruction of what must plausibly have been the author's view based on those scattered instances when we were actually paying attention.

I'd guess B, but I don't really know. If B is true, that suggests that better techniques to retain or capture attention might have a dramatic effect on uptake.

We could do more beeping, more systematically, perhaps connected with comprehension measures, and really try to find this out. But of course, that's kind of hard to justify when the talk itself isn't about experience sampling.

Anecdotally, I've noticed two things that really compel an audience's attention. One is a novel, unpredicted physical event: A cat wanders onstage, or you drop your coffee mug. It's disheartening how much more fascinating the audience finds your spontaneous little mishap than your carefully prepared lecture! The other is the pause. If you just stop talking for a few seconds to gather your thoughts—fiddling with your notes or projector doesn't count—it's amazing how the audience seems to reconvene its attention. Eyes come to you, rising from notepads and laptops, leaving the PowerPoint slide and the exit door and the backs of neighbors' coats. The audience almost holds its breath. For a moment, you can be nearly as fascinating as a falling coffee mug.

49 Why Metaphysics Is Always Bizarre

Bizarre views are a hazard of metaphysics. The metaphysician starts, seemingly, with some highly plausible initial commitments or commonsense intuitions—that there is a prime number between two and five, that she could have had eggs for breakfast, that squeezing the clay statue would destroy the statue but not the lump of clay. She thinks long and hard about what, exactly, these claims imply. In the end, she finds herself positing a realm of abstract Platonic entities, or the real existence of an infinite number of possible worlds, or a huge population of spatiotemporally coincident things on her mantelpiece.[14] I believe that there isn't a single broad-ranging exploration of fundamental issues of metaphysics that doesn't ultimately entangle its author in seeming absurdities. Rejection of these seeming absurdities then becomes the commonsense starting point of a new round of metaphysics, by other philosophers, which in turn generates a complementary bestiary of metaphysical strangeness. Thus are philosophers happily employed.

I see three possible explanations why philosophical metaphysics is never thoroughly commonsensical:

First possible explanation. A thoroughly commonsensical metaphysics wouldn't sell. It would be too obvious, maybe. Or maybe it would lack a kind of elegance or theoretical panache. Or maybe it would conflict too sharply with the sometimes uncommonsensical implications of empirical science.

The problem with this explanation is that there should be at least a small market for a thoroughly commonsensical metaphysics, even if that metaphysics is gauche, tiresome, and scientifically stale. Common sense might not be quite as fun as Nietzsche's eternal recurrence or Leibniz's windowless monads or as scientifically current as [insert ever-changing example], but a commonsense metaphysics ought to be attractive to at least a certain portion of philosophers. At least it ought to command attention as a foil. It shouldn't be so down-market as to be entirely invisible.

Second possible explanation. Metaphysics is very difficult. A thoroughly commonsensical metaphysics is out there to be discovered; we simply haven't found it yet. If all goes well, someday someone will piece it together, top to bottom, with no serious violence to common sense anywhere in the system.

I fear this is wishful thinking against the evidence. The greatest philosophers in history have worked at this for centuries, failing time and time again. Often, indeed, the most thorough metaphysicians—Leibniz, David Lewis—are the ones who generate the most stunningly strange systems.[15] It's not as though we've made slow progress toward ever more commonsensical views and are awaiting a few more pieces to fall into place. There is no historical basis for the hope that a well-developed commonsense metaphysics will eventually arrive.

Third possible explanation. Common sense is incoherent in matters of metaphysics. Contradictions thus inevitably flow from it, and no coherent metaphysical system can adhere to it all. Although (as I also suggest in other chapters) ordinary common sense serves us fairly well in practical maneuvers through the social and physical world, common sense has proven an unreliable guide in cosmology, probability theory, microphysics, neuroscience, macroeconomics, evolutionary biology, structural engineering, medicine, topology . . . If, as it seems to, metaphysics more closely resembles these latter endeavors than it resembles reaching practical judgments about picking berries and kissing, we might reasonably doubt the dependability of common sense as a guide to metaphysics.[16] Undependability doesn't imply incoherence, of course. But it seems a natural next step in this case, and it would neatly explain the historical facts at hand.

On the first explanation, we could easily enough invent a thoroughly commonsensical metaphysics if we wanted one, but we don't want one. On the second explanation, we do want one, or enough of us do, but we haven't yet managed to construct one. On the third explanation, we can't have one. The third explanation best fits the historical evidence and best acknowledges the likely epistemic limits of everyday human cognition.

∽

Common sense might be culturally variable. So whose common sense is at issue in this argument? I doubt it matters. All metaphysical systems in the philosophical canon, Eastern and Western, ancient and modern, I'm inclined to think, conflict both with the common sense of their milieu and with current Western Anglophone common sense. Eternal recurrence, windowless monads, Plato's Forms, and elaborate Buddhist systems of no-self and dependent origination were never part of any society's common sense.

Let me be clear also about the scope of my claim. It concerns only careful, broad-ranging explorations of fundamental metaphysical issues, especially issues around which seeming absurdities tend to congregate: mind and body, causation, identity, the catalogue of entities that really exist. Some skating treatments and some deep treatments of narrow issues might escape the charge.

Common sense changes. Heliocentrism used to defy common sense, but it no longer does. Maybe if we finally get our metaphysics straight, and then teach it patiently enough to generations of students, sowing it deeply into our culture, eventually people will say, "Ah yes, of course, windowless monads and eternal recurrence, what could be more plain and obvious to the common fellow?"

One can always dream!

∾

Some of you might disagree about the existence of the phenomenon I aim to explain. You'll think there is a thoroughly commonsensical metaphysics already on the market. Okay, so who might count as a thoroughly commonsensical metaphysician?

Aristotle, I've sometimes heard. Or Scottish "common sense" philosopher Thomas Reid. Or G. E. Moore, famous for his "Defence of Common Sense." Or "ordinary language" philosopher P. F. Strawson. Or the later Wittgenstein. But Aristotle didn't envision himself as developing a commonsensical view. In the introduction to the *Metaphysics*, he says that the conclusions of sophisticated inquiries such as his own will often seem "wonderful" to the untutored and contrary to their initial opinions, and he sees himself as aiming to distinguish the true from the false in common opinion.[17] Moore, though fierce in wielding common sense against his foes, seems unable to preserve all commonsense opinions when he develops his positive views in detail, for example, in his waffling about "sense-data."[18] Strawson struggles similarly, especially in his 1985 book, in which he can find no satisfactory account of mental causation. Wittgenstein does not commit to a detailed metaphysical system. Despite frequently championing the idea of "common sense" philosophy, Reid acknowledges that in some areas common sense goes badly wrong and his opinions conflict with those of "the vulgar." He argues, for example, that without the constant intervention of immaterial souls, causation is impossible and objects can't even cohere into stable shapes.[19]

Since I can't be expert in the entire history of global philosophy, maybe there's someone I've overlooked—a thorough and broad-ranging metaphysician who nowhere violates the common sense at least of their own culture. I welcome the careful exploration of other possible counterexamples to my generalization.

My argument is an empirical explanatory or "abductive" one. The empirical fact to be explained is that across the entire history of philosophy, all well-developed metaphysical systems defy common sense. Every one of them is in some respect jaw-droppingly bizarre. The best explanation of this striking empirical fact is that people's commonsensical metaphysical intuitions form an incoherent set.

∽

What should we conclude from this? Not, I think, that common sense must be abandoned. It's too essential to philosophical projects—common sense, or at least something that resembles it: pretheoretical intuition, a prior sense of plausibility, culturally shared common ground, a set of starting points that we reject only reluctantly. One has to start somewhere. But we shouldn't be surprised if despite starting commonsensically, we find ourselves, after sufficient inquiry, stuck having to choose among competing bizarrenesses.

When I was at the University of California, Berkeley, in the 1990s, the philosophy lounge had a billboard on which we graduate students posted philosophical humor. Among the items that lived a span upon that board was a newspaper clipping in which a French coiffeur claims to be not a barber, but rather a "philosopher of hair." The humor in this, presumably, derives from the seemingly pretentious strangeness of a barber describing himself as a philosopher of hair. Philosophers, one might think, normally work in philosophy departments, or sit on lonely hills, or stew profoundly in St. Petersburg basements; they don't stand behind people's chairs with scissors. Hair doesn't seem like the right kind of thing to get all philosophical about, much less to build an identity as a philosopher around.

But why not? Our society reveres hair. We devote enormous time and money to it! It's intellectual snobbery to think that hair styling is an art below philosophical notice. Aren't philosophers also supposed to be interested in Beauty, right alongside Truth and Morality? If a good pair of thinning shears helps with Beauty, let's celebrate it.

Moreover, the following are recognizably philosophical questions:

1. What exactly is a haircut? For example, what distinguishes a haircut from a trim or a styling?

2. Is a good haircut timelessly good, or does haircut's quality depend on the currents of fashion?

3. Must a haircut please its recipient to be good? Or could a haircut be objectively great although its recipient hates it?

4. Should a haircut's nature and quality be judged in part by the hairdresser's intent? Or is it more of a "strict liability" thing, such that the haircut's nature and quality depend entirely on the state of the hair on the head (and maybe surrounding fashion and the recipient's desires) but not at all on the hairdresser's intentions?

5. How important is it to have a good haircut, compared to other things one might value in life? Assuming it is important to have a good haircut, *why* is it important?

These questions resemble questions one sees in other areas of philosophy, especially aesthetics, and yet they aren't merely derivative of those other questions. The answers will involve factors particular to hair and won't follow straightaway from one's general stance about the role of authorial intent in literature, what grounds quality judgments about museum-style paintings, and so on. Our French philosopher of hair, as I imagine him, overflows with passionate opinions about these issues. ("You dislike your haircut? You know nothing!")

I care that there's a philosophy of hair partly because I care that we not misconstrue philosophy as a subject area. Philosophy should not be conceptualized as reflection on a particular set of specific, "profound" topics. Rather, philosophy is a style of thinking, a willingness to plunge in to consider the most fundamental ontological, normative, conceptual, and theoretical questions about anything. Any topic—the mind, language, physics, ethics, hair, Barbie dolls, carpentry, auto racing, garden snails, the game of dreidel—can be approached philosophically. For all x, there's a philosophy of x.

51 Obfuscatory Philosophy as Intellectual Authoritarianism and Cowardice

I've been told that Kant and Hegel were poor writers whose impenetrable prose style is incidental to their philosophy. I've also been told that their views are so profound as to defy expression in terms comprehensible even to smart, patient, well-educated people who are not specialists in the philosophy of the period. I've heard similar things about Laozi, Heidegger, Plotinus, and Derrida. (I won't name any living philosophers.) I don't buy it.

Philosophy is not wordless profound insight. Philosophy is prose. Philosophy happens not in numinous moments of personal genius, but in the creation of mundane sentences. It happens on the page, in the pen, through the keyboard, in dialogue with students and peers, and to some extent but only secondarily in private inner speech. If what exists on the page is not clear, the philosophy is not clear. Philosophers, like all specialists, profit from a certain amount of jargon, but philosophy need not become a maze of jargon. If private jargon doesn't regularly touch down in comprehensible public meanings, one has produced not philosophy, but only hazy words of indeterminate content. There are always gaps, confusions, indeterminacies, hidden assumptions, and failures of clarity, even in the plainest philosophical writers, like Mozi, Descartes, Hume, and David Lewis. Thus, these philosophers present ample interpretative challenges. But the gaps, confusions, indeterminacies, and hidden assumptions lie only one step behind the visible prose, available to anyone who looks conscientiously for them, not sliding away into a nebulous murk.

For a philosopher who can convince readers to take him seriously (given the exemplars, let's say "him"), obfuscation yields three illegitimate benefits. First, he intimidates the reader, and through intimidation, dons a mantle of undeserved intellectual authority. Second, he disempowers potential critics by having a view of such indeterminate form that any criticism can be attributed to misinterpretation. Third, he exerts a fascination on the kind of reader who enjoys the puzzle-solving aspect of interpretation, thus drawing from that reader more attention than the quality of his ideas may merit (though this third benefit may be offset by alienating readers with a low tolerance for lack of clarity). Philosophers of this type exhibit a kind of intellectual authoritarianism, with themselves as the assumed authority whose words we must spend time puzzling out. And simultaneously they lack intellectual courage: the courage to make plain claims that could be proven wrong, supported by plain arguments that could be proven fallacious. These three features synergize: If a critic thinks she has finally located a sound criticism, she can be accused of failing to solve the fascinating interpretative puzzle of the philosopher's superior genius.

Few philosophers, I suspect, deliberately aim to be obfuscatory. But I am inclined to believe that some are attuned to its advantages as an effect of their prose style and for that reason don't bother to write comprehensibly. Maybe they find their prose style shaped by audience responses: When they write clearly, they are dismissed or refuted; when they produce a fog of words that hint of profound meaning underneath, they earn praise. Maybe they are themselves to some extent victims—victims of a subculture, or a circle of friends, or an intended audience, that regards incomprehensibility as a sign of brilliance and so demands it in their heroes.[20]

52 Kant on Killing Bastards, Masturbation, Organ Donation, Homosexuality, Tyrants, Wives, and Servants

Immanuel Kant is among the best-respected, best-loved philosophers who has ever lived. His contributions to ethics, metaphysics, epistemology, and aesthetics have helped structure all four of those fields in Europe and the Americas for over two centuries. In the *Philosopher's Index* abstracts, Kant* ("*" is a truncation symbol) appears more frequently than similar searches for Plato, Aristotle, Hume, Confucius, Aquinas, or any other philosopher whose name I've tried. Philosophy departments even advertise specifically for specialists in Kant's philosophy—a treatment that no other philosopher receives even a quarter as frequently.[21]

Kant's most famous writings are notoriously abstract and difficult to understand. That's part, I suspect, of his appeal: Kant interpretation can be a fun puzzle, and his abstractions invite fleshing out with plausible, attractive details.

When Kant himself fleshes out the details, it's often not so pretty.

For example, in *The Metaphysics of Morals* (1797/1996; not to be confused with the more famous, more abstract, and somewhat earlier *Groundwork for the Metaphysics of Morals*), Kant expresses the following views:

1. Wives, servants, and children are possessed in a way akin to our possession of objects. If they flee, they must be returned to the owner if he demands them, without regard for the cause that led them to flee. (See especially pages 278, 282–284 [original pagination].) Kant does acknowledge that the owner is not permitted to treat these people as mere objects to "use up," but this appears to have no bearing on the owner's right to demand their return. Evidently, if such an owned person flees to us from an abusive master, we may admonish the master for behaving badly while we return what is rightly his.

2. Homosexuality is an "unmentionable vice" so wrong that "there are no limitations whatsoever that can save [it] from being repudiated completely" (277).

3. Masturbation is in some ways a worse vice than the horror of murdering oneself and "debases [the masturbator] below the beasts." Kant writes:

> But it is not so easy to produce a rational proof that unnatural, and even merely unpurposive, use of one's sexual attribute is inadmissible as being a violation of duty to oneself (and indeed, as far as its unnatural use is concerned, a violation in the highest degree). The ground of proof is, indeed, that by it a man surrenders his personality (throwing it away), since he uses himself as a means to satisfy an animal impulse. But this does not explain the high degree of violation of the humanity in one's own person by such a vice in its unnaturalness, which seems in terms of its form (the disposition it involves) to exceed even murdering oneself. It consists, then, in this: That a man who defiantly casts off life as a burden is at least not making a feeble surrender to animal impulse in throwing himself away. (425)

4. On killing bastards:

> A child that comes into the world apart from marriage is born outside the law (for the law is marriage) and therefore outside the protection of the law. It has, as it were, stolen into the commonwealth (like

contraband merchandise), so that the commonwealth can ignore its existence (since it rightly should not have come to exist in this way), and can therefore also ignore its annihilation. (336)

On the face of it, similar reasoning might seem to apply to people who enter a country illegally. As far as I'm aware, though, Kant doesn't address that issue.

5. On organ donation:

> To deprive oneself of an integral part or organ (to maim oneself)—for example, to give away or sell a tooth to be transplanted into another's mouth . . . are ways of partially murdering oneself . . . cutting one's hair in order to sell it is not altogether free from blame. (423)

6. Servants and women "lack civil personality and their existence is, as it were, only inherence" and thus should not be permitted to vote or take an active role in the affairs of state (314–315).

7. Under no circumstances is it right to resist the legislative head of state or to rebel on the pretext that the ruler has abused his authority (319–320). Of course, the ruler is *supposed* to treat people well—but (as with wives and servants under abusive masters) there appears to be no legitimate means of escape if he does not.

These views are all, I hope you will agree, odious.[22] So too, is Kant's racism, which doesn't show itself so clearly in *The Metaphysics of Morals* but is painfully evident in other of his writings, for example, "Of the Different Human Races," in which he argues that the Negro, biologically, is "lazy, soft, and trifling" ([1775] 2007, 438), and "On the Feeling of the Beautiful and Sublime," in which he asserts that the "Negroes of Africa have by nature no feeling that rises above the ridiculous" ([1764] 2007, 253).[23]

You might say, so what? Kant was a creature of his time, as are we all. No one is a perfect discoverer of moral truths. In two centuries, John Rawls, Peter Singer, Martha Nussbaum, and Bernard Williams might look similarly foolish in some of their opinions (if they don't already).

Well, sure! Maybe that's comforting to know. And yet I don't think that all ethicists' worldviews age equally badly. There's a humaneness and anachronistic egalitarianism that I think I hear in the ancient Chinese philosopher Zhuangzi and in the sixteenth-century French philosopher Montaigne that has aged better, to my ear.[24]

Some interpreters of Kant ask the reader for considerable patience and deference to his genius. It should be clear from the passages above, though, that Kant's arguments do not always deserve patience and deference. When reading a passage of Kant's with which you are inclined to disagree, bear in mind that among the interpretive possibilities is this: He's just being a vile, boneheaded doofus.

From our cultural distance, it is evident that Kant's arguments against masturbation, for the return of wives to abusive husbands, and so on, are shoddy stuff. This justifies the suspicion that other parts of Kant, too, might contain shoddy arguments, even if those arguments are too abstract to generate a vividly odious conclusion that alerts us to the shoddiness. I'd suggest that among the candidates for being shoddy work, incoherent and bad, are the "transcendental deduction," which stands at the heart of Kant's *Critique of Pure Reason* ([1781/1787] 1998) and defies consensus interpretation, and Kant's claim, near the heart of his ethics, that his three seemingly obviously nonequivalent formulations of the "categorical imperative" are in fact equivalent.[25] For the reader unfamiliar with the transcendental deduction and the formulations of the categorical imperative, suffice to say that these are among the most famous and influential aspects of Kant's work and consequently among the most famous and influential bits of philosophy done by anyone ever.

I might be entirely wrong in my suspicions about the transcendental deduction and the three formulations. It's perfectly reasonable to think that I am probably wrong! Interpreters have put quite a bit of effort into trying to make sense of them, and these pieces of Kant's work have been influential and even inspirational to many subsequent philosophers. How could such influential, widely admired work be rotten? From a bird's-eye view, so to speak, I think my suspicions must be wrong. But from a worm's-eye view, looking directly at what's on the page, well . . .

Kant specialists will tend to disagree with my negative opinion of the transcendental deduction and of Kant's claim of the equivalence of the three formulations of the categorical imperative. Should I defer to them? You'd think they'd know, if anyone does. Yet I worry that a person does not embark on becoming a Kant specialist without already having a tendency to give Kant more trust and charity than he may deserve. Continuing the long journey far into Kant scholarship might then further aggravate the specialist's initial excessive charity and trust: After dedicating years of one's career to Kant, it might be difficult not to see his work as worth the immense effort one has poured into him. In disputes about the quality of Kant's work, Kant specialists are not neutral parties.

If you'll forgive me, here's a very uncharitable theory of Kant: He is a master at promising philosophers what they long for—such as a decisive refutation of radical skepticism or a proof that it's irrational to be immoral—and then effusing a haze of words, some confident statements, some obscure patches of seemingly relevant argumentation, some intriguing suggestions, with glimmers enough of hope that readers can convince themselves that a profound solution lies beneath, if only they understood it.[26]

53 Nazi Philosophers, World War I, and the Grand Wisdom Hypothesis

As described in chapter 4, I've done a fair bit of empirical research on the moral behavior of ethics professors. My collaborators and I have consistently found that ethicists behave no better than socially comparable nonethicists. However, the moral violations that we've examined have mostly been minor: stealing library books, neglecting student emails, littering, forgetting to call mom. Some behaviors are arguably much more significant—donating large amounts to charity, vegetarianism— but there's certainly no consensus about the moral importance of those things. Sometimes I hear the objection that the moral behavior I've studied is all trivial stuff: that even if ethicists behave no better in day-to-day ways, on issues of great moral importance—decisions that reflect on one's overarching world-view, one's broad concern for humanity, one's general moral vision—professional ethicists, and professional philosophers in general, might show greater wisdom. Call this the *Grand Wisdom Hypothesis*.

Now let's think about Nazis. Nazism is an excellent test case of the Grand Wisdom Hypothesis, since pretty much everyone now agrees that Nazism is extremely morally odious. Germany had a robust philosophical tradition in the 1930s, and excellent records are available on individual professors' participation in or resistance to the Nazi movement. So we can ask: Did a background in philosophical ethics serve as any kind of protection against the moral delusions of Nazism? Or were ethicists just as likely to be swept up in noxious German nationalism as were others of their social class? Did reading Kant on the importance of treating all people as "ends in themselves" help philosophers better see the errors of Nazism, or did philosophers instead tend to appropriate Kant for anti-Semitic and expansionist purposes?

Heidegger's involvement with Nazism is famous and much discussed, but he's only one data point. There were also, of course, German philosophers who opposed Nazism, possibly partly—if the Grand Wisdom Hypothesis is correct—because of their familiarity with theoretical ethics. My question is quantitative: Were philosophers as a group *any more likely* than other academics to oppose Nazism or any less likely to be enthusiastic supporters? I am not aware of any careful quantitative attempts to address this question.

There's a terrific resource on ordinary German philosophers' engagement with Nazism: George Leaman's (1993) *Heidegger im Kontext*, which includes a complete list of all German philosophy professors from 1932 to 1945 and provides summary data on their involvement with or resistance to Nazism. In Leaman's data set, I count 179 philosophers with *habilitation* in 1932 when the Nazis started to ascend to power, including *dozents* and *ausserordentlichers* but not assistants. (*Habilitation* is an academic achievement beyond the doctorate, with no equivalent in the Anglophone world, but roughly comparable in its requirements to gaining tenure in the United States.) I haven't attempted to divide these philosophers into ethicists and nonethicists, since the ethics/nonethics division wasn't as sharp then as it is now in twenty-first century Anglophone

philosophy. (Consider Heidegger again. In a sense he's an ethicist, since he writes among other things on the question of how
one should live, but his interests range broadly.) Of these 179
philosophers, 58 (32 percent) joined the Nazi Party.[27] This com-
pares with estimates of about 21–25 percent Nazi Party membership among German professors as a whole.[28] Philosophers were
thus not underrepresented in the Nazi Party.

To what extent did joining the Nazi Party reflect enthusiasm for its goals versus opportunism versus a reluctant decision under pressure? I think we can assume that membership
in either of the two notorious Nazi paramilitary organizations,
the *Sturmabteilung* (Storm Detachment, SA) or the *Schutzstaffel*
(Protection Squadron, SS), reflects either enthusiastic Nazism or
an unusual degree of self-serving opportunism: Membership in
these organizations was by no means required for continuation
in a university position. Among philosophers with habilitation
in 1932, 2 (1 percent) joined the SS and another 20 (11 percent)
joined (or were already in) the SA (one philosopher joined both),
percentages approximately similar to the overall academic participation in these organizations. I suspect that this estimate
substantially undercounts enthusiastic Nazis, since a number of
philosophers (including briefly Heidegger) appear to have gone
beyond mere membership to enthusiastic support through their
writings and other academic activities, despite not joining the SA
or SS. One further possible measure is involvement with Alfred
Rosenberg, the notorious Nazi racial theorist. Combining SA and
SS members and Rosenberg associates yields a minimum of 30
philosophers (17 percent) on the far right side of Nazism—not
even including those who received their posts or habilitation
after the Nazis rose to power (and thus perhaps partly because of
their Nazism). By 1932, Hitler's *Mein Kampf* was widely known
and widely circulated, proudly proclaiming Hitler's genocidal

aims. Almost a fifth of professional philosophers thus embraced a political worldview that is now rightly regarded by most as a paradigm example of evil.

Among philosophers who were not party members, 22 (12 percent) were "Jewish" (by the broad Nazi definition) and thus automatically excluded from party membership. Excluding these from the total leaves 157 non-Jewish philosophers with habilitation before 1933. The 58 Nazis thus constituted 37 percent of established philosophers who had the opportunity to join the party. Of the remainder, 47 (30 percent) were deprived of the right to teach, imprisoned, or otherwise severely punished by the Nazis for Jewish family connections or political unreliability. (This second number does not include five philosophers who were Nazi Party members but also later severely penalized.) It's difficult to know how many of this group took courageous stands versus found themselves intolerable for reasons outside of their control. The remaining 33 percent we might think of as "coasters"—those who neither joined the party nor incurred severe penalty. Most of these coasters had at least token Nazi affiliations, especially with the *Nationalsozialistische Lehrerbund* (NSLB, the Nazi organization of teachers), but NSLB affiliation alone probably did not reflect much commitment to the Nazi cause.

If joining the Nazi Party were necessary for simply getting along as a professor, membership in the Nazi Party would not reflect much commitment to Nazism. The fact that about a third of professors could be coasters suggests that token gestures of Nazism, rather than actual party membership, were sufficient, as long as one did not actively protest or have Jewish affiliations. Nor were the coasters mostly old men on the verge of retirement (though there was a wave of retirements in 1933, the year the Nazis assumed power). If we include only the subset of 107 professors who were not Jewish, received habilitation before 1933, and continued to teach past 1940, we still find 30 percent coasters (or 28 percent, excluding two emigrants).

The existence of so many unpunished coasters shows that philosophy professors were not forced to join the Nazi Party. Nevertheless, a substantial proportion did so voluntarily, either out of enthusiasm or opportunistically for the sake of career advancement. A substantial minority, at least 19 percent of the non-Jews, occupied the far right of the Nazi Party, as reflected by membership in the SS or SA or association with Rosenberg. It is unclear whether pressures might have been greater on philosophers than on those in other disciplines, but there was substantial ideological pressure in many disciplines: There was also Nazi physics (no Jewish relativity theory, for example), Nazi biology, Nazi history, and so on. Given the possible differences in pressure and the lack of a data set strictly comparable to Leaman's for the professoriate as a whole, I don't think we can conclude that philosophers were especially more likely to endorse Nazism than were other professors. However, I do think it is reasonable to conclude that they were not especially *less* likely.

Nonetheless, given that about a third of non-Jewish philosophers were severely penalized by the Nazis (including one executed for resistance and two who died in concentration camps), it remains possible that philosophers are overrepresented among those who resisted or were ejected. I have not seen quantitative data that bear on this question.

そ

In doing background reading for the analysis I've just presented, I was struck by the following passage from Fritz Ringer's 1969 classic *Decline of the German Mandarins*:

> Early in August of 1914, the war finally came. One imagines that at least a few educated Germans had private moments of horror at the

slaughter which was about to commence. In public, however, German academics of all political persuasions spoke almost exclusively of their optimism and enthusiasm. Indeed, they greeted the war with a sense of relief. Party differences and class antagonisms seemed to evaporate at the call of national duty . . . intellectuals rejoiced at the apparent rebirth of "idealism" in Germany. They celebrated the death of politics, the triumph of ultimate, apolitical objectives over short-range interests, and the resurgence of those moral and irrational sources of social cohesion that had been threatened by the "materialistic" calculation of Wilhelmian modernity.

On August 2, the day after the German mobilization order, the modernist [theologian] Ernst Troeltsch spoke at a public rally. Early in his address, he hinted that "criminal elements" might try to attack property and order, now that the army had been moved from the German cities to the front. This is the only overt reference to fear of social disturbance that I have been able to discover in the academic literature of the years 1914–1916 . . . the German university professors sang hymns of praise to the "voluntary submission of all individuals and social groups to this army." They were almost grateful that the outbreak of war had given them the chance to experience the national enthusiasm of those heady weeks in August. (180–181)

With the notable exception of Bertrand Russell (who lost his academic post and was imprisoned for his pacifism), philosophers in England appear to have been similarly enthusiastic. Ludwig Wittgenstein never did anything so cheerily, it seems, as head off to fight as an Austrian foot soldier. Alfred North Whitehead rebuked his friend and coauthor Russell for his opposition to the war and eagerly sent off his sons North and Eric. (Eric Whitehead died.) French philosophers appear to have been similarly enthusiastic. It's as though, in 1914, European philosophers rose as one to join the general chorus of people proudly declaring, "Yay! World war is a great idea!"

If there is anything that seems, in retrospect, plainly, head-smackingly obviously *not* to have been a great idea, it was World

War I, which destroyed millions of lives to no purpose. At best, it should have been viewed as a regrettable, painful necessity in the face of foreign aggression that hopefully could soon be diplomatically resolved, yet that seems rarely to have been the mood of academic thought about war in 1914. Philosophers at the time were evidently no more capable of seeing the downsides of world war than was anyone else. Even if those downsides were, in the period, not entirely obvious upon careful reflection—the glory of Bismarck and all that?—with a few rare and ostracized exceptions, philosophers and other academics showed little of the special foresight and broad vision required by the Grand Wisdom Hypothesis.

Here's a model of philosophical reflection on which philosophers' enthusiasm for World War I is unsurprising: Philosophers— and everyone else—possess their views about the big questions of life for emotional and sociological reasons that have little to do with their philosophical theories and academic research. They recruit Kant, Mill, Locke, Rousseau, and Aristotle only after the fact to justify what they would have believed anyway. Moral and political philosophy is nothing but post hoc rationalization.

Here's a model of philosophical reflection on which philosophers' enthusiasm for World War I is, in contrast, surprising: Reading Kant, Mill, Locke, Rousseau, Aristotle, and so on helps induce a broadly humanitarian view, helps you see that people everywhere deserve respect and self-determination, moves you toward a more cosmopolitan worldview that doesn't overvalue national borders, helps you gain critical perspective on the political currents of your own time and country, and helps you better see through the rhetoric of demagogues and narrow-minded politicians.

Both models are of course too simple.

☙

When I was in Berlin in 2010, I spent some time in the Humboldt University library, browsing philosophy journals from the Nazi era. The journals differed in their degree of alignment with the Nazi worldview. Perhaps the most Nazified was *Kant-Studien*, which at the time was one of the leading German-language journals of general philosophy (not just a journal for Kant scholarship). The old issues of *Kant-Studien* aren't widely available, but I took some photos. Below, Sascha Fink and I have translated H. Heyse's preface to *Kant-Studien*, volume 40 (1935):

> *Kant-Studien*, now under its new leadership that begins with this first issue of the fortieth volume, sets itself a new task: to bring the new will, in which the deeper essence of the German life and the German mind is powerfully realized, to a breakthrough in the fundamental questions as well as the individual questions of philosophy and science.
>
> Guiding us is the conviction that the German Revolution is a unified metaphysical act of German life, which expresses itself in all areas of German existence, and which will therefore—with irresistible necessity—put philosophy and science under its spell.
>
> But is this not—as is so often said—to snatch away the autonomy of philosophy and science and give it over to a law alien to them?
>
> Against all such questions and concerns, we offer the insight that moves our innermost being: that the reality of our life, that shapes itself and will shape itself, is deeper, more fundamental, and more true than that of our modern era as a whole—that philosophy and science, which compete for it, will in a radical sense become liberated to their own essence, to their own truth. Precisely for the sake of truth, the struggle with modernity—maybe with the basic norms and basic forms of the time in which we live—is necessary. It is—in a sense that is alien and outrageous to modern thinking—to recapture the form in which the untrue and fundamentally destroyed life can win back its innermost truth—its rescue and salvation. This connection of the German life to fundamental forces and to the original truth of Being and its order—as has never been attempted in the same

depth in our entire history—is what we think of when we hear that word of destiny: a new Reich.

If on the basis of German life German philosophy struggles for this truly Platonic unity of truth with historical-political life, then it takes up a European duty. Because it poses the problem that each European people must solve, as a necessity of life, from its own individual powers and freedoms.

Again, one must—and now in a new and unexpected sense, in the spirit of Kant's term, "bracket knowledge" [*das Wissen aufzuheben*]. Not for the sake of negation: but to gain space for a more fundamental form of philosophy and science, for the new form of spirit and life [*für die neue Form . . . des Lebens Raum zu gewinnen*]. In this living and creative sense is *Kant-Studien* connected to the true spirit of Kantian philosophy.

So we call on the productive forces of German philosophy and science to collaborate in these new tasks. We also turn especially to foreign friends, confident that in this joint struggle with the fundamental questions of philosophy and science, concerning the truth of Being and life, we will not only gain a deeper understanding of each other, but also develop an awareness of our joint responsibility for the cultural community of peoples.

—H. Heyse, Professor of Philosophy, University of Königsberg

☙

Is it just good cultural luck—the luck of having been born into the right kind of society—that explains why twenty-first-century Anglophone philosophers reject such loathsome worldviews? Or is it more than luck? Have we somehow acquired better tools for rising above our cultural prejudices?

Or—as I'll suggest in chapter 58—ought we to entirely refrain from self-congratulation, whether for our luck or our skill? Maybe we aren't so different, after all, from the early-twentieth-century Germans. Maybe we have our own suite of culturally shared, heinous moral defects, invisible to us or obscured by a fog of bad philosophy.

In 2016, Peter Adamson, host of the podcast *History of Philosophy without Any Gaps*, posted twenty "Rules for the History of Philosophy." Mostly they are fine rules. I want to quibble with one.

Like almost every historian of philosophy I know, Adamson recommends that we be "charitable" to the text. Here's how he puts it in "Rule 2: Respect the text":

> This is my version of what is sometimes called the "principle of charity." A minimal version of this rule is that we should assume, in the absence of fairly strong reasons for doubt, that the philosophical texts we are reading make sense . . . [It] seems obvious (to me at least) that useful history of philosophy doesn't involve looking for inconsistencies and mistakes, but rather trying one's best to get a coherent and interesting line of argument out of the text. This is, of course, not to say that historical figures never contradicted themselves, made errors, and the like, but our interpretations should seek to avoid imputing such slips to them unless we have tried hard and failed to find a way of resolving the apparent slip.

At a first pass, it seems like a good idea, if at all possible, to avoid imputing contradictions and errors and to seek a coherent, sensible interpretation of historical texts. This is how, it seems, to best "respect the text."

To see why I think charity isn't as good an idea as it initially seems, let me first mention my main reason for reading history of philosophy: It's to gain a perspective, through the lens of distance, on my own philosophical views and presuppositions, and on the philosophical attitudes and presuppositions of twenty-first century Anglophone philosophy generally. Twenty-first century Anglophone philosophers, for example, tend to assume that the world is wholly material—or if they reject that view, they tend to occupy one of a few well-known alternative positions (e.g., Christian theism, naturalistic "property dualism"). I'm inclined to accept the majority's materialism. Reading the history of philosophy reminds me that a wide variety of other views have been taken seriously over time. Similarly, twenty-first century Anglophone philosophers tend to favor a certain species of liberal ethics, with an emphasis on individual rights and comparatively little deference to traditional rules and social roles—and I tend to favor such an ethics too. But it's good to be vividly aware that historically important thinkers have often had very different moral opinions, which they felt they could adequately justify. Reading culturally distant texts reminds me that I am a creature of my era, with views that have been shaped by contingent social factors.

Others might read history of philosophy with very different aims, of course.

Question: If my main aim in reading history of philosophy is to appreciate the historical diversity of philosophical views, what is the most counterproductive thing I could do when confronting a historical text?

Answer: Interpret the author as endorsing a view that is familiar, "sensible," and similar to my own and my colleagues'.

Historical texts, like all philosophical texts—but more so, given our linguistic and cultural distance—tend to be difficult and ambiguous. Therefore, they will admit of multiple interpretations. Suppose, then, that a text admits of four possible interpretations, A, B, C, and D, of which interpretation A is the least challenging, least weird, and most sensible, and interpretation D is the most challenging, weirdest, and least sensible. A simple application of the principle of charity seems to recommend that we favor the sensible, pedestrian interpretation A, the interpretation that, in our view, makes the most sense and avoids the most errors. However, weird and wild interpretation D might be the one we would learn most from taking seriously, challenging our presuppositions more deeply and giving us a more helpfully divergent perspective. This is one reason to favor interpretation D. Call this the *Principle of Anticharity*.

This way of defending anticharity might seem bluntly instrumentalist. What about historical accuracy? Don't we want the interpretation that's most likely to be the *correct* interpretation?

Bracketing postmodern views that reject truth in textual interpretation, I have four responses to that concern:

1. Being anticharitable doesn't mean that anything goes. You still want to respect the surface of the text. If the author says *p*, you don't want to attribute the view that not-*p*. In fact, it is the more "charitable" views that are likely to interpret an author's claims other than at face value: "Kant seems to say that it's permissible to kill children who are born out of wedlock, but really a charitable, sensible interpretation in light of X, Y, and Z is that he really meant . . ." In one way, it is actually more respectful to texts *not* to be too charitable and to interpret the text superficially at face value. After all, *p* is what the author literally said.

2. What seems "coherent" and "sensible" is culturally variable. You might reject excessive charitableness, while still wanting to limit allowable interpretations to one among several sensible and coherent ones. But this might already be too limiting. It might not seem "coherent" to us to embrace a contradiction, but some philosophers in some traditions seem happy to accept some bald contradictions.[29] It might not seem sensible to think that the world is nothing but a flux of ideas, the existence of rocks depending on the states of immaterial spirits, so in the spirit of charity, if there's any ambiguity, you might prefer an interpretation that you find less metaphysically peculiar. But metaphysical idealism is now at a low ebb by world historical standards, so this strategy might lead you away from rather than toward interpretive accuracy.

3. Philosophy is hard and philosophers are stupid. This human mind is not well designed for figuring out philosophical truths. Timeless philosophical puzzles tend to kick our collective butts. Sadly, this is going to be true of your favorite philosopher too. The odds are good that this philosopher, being a flawed human like you and me, made mistakes, fell into contradictions, changed opinions, and failed to see what seem in retrospect to be obvious consequences and counterexamples. Great philosophers can be great fools, and indeed the foolishness of rejecting assumptions that are widespread in your culture, without appreciating the alarming consequences for other views you hold, is sometimes exactly what propels philosophy forward. (An example might be Kant's egalitarian abstract ethics alongside his inegalitarian views on race, class, and gender; see chapter 52.) Respecting the text and respecting the person means, in part, not trying too hard to smooth this kind of thing away. The warts can even be part of the loveliness. Noticing them in your favorite philosopher can

also be tonic against excessive hero worship and a reminder of your own likely warts and failings.

4. Some authors might not even *want* to be interpreted as having a coherent, stable view. Zhuangzi, Montaigne, Nietzsche, and the later Wittgenstein all might be interpreted as expressing philosophical opinions that they don't expect to form an entirely coherent set.[30] If so, attempting "charitably" to stitch together a coherent picture might be a failure to respect the philosopher's own aims and intentions as expressed in the text.

I prefer uncharitable interpretation and the naked wartiness of the text. Refuse to hide the weirdness and the plain old wrongness and badness. Refuse to dress the text in sensible twenty-first century garb.

Imagine an essay manuscript: version A. Monday morning, I read through version A. I'm not satisfied. Monday, Tuesday, Wednesday, I revise and revise—cutting some ideas, adding others, tweaking the phrasing, trying to perfect the manuscript. Wednesday night I have the new version, version B. My labor is complete. I set it aside.

Three weeks later, I reread the manuscript—version B, of course. It lacks something. The ideas I had made more complex seem now too complex. They lack vigor. Conversely, what I had simplified for version B now seems flat and cartoonish. The new sentences are clumsy, the old ones better. My first instincts had been right, my second thoughts poor. I change everything back to the way it was, one piece at a time, thoughtfully. Now I have version C—word-for-word identical to version A.

To your eyes, version A and version C look the same, but I know them to be vastly different. What was simplistic in version A is now, in version C, elegantly simple. What I overlooked in version A, version C instead subtly finesses. What was rough prose in version A is now artfully casual. Every sentence of version C is deeper and more powerful than in version A. A journal would rightly reject version A but rightly accept version C.[31]

Once upon a time, there was a graduate student at University of California, Riverside, who I will call Student X. The general sense among the faculty was that Student X was particularly promising. For example, after a colloquium at which the student had asked a question, one faculty member expressed to me how impressive the student was. That remark surprised me, because I had thought the student's question had actually been rather poor. But it occurred to me that the question had seemed, superficially, to be smart. That is, if you didn't think too much about the content but rather just about the tone and delivery, you probably would get a strong impression of smartness. In fact, my overall view of this student was that he was about average—neither particularly good nor particularly bad—but that he was a master of *seeming smart:* He had the confidence, the delivery, the style, all the paraphernalia of smartness, without an especially large dose of the actual thing.

Mostly, I've noticed, it's white men from upper- and upper-middle-class backgrounds who are described in my presence as "seeming smart." It's really quite a striking pattern. (I've been keeping a tally since I first became interested in the phenomenon.) This makes sense, in a way. When the topic of conversation is complex and outside of one's specific expertise—in other words, most of philosophy, even for most professional philosophers—seeming smart is probably to a large extent about activating people's *associations* with intelligence as one discusses that topic. This can be done through poise, confidence (but not defensiveness), giving a moderate amount of detail but not too much, and providing some frame and jargon, and also, I suspect, unfortunately, in part by having the right kind of look and physical bearing, a dialect that is associated with high education levels, the right prosody (e.g., not the "Valley girl" habit of ending sentences with a rising intonation), the right body language. If you want to "seem smart," it helps immensely, I think, to just *sound* right, to have a "smart professor voice" in your toolkit, to be comfortable in an academic setting, to just strike the listener at a gut level as someone who belongs. Who will tend to have those tools and habits and feelings of confidence, and who will feel like someone who naturally belongs, and who will strike those in power as "one of us"? Unsurprisingly, it's typically the people who culturally resemble those who hold the majority of academic power. Me, for example: the white male professor's kid from an affluent suburb who went to Stanford. But philosophy as a discipline shouldn't be so dominated by my social group. The kid from the inner city whose parents never went to college will also have some interesting things to say, even if she's not so good at "professor voice."

℘

Student X actually ended up doing very well in the program and writing an excellent dissertation. He rose to his teachers' expectations—as students often do.[32] His terrific skill at seeming smart paid off handsomely in attracting positive attention and his professors' support and confidence, which probably helped him flourish over the long haul of the doctoral program. Conversely, the students not as good at the art of seeming smart often sink to their teachers' low expectations—frustrated, ignored, disvalued, criticized, made to feel not at home, as I have also seen.

I hereby renew my resolution to view skeptically all judgments of "seeming smart." Let's try to appreciate instead the value and potential in young scholars who seem superficially not to belong, who seem to be awkward and foolish and out of their depth, but who have somehow made it into the room anyway. They've probably fought a few more battles to get there, and they might have something different and interesting to say, if we're game to listen.

Academic philosophers tend to have a narrow view of what constitutes valuable philosophical research. Hiring, tenure, promotion, and prestige depend mainly on one's ability to produce journal articles in a particular theoretical, abstract style, mostly in reaction to a small group of canonical and recently influential thinkers, for a small readership of specialists. We should broaden our vision.

Consider the historical contingency of the journal article, a late-nineteenth-century invention. Even as recently as the middle of the twentieth century, influential philosophers in western Europe and North America did important work in a much broader range of genres: the fictions and difficult-to-classify reflections of Sartre, Camus, and Unamuno; Wittgenstein's cryptic fragments; the peace activism and popular writings of Bertrand Russell; John Dewey's work on educational reform. Popular essays, fictions, aphorisms, dialogues, autobiographical reflections, and personal letters have historically played a central role in philosophy. So also have public acts of direct confrontation with the structures of one's society: Socrates' trial and acceptance of the lethal hemlock, Confucius's inspiring personal correctness. It was really only with the generation hired to teach the baby boomers in the 1960s and 1970s that academic philosophers' conception of philosophical work became narrowly focused on the technical journal article.

In the twenty-first century, we have an even wider selection of media available to us. Is there reason to think that journal articles are uniformly better for philosophical reflection than videos, interactive demonstrations, blog posts, or multiparty conversations in social media? A conversation on Facebook, if good participants bring their best to the enterprise, has the potential to be a philosophical creation of the highest order, with a depth and breadth beyond the capacity of any individual philosopher to create. A video game could illuminate, critique, and advance a vision of worthwhile living, deploying sight, hearing, emotion, and personal narrative as well as (why not?) traditional verbal exposition—and it could potentially do so with all the freshness of thinking, all the transformative power, and all the expository rigor of Aristotle, Xunzi, or Hume. Academic philosophers are paid to develop expertise in philosophy, to bring that expertise into the classroom, and to contribute that expertise to society in part by advancing philosophical knowledge. A wide range of activities fit within that job description.

Every topic of human concern is open to philosophical inquiry—not only subjects well represented in journals, such as the structure of propositional attitudes and the nature of moral facts, but also how one ought to raise children and what makes a haircut good (chapter 50). Writing and responding to journal-article-length expository arguments by fellow philosophers is only one possible method of inquiry. Engaging with the world, trying out one's ideas in action, seeing the reactions of nonacademics, exploring ideas in fiction and meditation—in these activities we can not only deploy knowledge but also cultivate, expand, and propagate that knowledge.

Philosophical expertise is not like scientific expertise. Although academic philosophers know certain literatures very well, on questions about the general human condition and what our fundamental values should be, knowledge of the canon gives academic philosophers no especially privileged wisdom. Nonacademics can and should be respected partners in the philosophical dialogue. Too exclusive a focus on technical journal articles excludes nonacademics from the dialogue—or maybe, better said, excludes us philosophers from nonacademics' more important dialogue. The academic journal article as it exists today is too limited in format, topic, method, and audience to deserve so centrally privileged a place in philosophers' conception of the discipline.

If one approaches popular writing only as a means of "dumbing down" preexisting philosophical ideas for an audience of nonexperts whose reactions one doesn't plan to take seriously, then one is squandering a great research opportunity. The popular essay can be a locus of philosophical creativity in which ideas are explored in hope of discovering new possibilities, advancing (and not just marketing) one's own thinking in a way that might strike professionals too as interesting. Analogously for government consulting, Twitter feeds, TED videos, and poetry.

A *Philosophical Review* article can be an amazing thing. But we should see journal articles in that style, in that type of venue, as only one of many possible forms of important, field-shaping philosophical work.

෨

The eight-hundred-word blog post deserves, I think, special praise, for three distinct reasons:

1. *Short, fat, tangled arguments.* In her 2015 Dewey lecture at the Pacific Division meeting of the American Philosophical

Association, philosopher of science Nancy Cartwright celebrated what she called "short, stocky, tangled" arguments over
"tall, skinny" arguments. Here's a tall, skinny, neat argument:

A

$A \rightarrow B$

$B \rightarrow C$

$C \rightarrow D$

$D \rightarrow E$

$E \rightarrow F$

$F \rightarrow G$

$G \rightarrow H$

$H \rightarrow I$

$I \rightarrow J$

Therefore, J. (Whew!)

And here's a short, fat, tangled argument:

A1	A2	A3
$A1 \rightarrow B$	$A2 \rightarrow B$	$A1 \rightarrow A3$
Therefore, B	$A2 \rightarrow A1$	$A3 \rightarrow A2$
	Therefore, B	$A3 \rightarrow B$
		Therefore, B.

The tall, lean argument carries you straight like an arrow shot
all the way from A to J. All the way from the fundamental
nature of consciousness to the reforms of Napoleon. (Yes,
I'm thinking of you, Georg Wilhelm Friedrich.[33]) All the way
from seven abstract Axioms to Proposition V.42: "Blessedness
is not the reward of virtue, but virtue itself; nor do we enjoy
it because we restrain our lusts; on the contrary, because we
enjoy it, we are able to restrain them." (Sorry, Baruch, I wish I
were more convinced![34])

In contrast, the short, fat, tangled argument takes you only from versions of A to B. But it does so in three ways, so that if one argument fails, the others remain. It does so without needing a long string of possibly dubious intermediate claims. And the different premises lend tangly sideways support to each other. I think here of the ancient Chinese philosopher Mozi's dozen arguments for impartial concern or the ancient Greek philosopher Sextus's many modes of skepticism.[35]

In areas like mathematics, tall, skinny arguments can work. Maybe the proof of Fermat's last theorem is one—long and complicated, but apparently sound. (Not that I would be any authority.) When each step is secure, tall arguments succeed and lift us to wonderful heights. But philosophy tends not to have such secure intermediate steps.

The human mind is great at determining an object's shape from its shading and also at interpreting a stream of incoming sound as a sly dig on someone's character. The human mind is horrible at determining the soundness of philosophical arguments and also at determining the soundness of most intermediate stages within philosophical arguments. (If these remarks sound familiar from my other chapters, that's part of the fat tangle I seek.) Tall, skinny philosophical arguments— this was Cartwright's point—will almost inevitably topple. Even the short arguments usually fail—as I believe they do in Mozi and Sextus—but at least they have a shot.

Individual blog posts are short. They are, I think, just about the right size for human philosophical cognition: five hundred to a thousand words, long enough to put some flesh on an idea, making it vivid (pure philosophical abstractions being almost impossible to evaluate for multiple reasons), long enough to introduce one or maybe two novel turns or connections, but short enough that the reader can reach the end without having lost track of the path there, keeping more or less the whole argument simultaneously in view.

In the aggregate, blog posts are fat and tangled: Multiple posts can drive toward the same conclusion from diverse angles and can lend sideways support to each other. I've written many posts, for example, that are skeptical of expert philosophical cognition—several of which have been adapted for this book. I've written many posts, some also adapted for this book, that are skeptical of moral self-knowledge, and also many that aim to express my wonder at the possible weirdness of the world. They synergize, perhaps, in conveying my overall philosophical perspective—but they do not stack up into a tall, topply tower. If some or even most of them fail individually, the general picture can still stand supported.

Of course, there's also something to be said for trying to build a ladder to the Moon. Maybe you'll be the one who finally gets there! Even if you don't, it might be quite a lovely ladder.

2. *The discipline of writing clearly for a broad audience.* Specialists love jargon. And for good reason: When you work a frequently with a concept or a tool, you want to have a specific name for it, and that specific name might not be part of the common language of nonspecialists. So stock analysts have their trailing P/E ratios and their EBITDAs, jazz musicians have their 9/8 time signatures and their A♭dim7s, and philosophers have their neutral monisms and their supererogation.

Specialists also love arguing about subsidiary issues four layers deep in a conversation no one else will understand. And for good reason: Those things matter, and when something works or doesn't work, especially if its success or failure is surprising, it's often because of some recondite detail: the previous quarter report reflects a huge legal liability that everyone knew was coming and makes the earnings look jumpy, the guitar sound will be fuller if the song is transposed into the key of E, which will open more strings. The last two journal articles I reviewed (at the time of writing this) concerned, in part, (a) whether the "rubber hand" illusion is a good objection to Rory Madden's argument that there can be no scattered subjects of consciousness and (b) whether Tamar Gendler's concept of "alief" can successfully save, from a certain type of objection concerning absentmindedness, the view that the disposition to phenomenally experience the judgment that p is sufficient for believing that p. (Don't ask.[36]) These are important issues. Pulling on these threads threatens to unravel some big theories. I recommended publication.

And yet the specialist can spend too much time neck deep in these issues, conversing with others who are also neck deep. Consequently, you can forget what is at stake—why the issues are interesting in the first place. You can lose yourself in picayune details and forget the big picture that those detailed arguments are supposed to be illuminating. Furthermore, you can lose sight of the presuppositions, idealizations, or philosophical background beliefs that are implicit in your shared specialists' jargon.

I have found it to be excellent philosophical discipline to regularly articulate what I care about for educated but non-specialist readers. It forces me to convey what's interesting or important in what I'm doing, and it forces me to examine my jargon. If a thousand words isn't enough space to clearly say what I'm doing, why it might be interesting, and what my core argument is, then I'm probably uncompassed in some philosophical forest, turning circles in the underbrush.

3. *Feedback and revisability.* If you're a big believer in philosophical expertise, then you might not put much stock in feedback

from nonexperts. No mathematician would value my feedback on a proof and rightly so; I don't have the expertise to comment competently. You could think the same thing is true in philosophy. Philosophical combatants deep in the trenches of arguments about neutral monism and supererogation might reasonably believe that nonexperts could have little of value to contribute to their exchange.

But I'm mistrustful of philosophical expertise, as you'll have gathered. Philosophers have *some* expertise, sure, and much more familiarity with some of the standard moves in their professional terrain—but the difference between Kant and our philosopher of hair (chapter 50) is, I believe, not nearly as great as sometimes advertised. If Kant had approached the women and servants around him as philosophical equals, expressing his ideas in plain language, they might have given him some good advice (chapter 52). In presenting ideas for a broad audience, one receives feedback from a broad range of people. Those people can often see your specialist's dicey presuppositions, which really ought to be challenged, and they can see connections to issues beyond your usual purview.

And then—even better—in a blog, you can *continue* the discussion, gain a better understanding of where they're coming from and how they react to your responses. You can reply in the comments section, maybe even revise the post or write an addendum, or you can try again in a different way next year when your mind circles back around to writing another post on the topic.

The blog post is therefore the ideal medium for philosophy! Several hundred to a thousand words: just the right length for a human-sized philosophical thought with some detail, not built too tall. A public medium, encouraging clarity and a sense of what's important, and potentially drawing feedback from a wide range of thoughtful people, both expert and nonexpert, in light of which you can revise and develop your view. It's how philosophy ought to be done.

Okay, I shouldn't be so imperialistic about it. Journal articles and books are good too, in their own way, for their own different purposes, since the detailed argumentative moves do often matter. And short stories, for their vividness and emotional complexity. And television shows. And interviews, and dialogues, and . . .

58 Will Future Generations Find Us Morally Loathsome?

Ethical norms change. Although reading Confucius doesn't feel like encountering some bizarrely alien moral system, some ethical ideas do shift dramatically over time and between cultures. Genocide and civilian-slaughtering aggressive warfare are now generally considered among the evilest things people can do, yet they appear to be celebrated in the Bible, and we still name children after Alexander "the Great."[37] Many seemingly careful thinkers, including notoriously Aristotle and Locke, wrote justifications of slavery.[38] Much of the world now recognizes equal rights for women, homosexuals, low-status workers, people with disabilities, and ethnic minorities.[39]

It's unlikely that we've reached the end of moral change. In a few centuries, people might view our current norms with the same mix of appreciation and condemnation with which we now view norms common in ancient China and early modern Europe. Indeed, future generations might find our generation to be loathsome in an especially vivid way, since we are the first generation creating an extensive video record of our day-to-day activities.

Let me highlight the vividness of video. I find it helpful—and intimidating—to imagine the microscope upon us. It's one thing to know, in the abstract, that Rousseau fathered five children with

a lover he regarded as too dull witted to be worth attempting to
formally educate and that he demanded against her protests that
their children be sent to (probably high mortality) orphanages.[40]
It would be quite another if we had baby pictures and video of
Rousseau's interactions with Thérèse. It's one thing to know, in
the abstract, that Aristotle had a wife and a life of privilege. It
would be quite another to watch video of him proudly enacting
elitist and patriarchal values we now find vile while pontificat-
ing on the ethics of the man of wisdom. Our consumerism, or
our casual destruction of the environment, or our neglect of the
sick and elderly—whatever vilenesses future generations might
detest in us will be available for viewing in vivid detail. By "our"
practices and values, I mean the typical practices and values of
readers living in early-twenty-first-century democracies—the
notional readership of this book.

Maybe climate change proves to be catastrophic: Crops fail,
low-lying cities are flooded, a billion desperate people are dis-
placed or malnourished or tossed into war. Looking back on
video of a philosopher of our era proudly stepping out of his
shiny, privately owned minivan across his beautiful irrigated
lawn in the summer heat into his large, chilly air-conditioned
house, maybe wearing a leather hat, maybe sharing McDonald's
ice cream cones with his kids—looking back, that is, on what I
(of course this is me) think of as a lovely family moment—might
this seem to some future Bangladeshi philosopher as vividly dis-
gusting as I suspect I would find, if there were video record of it,
Heidegger's treatment of his Jewish colleagues?

 App

If we are currently at the moral pinnacle, any change will be
a change for the worse. Future generations might condemn
our mixing of the races, for example. They might wince to see

video of interracial couples walking together in public with their mixed-race children. Or they might loathe clothing customs they view as obscene. However, I feel comfortable saying that they'd be wrong to condemn us, if those were the reasons why. Only by an unusual exertion of imagination can I muster any real doubt about the moral permissibility of our culture's interracial marriage and tank tops.

But it seems unlikely that our culture is at the moral pinnacle, and thus it seems likely that future generations will have some excellent moral reasons to condemn us. More likely than our being at the moral pinnacle, it seems to me, is either that (a) there has been a slow trajectory toward better values over the centuries (as recently argued by Steven Pinker[41]) and that the trajectory will continue, or alternatively that (b) shifts in value are more or less a random walk up, down, and sideways, in which case it would be unlikely chance if we happened to be at peak right now. I am assuming here the same kind of nonrelativism that most people assume in condemning Nazism and in thinking that it constitutes genuine moral progress to recognize the equal moral status of women and men.

It doesn't *feel* like we're wrong, I assume, for those of us who share the values we currently find ordinary. It probably feels as though we are applying our excellent minds excellently to the matter, with wisdom and good sense. But might we sometimes be using philosophy to justify the twenty-first-century college-educated North American's moral equivalent of keeping slaves and oppressing women? Is there some way to gain some insight into this possibility—some way to get a temperature reading, so to speak, on our unrecognized evil?

Here's one thing I don't think will work: relying on the ethical reasoning of the highest-status philosophers in our society.

If you've read my chapters on Kant, Nazi philosophers, and the morality of ethics professors, you'll know why I say this.

ᴄᴏ

I'd suggest, or at least I'd hope, that if future generations rightly condemn us, it won't be for something we'd find incomprehensible. It won't be because we sometimes chose blue shirts over red ones or because we like to smile at children. It will be for things that we already have an inkling might be wrong and that some people do already condemn as wrong. As Michele Moody-Adams emphasizes in her discussion of slavery and cultural relativism, in every slave culture there were always *some* voices condemning the injustice of slavery—among them, typically, the slaves themselves.[42] As a clue to our own evil, we might look to minority moral opinions in our own culture.

I tend to think that the behavior of my social group is more or less fine, or at worst forgivably mediocre (chapters 4 and 8), and if someone advances a minority ethical view I disagree with, I'm philosopher enough to concoct some superficially plausible defenses. But I worry that a properly situated observer might recognize those defenses to be no better than Hans Heyse's defense of Nazism (chapter 53) or Kant's justification for denying servants the vote (chapter 52).

I find myself, as I write this final chapter, rereading the epilogue of Moody-Adams's 1997 book, *Fieldwork in Familiar Places*. Moody-Adams suggests that we can begin to rise beyond our cultural and historical moral boundaries through moral reflection of the right sort: moral reflection that involves . . . well, I'm going to bullet-point the list to slow down the presentation of it, since the list is so good:

- self-scrutiny
- vivid imagination

- a wide-ranging contact with other disciplines and traditions
- a recognition of minority voices
- serious engagement with the concrete details of everyday moral inquiry

(This list, I should clarify, is what I extract from Moody-Adams's remarks, which are not presented in exactly these words or in a list format.)

Instead of a narrow or papier-mâché seminar-room rationalism, we should treasure insight from the entire range of lived experience and from perspectives as different as possible from our own, in a spirit of open-mindedness and self-doubt. Here lies our best chance of repairing our probable moral myopia.

If I have an agenda in this book, it's less to defend any specific philosophical thesis than to philosophize in a manner that manifests these virtues.

☙

There's one thing missing from Moody-Adams's lovely list, though, or maybe it's a cluster of related things. It's wonder, fun, and a sense of the incomprehensible bizarreness of the world. We should have those in our vision of good philosophy too! Moral open-mindedness is not, I think, entirely distinct from epistemic and metaphysical open-mindedness. They mix (I hope) in this book. I think I see them mixing, too, in two of my favorite philosophers, the great humane skeptics Zhuangzi and Montaigne.

Uncomfortably self-critical reflections on excuses and jerkitude—they're apt to wear us down, and too much thinking of that sort might reinforce the exact type of moral rationalization we hope to avoid. When we need a break from moral self-doubt, and some fun, we can cast ourselves into a different sort of doubt. We can spend some time—you and me together if you like—dreaming of cute AI and zombie robots.

Acknowledgments

The following chapters appeared first in venues other than my blog, and have been somewhat revised for inclusion in this book: "A Theory of Jerks," "Cheeseburger Ethics (or How Often Do Ethicists Call Their Mothers?)," and "We Would Have Greater Moral Obligations to Conscious Robots than to Otherwise Similar Humans " in *Aeon Magazine*; "Should Your Driverless Car Kill You So Others May Live?," "Dreidel: A Seemingly Foolish Game That Contains the Moral World in Miniature," "Does It Matter If the Passover Story Is Literally True?," "What Happens to Democracy When the Experts Can't Be Both Factual and Balanced?," and part of "Blogging and Philosophical Cognition" in the *Los Angeles Times*; "Cute AI and the ASIMO Problem" in Schwitzgebel and Garza 2015; "Why Metaphysics Is Always Bizarre" in Schwitzgebel 2014b; and both "The Happy Coincidence Defense and The-Most-You-Can-Do Sweet Spot" and "Is It Perfectly Fine to Aim for Moral Mediocrity?" in Schwitzgebel 2019. "Is the United States Literally Conscious" is an abbreviated version of Schwitzgebel 2015a.

So many people have given me helpful comments and suggestions on the topics of these chapters, in person and on social media and by email or instant messages and during presentations and interviews and telephone conversations and video calls (and even a couple of helpful old-fashioned pieces of mail about my op-ed on Passover traditions) that it would require a superhuman memory to properly thank everyone who deserves it. So I'll just mention some names of people who saliently came to mind as I was revising and updating, for having said something memorably helpful on one or more of the chapters. My embarrassed apologies—especially embarrassed in light of what I say about forgetting in chapter 2!—to the many I unfairly omit. Thank you, Peter Adamson, Nick Alonso, Roman Altshuler, Gene Anderson, Nomy Arpaly, Yuval Avnur, Uziel Awret, John Baez, Nick Baiamonte, Dave Baker, Scott Bakker, Zach Barnett, Jon Baron, John Basl, Howard Berman, Daryl Bird, Izzy Black, Reid Blackman, Ned Block, Daniel Bonevac, Nick Bostrom, Kurt Boughan, "Brandon" (on Kant), Richard Brown, Tim Brown, Wesley Buckwalter, Nick Byrd, Joe Campbell, Sean Carroll, David Chalmers, Myisha Cherry, chinaphil, Michel Clasquin-Johnson, Brad Cokelet, Mich Curria, Leif Czerny, Helen De Cruz, Rolf Degen, Dan Dennett, Keith DeRose, Cory Doctorow, Fred Dretske, David Duffy, Kenny Easwaran, Aryeh Englander, Daniel Estrada, Sascha Fink, John Fischer, Owen Flanagan, Kirk Gable, Julia Galef, Mara Garza, Dan George, David Glidden, Peter Godfrey-Smith, Sergio Graziosi, Jon Haidt, Rotem Hermann, Joshua Hollowell, Russ Hurlburt, Anne Jacobson, Aaron James, Eric Kaplan, Jonathan Kaplan, Kim Kempton, Jeanette McMullin King, Peter Kirwan, Roxana Kreimer, Ed Lake, Juliet Lapidos, Chris Laursen, Amod Lele, Neil Levy, P. D. Magnus, Angra Mainyu, Pete Mandik, Josh May, Randy Mayes, Joshua Miller, Ethan Mills, Kian Mintz-Woo, Alan Moore, Daniel Nagase, Eddy Nahmias, Adam Pautz, Steve Petersen, Benjamin Philip, Bryony Pierce, Peter Railton, Paul Raymont, Kris Rhodes, Sam Rickless, Regina Rini, Rebecca Roache, Josh Rust, Colleen Ryan, Sandy Ryan, Callan S., Susan Schneider,

David Schwitzgebel, Kate Schwitzgebel, Lisa Shapiro, Henry Shevlin, Justin Smith, Nichi Smith, David Sobel, Dan Sperber, Eric Steinhart, Charlie Stross, Olufemi Taiwo, Yvonne Tam, June Tangney, Valerie Tiberius, Justin Tiwald, Clinton Tolley, Shelley Tremain, David Udell, Bryan Van Norden, Dan Weijers, Nathan Westbrook, Eric Winsberg, Charles Wolverton, Mark Wrathall, Aaron Zimmerman, and of course the cognitively diverse group mind Anonymous.

For comments on the whole draft, I am especially grateful to Linus Huang, P. J. Ivanhoe, Jeremy Pober, Cati Porter, and most of all my wife Pauline Price, ever patient, tolerant, critical, and forgiving. This book is the joint project of our coauthored lives.

Notes

1 Jerks and Excuses

1. Yankovic 2006; Temple 1959, as cited in Schwitzgebel 2014a.

2. *Etymology Online*, https://www.etymonline.com/word/jerk (accessed June 21, 2018); and *Oxford English Dictionary* online, http://www.oed .com/ (accessed June 21, 2018); Barnhart 1988.

3. Nietzsche (1887) 1998, I.4–5, 12–14.

4. Frankfurt (1986) 2005; James 2012.

5. James 2012, 5.

6. Lilienfeld and Andrews 1996; Paulhus and Williams 2002; Blair, Mitchell, and Blair 2005.

7. On Machiavellianism and narcissism, see Christie and Geis 1970; Fehr, Samsom, and Paulhus 2013; Miller and Campbell 2008; and Jones and Paulhus 2014.

8. Vazire 2010; also John and Robins 1993 and Gosling et al. 1998.

9. Arendt 1963, 114. For a very different portrayal of Eichmann in which he might have only strategically feigned ignorance, see Stang-neth 2014.

10. I had heard that Michelangelo said this, but no such luck: O'Toole 2014.

11. GiveWell, for example, estimates that effective malaria programs cost about two thousand dollars per life saved. https://www.givewell. org/giving101/Your-dollar-goes-further-overseas (accessed June 21, 2018). See also the discussion in Singer 2009, chap. 6.

12. Doctors report smoking at rates substantially lower than do members of other professions. However, the data on nurses are mixed, and the self-reports of doctors are probably compromised to some extent by embarrassment (Squier et al. 2006; Jiang et al. 2007; Sezer, Guler, and Sezer 2007; Smith and Leggat 2007; Bazargan et al. 2009; Frank and Segura 2009; Sarna et al. 2010; Shaikh et al. 2015; though see also Abdullah et al. 2013). Studies of doctors' general health practices are mixed but confounded by issues of convenience, embarrassment, high professional demands, and the temptation to self-diagnose and self-treat (Richards 1999; Kay, Mitchell, and Del Mar 2004; Frank and Segura 2009; George, Hanson, and Jackson 2014).

13. Sluga 1993; Young 1997; Faye (2005) 2009; Gordon 2014.

14. With the exception of the Nazi study, which was never formally published and appeared only as a blog post (included here in chapter 53), these studies are summarized in Schwitzgebel and Rust 2016. Philipp Schoenegger and his collaborators have recently replicated several of our findings among German-language philosophers (personal communication), although the results on vegetarianism appear to be rather different, perhaps because of US-German cultural differences, changes in attitude in the ten years between 2008 and 2018, or both.

15. Schwitzgebel and Rust 2014, sec. 7.

16. Schwitzgebel and Rust 2014, sec. 10.

17. Singer (1975) 2009.

18. Cialdini, Reno, and Kallgren 1990; Cialdini et al. 2006; Schultz et al. 2007; Goldstein, Cialdini, and Griskevicius 2008; Bicchieri and Xiao 2009; Bicchieri 2017. The most widely replicated of these findings is that home energy conservation practices shift depending on what people learn about their neighbors' conservation practices: Allcott 2011; Ayres, Raseman, and Shih 2013; Karlin, Zinger, and Ford 2015.

19. Mazar and Zhong 2010; Brown et al. 2011; Jordan, Mullen, and Murnighan 2011; Conway and Peetz 2012; Clot, Grolleau, and Ibanez 2013; Cornelissen et al. 2013; Susewind and Hoelzl 2014; Blanken, van de Ven, and Zeelenberg 2015; Mullen and Monin 2016. However, see Schwitzgebel 2019 for some hesitations about effect size and replicability.

20. This is why I find it so interesting, for example, to examine Kant's *Metaphysics of Morals* alongside his more abstract ethical works. See chapter 52.

21. See Haidt 2012 for an interpretation of Josh's and my work along roughly these lines, and see Rust and Schwitzgebel 2015 for discussion of that and several other alternative interpretations.

22. In many theoretical discussions (e.g., Schroeder 2004; Moore [2004] 2013; Berridge and Kringelbach 2013), pleasure and displeasure are treated as having similar motivational weight, but this doesn't seem phenomenologically correct to me. (This issue is distinct from the question of whether pleasure and pain are distinct dimensions of experience that are capable of being experienced simultaneously.)

23. Nuanced readings of Stoicism and Buddhism normally acknowledge that the aim is not the removal of all hedonically valenced states, but rather the cultivation of a certain type of calm positive state of joy or tranquility (e.g., Epictetus [1st c. CE] 1944; Hanh [1998] 2015). Smart (1958) critiques a version of "negative utilitarianism," drawn partly from Popper (1945) 1994 (548–549), in which relieving suffering has more moral value than increasing pleasure by a similar amount. However, negative utilitarianism is rarely endorsed. Griffin (1979) suggests similarly that a small amount of unhappiness may be much more undesirable than a fairly large amount of happiness is desirable.

24. The classic treatments of "loss aversion" are Tversky and Kahneman 1991, 1992. The huge subsequent literature in psychology and experimental economics is, I understand, broadly confirmatory, though I have not yet managed to read quite all of it.

25. At least nonderivatively. Bentham (1781) 1988. Such psychological or motivational hedonism is now rarely accepted. Influential critiques

include Hume's ([1751] 1975, app. II) discussion of "self-love," Nozick's (1974) "experience machine" thought experiment, Sober and Wilson's (1998) discussion of the evolutionary bases of altruism, and Batson's long series of psychological experiments on altruistic motivation (summarized in Batson 2016). For a recent defense of motivational hedonism, see Garson 2016.

26. For some (nondecisive) evidence of this, see Kahneman et al. 2004; Margolis and Myrskylä 2011; and Hansen 2012; for a critical perspective, see Herbst and Ifcher 2016.

27. See Parfit's (1984) classic distinction between hedonic, desire-fulfillment, and objective-list theories of well-being. For a review of the literature on well-being, see Crisp (2001) 2017; for a recent defense of prudential hedonism, see Feldman 2004. Three prominent objections against prudential hedonism are the "happy swine" objection (that life is not better for an enormously happy pig than for a person with a mix of ups and downs; see the discussion in Bramble 2016), Nozick's (1974) "experience machine" objection (that it would be worse to be unwittingly trapped in an experience machine generating all sorts of fake experiences and consequent real pleasures than to live a real life), and the idea that betrayal behind your back harms you even if you never learn about it or have any bad experiences as a result (Nagel 1979; Fischer 1997).

28. This is widely accepted in the dream literature, matches the personal experiences of the people I've discussed it with, and follows from a common model of dream recall on which shortly after waking the attempt to recall one's dreams consolidates them into long-term memory. However, as noted in Aspy, Delfabbro, and Proeve 2015, direct and rigorous empirical evidence in support of this conclusion is thin.

29. The classic treatment of lucid dreaming is LaBerge and Rheingold 1990.

30. I remember chatting with someone about these matters at a conference a few weeks before the original post in 2012. In the fog of memory, I couldn't even then recall exactly who it was or to what extent these thoughts originated from me as opposed to my interlocutor, and subsequent inquiries have proved fruitless. Apologies, then, if they're due.

31. Mengzi (4th c. BCE) 2008, section 7A15.

32. Mengzi (4th c. BCE) 2008, section 1A7.

33. I owe this point to Yvonne Tam.

34. I discuss this issue at length in Schwitzgebel 2007.

35. Rousseau (1762) 1979, 235.

36. Confucius (5th c. BCE) 2003, section 15.24. Because of its negative phasing "do not . . . ," this is sometimes referred to as the "Silver Rule."

37. Mozi (5th c. BCE) 2013; Xunzi (3rd c. BCE) 2014. However, Mozi does have an argument for impartial concern that starts by assuming that one is concerned for one's parents (see Mozi, chap. 16).

38. Schwitzgebel 2019.

39. Susan Wolf famously argues that sainthood "does not constitute a model of personal well-being toward which it would be particularly rational or good or desirable for a human being to strive" (1982, 419). What I mean to be discussing here is not sainthood in Wolf's strong sense, but only moral excellence of the more pedestrian sort—the excellence, perhaps, of the few most overall morally excellent people you personally know.

40. In the philosophical lingo, your actual and hypothetical choices reveal what you are aiming for *de re* (i.e., what state of affairs in the world you are really guiding your actions toward), which might be different from what you are aiming for *de dicto* (i.e., what sentence you would endorse to describe what you are aiming for). Or something like that. On the de re/de dicto distinction in general, see McKay and Nelson (2010) 2014. For a discussion of its application to moral cases, see Arpaly 2003.

41. See, for example, the essays in Bloomfield 2008.

42. For a review, see Langlois et al. 2000.

43. See references in note 19.

44. See, for example, Erin Faith Wilson's (2017) list of seventeen antigay activists and preachers whose homosexual affairs were exposed between 2004 and 2017.

45. Mikkelson and Evon (2007) 2017. Nota bene: If Gore were saying, "We need top-down regulation, but until that comes, individuals should feel free to consume as luxuriously as they wish," then his luxurious consumption would not be evidence of hypocrisy.

46. Optimistic self-illusions: Taylor and Brown 1988; Shepperd et al. 2013. End-of-history thinking: Quoidbach, Gilbert, and Wilson 2013, though see Ellenberg 2013 for a critique.

47. Batson 2016, 25–26.

48. LeCun, Bengio, and Hinton 2015; Silver et al. 2016; for comparison and contrast with human cognitive architecture, see Lake et al. 2017.

49. Wheatley and Haidt 2005; Schnall et al. 2008; and Eskine, Kacinik, and Prinz 2011; for a review and meta-analysis, see Landy and Goodwin 2015.

50. Baron 1997.

51. Haidt 2012.

52. In ethics, see McDowell 1985; Railton 1986; Brink 1989; Casebeer 2003; and Flanagan, Sarkissian, and Wong 2008.

53. Kruger and Dunning 1999.

54. I haven't found a systematic discussion of cases in which Dunning-Kruger doesn't apply, though Kahneman and Klein 2009 is related.

55. Taylor and Brown 1988; Sedikides and Gregg 2008; Shepperd et al. 2013.

56. On self-enhancement, see references in note 55. On low correlation, see references in notes 53 and 54.

57. In Schwitzgebel 2007, I argue that Xunzi's and Hobbes's models of moral education fit this pattern.

58. In Schwitzgebel 2007, I argue that Mengzi's and Rousseau's models of moral education fit this pattern. See also Ivanhoe (1990) 2002 on the metaphor of cultivation in the Confucian tradition. I also read most of the foundational figures in twentieth-century moral psychology as endorsing this type of approach, including Piaget ([1932] 1975),

Kohlberg (1981), and Damon (1988). See also Baumrind 1971 on the "authoritative" parenting style.

59. Here, and in most of my examples, names are chosen randomly from names of former students in my lower-division classes, excluding Jesus, Mohammed, and very unusual names. For unnamed characters, the gender is the opposite of the named characters', to improve pronoun clarity.

60. For example, Damon 1988; de Waal 1996; Haidt 2012; and Bloom 2013.

II Cute AI and Zombie Robots

1. Respondents in one survey (Bonnefon, Shariff, and Rahwan 2016) reported a median 50 percent likelihood of purchasing an autonomous vehicle programmed to save its passengers even at the cost of killing ten times as many pedestrians, compared to a median 19 percent likelihood of purchasing one programmed to minimize the total number of deaths even if it meant killing the respondent and a family member.

2. I originally published the reflections included in this chapter in the *Los Angeles Times* in 2015, while Google was actively making the case for "self-certification" in California. Google and Tesla were threatening to move testing out of California to more lenient states if the California Department of Motor Vehicles didn't relax its attitude. It appears that they subsequently convinced the department to permit self-certification rather than make the algorithms and standards public or have them at least evaluated by an independent regulator (McFarland 2017). However, it's not yet too late for federal regulators to step in, to reduce the race-to-laxity competition among the states.

3. Clark 2008.

4. Weizenbaum 1976.

5. Darling 2017; Vedantam 2017.

6. Johnson 2003; Meltzoff et al. 2010; Fiala, Arico, and Nichols 2012.

7. But see references in note 20 for an alternative view.

8. Snodgrass and Scheerer 1989.

9. Bryson 2010, 2013.

10. For further discussion, see Schwitzgebel and Garza 2015. Jeremy Pober has argued in personal communication that artificial selection in dog breeding might partly violate the Emotional Alignment Design Policy by creating dogs that solicit emotional reactions disproportionate to their real moral status—in contrast to, say, coyotes. On the other hand, according to the reasoning of chapter 19 (as also observed by Jeremy), we might owe dogs special moral consideration, more than we owe to coyotes, because of the role we have played in shaping them.

11. This chapter was inspired by a conversation with Cory Doctorow about how a child's high-tech rented eyes might be turned toward favored products in the cereal aisle.

12. Especially Asimov 1950, 1976. See Petersen 2012 for a philosophical essay defending this solution.

13. Adams (1980) 2002, 224.

14. Adams (1980) 2002, 225. Note the pronoun change from "it" to "he" after the the animal winks at Arthur.

15. As usual, the *Stanford Encyclopedia of Philosophy* is an excellent starting place for general reviews: Sinnott-Armstrong (2003) 2015; Hursthouse and Pettigrove (2003) 2017; Johnson and Cureton (2004) 2016.

16. However, in Schwitzgebel and Garza, forthcoming, my coauthor and I argue that the deontological concern here is closest to the root issue.

17. Asimov 1976; Snodgrass and Scheerer 1989; Sparrow 2004; Basl 2013; Bostrom and Yudkowsky 2014.

18. Shelley (1818) 1965, 95.

19. Searle 1980, 1992.

20. See Schwitzgebel 2014b for my defense of the medium-term dubiety of any general theory of consciousness that applies broadly across

possible types of natural and artificial beings. I assume that consciousness is required for human-level moral considerability. Kate Darling
(2016), Daniel Estrada (2017), and Greg Antill (in a noncirculating draft
article) have argued (each on different grounds) that AI need not even
be potentially conscious to deserve at least some moral consideration.

21. For more extended discussion of these issues, see Schwitzgebel and
Garza 2015, forthcoming.

22. Nozick 1974.

23. Sparrow 2004; in short story format: Schwitzgebel and Bakker 2013.

24. By random chance, it is a heterosexual marriage. See note 59 in part I
on my policy for choosing names in philosophical examples.

25. For more detailed philosophical treatments of simulated and virtual
worlds, see Bostrom 2003; Chalmers (2003) 2010, 2017; Steinhart 2014;
and Schwitzgebel, forthcoming. For a science-fictional portrayal of such
worlds, with philosophical consequences in plain view, see Egan 1994,
1997.

26. Bostrom 2003.

27. Chalmers (2003) 2010. See also Steinhart 2014. The famous entre-
preneur Elon Musk endorses the possibility in a 2016 interview: https://
www.youtube.com/watch?v=2KK_kzrJPS8.

28. Chalmers does not specifically discuss dream scenarios, but I see
no reason to think he would treat such scenarios differently as long as
they met fairly stringent conditions of stability and shared collective
experience.

29. See also Nick Bostrom, personal communication publicly shared
with permission as "Bostrom's Response to My Discussion of the Simulation Argument," *The Splintered Mind* (blog), September 2, 2011. http://
schwitzsplinters.blogspot.com/2011/09/bostroms-response-to-my
-discussion-of.html.

30. For a more detailed defense of sim-based skepticism and cosmological skepticism, see Schwitzgebel 2017.

31. See Schneider 2019. On philosophical "zombies" see Kirk (2003) 2015. I use "zombie" here in a somewhat looser sense than is orthodox: My zombies need not be exactly like us in all physical respects.

32. Block (1978) 2007, (2002) 2007; Searle 1980, 1984.

33. See Schneider 2019, chap. 4.

34. Descartes (1641) 1984. For an extended argument that introspection even of current conscious experience is highly untrustworthy, see Schwitzgebel 2011, especially chap. 7.

35. This might follow from the well-known Integrated Information Theory of Consciousness (Oizumi, Albantakis, and Tononi 2014).

36. For related arguments, but with the opposite conclusion, see Cuda 1985 and Chalmers 1996, chap. 7. For helpful discussion of Schneider's chip test, thanks to David Udell.

III   Regrets and Birthday Cake

1. See Heschel 2003 for details of the story.

2. I transcribed this quote from an old California Lutheran University newspaper clipping, but I can no longer find the original source.

3. For example, Skinner (1948) 1972; Leary (1988) 2003.

4. As famously portrayed in *One Flew Over the Cuckoo's Nest* (Kesey 1962).

5. In the psychology literature, this is called "conversational shadowing." In his career as a psychologist, my father was involved in some early shadowing studies: Schwitzgebel and Taylor 1980.

6. Here was I was influenced by Harry Frankfurt's lectures and discussions at the University of California, Riverside, some of which became Frankfurt 2004.

7. McGeer 1996. See also Zawidzki 2013.

8. On cognitive dissonance: Festinger 1957; Cooper 2007. Relatedly, in "choice blindness" studies, people choose one response and through sleight of hand, the experimenter makes it appear as though they had

chosen the opposite response. Participants often don't notice the swap and even justify their "choice" with reasons indistinguishable from the types of reasons that are given for ordinary choices: Johansson et al. 2006; Hall, Johansson, and Strandberg 2012.

9. Timmer, Westerhof, and Dittmann-Kohli 2005. Ware 2011 is a popular discussion based on the author's experiences in elder care, which better fits the standard picture.

10. Adams (1980) 2002, 163.

11. Roese and Vohs 2012.

12. The final words of a death row inmate who was not given the dignity of a careful fulfillment of his requested last meal (Melton 2009, 90).

13. Sacks 1985; Bruner 1987; Dennett 1992; Fischer 2005; Velleman 2005.

14. See *The Essential Herodotus* (Herodotus [5th c. BCE] 2017, especially bk. I [30–32], 15–17, and bk. I [86], 38–40).

15. Roache 2015, 2016.

16. Roache 2015, at 31:20.

17. Carlin 1972. Evidently, there was no official list, but I can attest that *I* never heard these words on US television in the 1970s, and broadcasters used to be fined for violations. Carlin was arrested for "disturbing the peace" when he performed his "Seven Words" act in Milwaukee in 1972 (Dimeo 2008). To be clear, despite my preference for reducing the usage of "fuck," I would not support arresting anyone for using it.

18. See https://trends.google.com/trends/?geo=US (accessed July 4, 2018). Usage has declined somewhat since peaking in 2015, but it's unclear whether that marks the beginning of a long-term trend. Similar increases, and 2015 peaks, show up in data from the UK, Canada, and Australia. Worldwide usage has almost doubled over the period.

IV Cosmic Freaks

1. Bradbury 1997–2000.

2. See also Bostrom 2014; Steinhart 2014; and Schneider 2019.

3. This is the orthodox "functionalist" view of consciousness: Levin (2004) 2013.

4. This is the "simulation" scenario, which I explore in more detail in chapters 21 and 22.

5. Gazzaniga 2005.

6. Ever since Chalmers 1996.

7. Since the whole affair is secret, there's no point in searching Koch's website for information on it. Sorry! In fact, I am revealing this episode now only because I trust that you will misinterpret it as fiction.

8. Example adapted from Block (1978) 2007.

9. For example, Putnam 1975; Burge 1979; Millikan 1984; and Dretske 1988, 1995.

10. See Moravec 1999; Kurzweil 2005; and Hilbert and López 2011. It is probably too simplistic to conceptualize the brain's connectivity as though all that mattered were neuron-to-neuron connections, but those who favor complex models of the brain's internal interactivity should, I think, for similar reasons, be drawn to appreciate complex models of the interactivity of citizens and residents of the United States.

11. As in Dennett 1991 and Metzinger 2003.

12. Few theorists have attempted to explain why they think that the United States isn't literally conscious. Giulio Tononi is one; see my responses in Schwitzgebel 2014c and Schwitzgebel 2015a (from which the present chapter is adapted). François Kammerer is another; see our exchange in Kammerer 2015 and Schwitzgebel 2016a. In Schwitzgebel 2015a, I also reply to objections via email from David Chalmers, Daniel Dennett, and Fred Dretske.

13. Boltzmann 1897; Gott 2008; Carroll 2010, 2017; De Simone et al. 2010; Crawford 2013; Boddy, Carroll, and Pollack 2016.

14. On "externalist" views of the mind, specific thought contents or even the presence of consciousness itself can require certain things to be factually true about one's history or environment, independent of any difference in one's current locally described brain structure. For

this chapter, I am assuming the falsity of externalism. Classic externalist arguments include Putnam 1975; Burge 1979; Millikan 1984; and Dretske 1995. For a review, see Lau and Deutsch (2002) 2014. For modest externalisms that require only a moderately large chunk of environment, we can modify the case to include random fluctuations of at least that size. Externalisms that require a substantial evolutionary history and thus stability over millions of years might be so much less likely as to require a different type of assessment of the relative probabilities. Even if we grant a version of externalism that disallows genuine thoughts about cosmology in freak systems, we might only have kicked the epistemic problem up a level, turning it into a problem about how we know that we are actually having thoughts about cosmology (possible only with the right history) instead of sham thoughts that only seem to have that content (as a freak might, on an externalist view of mental content; adapting McKinsey's [1991] well-known challenge to externalism).

15. Boddy, Carroll, and Pollack 2016.

16. De Simone et al. 2010.

17. The classic presentation is Putnam 1981.

18. Descartes (1641) 1984.

19. See Schwitzgebel 2017 for a fuller version of this argument, as well as a parallel argument concerning the skeptical worry that you might currently be dreaming.

20. Gott 2008; Tegmark 2014.

21. Davenport and Olum 2010; Crawford 2013; and Carroll 2017.

22. The example is originally from Davidson 1987. See also Dretske 1995; Neander 1996; and Millikan 2010.

23. The classic source of transporter puzzles about personal identity is Parfit 1984. For a recent discussion, see Langford and Ramachandran 2013.

24. I further develop this thought experiment in Schwitzgebel 2015b.

25. Greene 2011; Tegmark 2014.

26. The classic statement of this principle is in Bondi (1952) 1960.

27. The name "butterfly effect" traces to Lorenz 1972 and was popularized in Gleick 1987. Wolfram (2002) traces mathematical proofs of the amplification of small effects back to James Clerk Maxwell in 1860 and Henri Poincaré in 1890.

28. Please don't think about Evil Emily.

29. Williams 1973. For the contrary case, see especially Fischer 1994 and Fischer and Mitchell-Yellin 2014. The thought behind this chapter is that Fischer's defense of immortality by appeal to "repeatable" pleasures is even stronger than it might seem, since forgetting is inevitable and every pleasure is repeatable upon forgetting.

30. Gaiman (1996) 1998, 81.

31. If you haven't yet read Borges's *Labyrinths* ([1962] 2007)—a translation of some of his most philosophical midcareer stories—I urge you to put this book down and pick up that one instead.

32. For a formal discussion of the physics and logic of recurrence, see Wallace 2015.

33. For a fictional exploration of some related themes, see Schwitzgebel 2016b.

34. Most of the material in this section is drawn from Chase 2002. For more details and fuller references, see Schwitzgebel 2018b.

35. Carruthers 1996, 2018; Dennett 1996; Strawson 2006; and Oizumi, Albantakis, and Tononi 2014.

V   Kant versus the Philosopher of Hair

1. Arpaly and Barnett 2017.

2. This is an empirical claim about what is usually the case. Sometimes Truth philosophers will strike upon a truth so weird and rarely recognized that others think that they can't really sincerely believe the position they advance. Such discoveries should, by their nature, be rare

among philosophers with realistic self-assessments. Of course, one such truth, once found, can become the centerpiece of a whole career.

3. Possible worlds really exist: Lewis 1986. All matter is conscious: Goff 2017. We're morally obliged to let humanity go extinct: Benatar 2006.

4. US consciousness: chapter 39 and Schwitzgebel 2015a. Bad introspectors: Schwitzgebel 2011. Short-lived AIs: chapter 22 and Schwitzgebel 2017. Freaks: chapter 40 and Schwitzgebel 2013.

5. In a comment on the blog post from which this chapter was drawn, Randy Mayes suggests that the Hair Splitter may be an even more common type, and Nichi Smith suggests the Hole Poker. Clearly there remains much important taxonomic work to be done.

6. I'm assuming you didn't just jump to chapter 47 after reading the Preface. If you did, you probably already trust your sense of fun, and so you don't need to read this chapter. But then, if you're like that, you probably aren't reading this note—unless you find notes fun, in which case you're some sort of *double* dork (just like me for writing this dorky note).

7. External world: Schwitzgebel and Moore 2015. Ethics books: Schwitzgebel 2009. Dreaming in black and white: Schwitzgebel 2011. Jerkitude: chapter 1. Self-ignorance: Schwitzgebel 2012. Bizarre aliens: Schwitzgebel 2015a. Babies: Schwitzgebel 1999.

8. If you mention the code phrase "philosophy dork," I will befriend you on my own social media. Hi!

9. Feynman and Leighton 1985, 173ff.

10. Karpel 2014. The rest of the Whedon quote also applies quite well to philosophy, I think:

> Some people will disagree, but for me if I've written a meaty, delightful, wonderful bunch of scenes and now I have to do the hard, connective, dog's body work of writing, when I finish the dog's body work, I'll have a screenplay that I already love. I used to write chronologically when I started, from beginning to end. Eventually I went, That's absurd; my heart is in this one scene, therefore I must follow it. Obviously, if you know you have a bunch of stuff to do, I have to lay out this, all this dull stuff, and I feel very uncreative but the clock is ticking. Then you do that and you choose to do that. But I always believe in

just have as much fun as you can so that when you're in the part that you hate there's a light at the end of the tunnel, that you're close to finished.

11. For methodological details see Hurlburt 2011.

12. At our most recent presentation of this material in Tucson in 2018, Russ and I noticed that quite unusually, in all three samples, the audience member reported content having to do with the lecture. I'm unsure whether this is a fluke, or some difference in the audience (though we didn't notice this in our previous presentation in Tucson), or because early in the presentation I had mentioned that audience members rarely reported attending to the content of the lectures (and thereby may have tainted the procedure).

13. Hurlburt 1979 and personal communication July 18, 2018, as well as my own experience in beeping studies in both the participant and the researcher roles.

14. For example, Frege (1884) 1953, (1918) 1956 (though see Reck 2005); Lewis 1986; and Yablo 1987.

15. Besides the strangeness of realism about possible worlds, which I've already mentioned, Lewis's view of consciousness is bizarre in ways that I don't think have been fully appreciated: See Schwitzgebel 2015c and Schwitzgebel 2014b, sec. 3.

16. Critiques of the role of common sense or philosophical intuition as a guide to metaphysics and philosophy of mind can be found in, for example, Churchland 1981; Stich 1983; Kornblith 1998; Dennett 2005; Ladyman and Ross 2007; and Weinberg et al. 2010. Hume ([1740] 1978) and Kant ([1781/1787] 1998) are also interesting on this issue. Even metaphilosophical views that treat metaphysics largely as a matter of building a rigorous structure out of our commonsense judgments often envision conflicts within common sense so that the entirety of common sense can't be preserved: for example, Ayer 1967 and Kriegel 2011.

17. Aristotle (4th c. BCE) 1928, 983a; θαυμαστόν: wonderful in the sense of tending to cause wonder, or amazing.

18. See Moore 1925 on common sense and Moore 1922, 1953, and 1957 on sense data.

19. Reid (1774–1778) 1995, (1788) 2010; though he says this mistake of the "vulgar" does them no harm: (1788) 2010, section IV.3.

20. See also Sperber 2010 on gurus. A fuller treatment of the topic would also mention the positive reasons for obscurity (some of which are nicely listed by "boomer" in an October 24, 2011, comment on the original blog post from which this chapter was adapted; https://schwitzsplinters .blogspot.com/2011/10/obfuscatory-philosophy-as-intellectual.html).

21. For example, in a June 19, 2018, search of the PhilJobs database from June 1, 2015, to June 18, 2018, I count 30 advertisements mentioning Kant*, three each for Plato* and Aquin*, two for Aristot*, and one for Confuc*.

22. For more charitable interpretations of these passages, a starting place might be the dozens of annoyed comments that my original post on this topic received on my blog (some with helpful references). I recommend checking it out for the other side of the story! https://schwitzsplinters .blogspot.com/2010/03/kant-on-killing-bastards-on.html.

23. For discussion of Kant's racism, see Mills 2005; Bernasconi 2011; and Allais 2016. Allais argues that on the issue of race, Kant is simply "not noticing obvious contradictions" in his thinking (20), illustrating that even great philosophers are liable to ordinary human self-deception. For more of my reflections on philosophers' capacity for rationalization, see Schwitzgebel and Ellis 2017.

24. Zhuangzi (4th c. BCE) 2009 and Montaigne (1580/1595) 1957. Admittedly, Montaigne is disappointing on gender.

25. Kant (1785) 1996.

26. For a much more charitable reading of one aspect of Kant, see Schwitzgebel, forthcoming.

27. A few joined the SA or SS but not the Nazi Party, but since involvement in one of these dedicated Nazi organizations reflects at least as much involvement in Nazism as does Nazi Party membership alone, I have included them in the total.

28. Jarausch and Arminger 1989.

29. See Priest, Berto, and Weber (1998) 2018.

30. For example, on contradictoriness in Zhuangzi: Schwitzgebel 2018a; Montaigne: Miernowski 2016; Nietzsche: Müller-Lauter (1971) 1999; and Wittgenstein: Pichler 2007.

31. I have undertaken several invisible revisions of this chapter to make it more consistent with chapters 51 and 54. I think you'll find it much better now.

32. This is called the "Pygmalion effect" in educational psychology. The classic study is Rosenthal and Jacobson (1968) 1992. For a recent review, see Murdock-Perriera and Sedlacek 2018.

33. Hegel (1807) 1977; on Hegel's reaction to Napoleon: Pinkard 2000, 246, 311. One Hegel expert has commented that this might be the first time he had heard Hegel's arguments associated with "tidy." However, this expert did not dispute that it is a long, tenuous path from Hegel's A to his J.

34. Spinoza (1677) 1994, 180.

35. Mozi (5th c. BCE) 2013, chap. 16; Sextus Empiricus (circa 200 CE) 1994, bk. I.

36. Or ask, I suppose, if you want. Update: Both articles have been accepted for publication and are available in advance versions: Chomanski 2018; Schiller 2018.

37. One instance of brutal slaughter by Alexander and his forces was after the famous siege of Tyre (Green [1972] 2013, chap. 7).

38. Aristotle is clearest about this in *Politics* ([4th c. BCE] 1995, bk. I [1254a–b], 6–7). Some scholars have charitably interpreted Locke as opposed to slavery, and others have interpreted him as defending it (Glausser 1990; Armitage 2004). I believe it is clear that in his *Second Treatise of Government* ([1689] 2016), Locke defends the capture and holding of slaves as long as master and slave are "at war" with each other, and justly so if the slavery results from a just war, while acknowledging that slavery should end as soon as master and slave enter into a "pact" (which might possibly not occur during the slave's lifetime). Locke writes, for example: "*Slaves*, who being Captives taken in a just

War, are by the Right of Nature subjected to the absolute Dominion and arbitrary Power of their Masters. These Men having, as I say, forfeited their Lives, and with it their Liberties, and lost their Estates; and being in the *State of Slavery*, not capable of any Property, cannot in that State be considered as any part of *Civil Society;* the chief end whereof is the Preservation of Property" ([1689] 2016, [sec. VII.86], 43; though in chap. 16 Locke confusingly seems to take back the part about forfeiting goods: [sec. XVI.182], 92). Locke also held part ownership in slave-trading enterprises and probably helped compose the 1669 Fundamental Constitutions of Carolina, which stated that "every freeman of Carolina shall have absolute power and authority over his negro slaves."

39. Steven Pinker (2011) makes this point vividly in terms of what he calls the "Rights Revolutions." However, his depiction of traditional, "nonstate" societies might be inaccurate, excessively emphasizing their violence: Ferguson 2013a, 2013b; Gómez et al. 2016.

40. See books VII and IX of Rousseau's *Confessions* ([1769] 1995, especially [bk. VII, 331–333], 278–279, and [bk. VII, 343–345], 289. On high mortality rates in French orphanages or "foundling homes" during the period, see Colón and Colón 2001, 323–324, 503–504. Colón and Colón remark that "for overtly abandoned infants being nursed in foundling homes, death was a predictable outcome" (503–504). Under the influence of new friends over a decade later, Rousseau made inquiries about the fate of his eldest child, seeking reunion. However, no record could be found.

41. Pinker 2011.

42. Moody-Adams 1997.

References

Abdullah, Abu S., Feng Qiming, Vivian Pun, Frances A Stillman, and Jonathan M. Samet. 2013. "A Review of Tobacco Smoking and Smoking Cessation Practices among Physicians in China." *Tobacco Control* 22:9–14.

Adams, Douglas. (1980) 2002. "The Restaurant at the End of the Universe." In *The Ultimate Hitchhiker's Guide to the Galaxy*, 145–309. New York: Random House.

Adamson, Peter. 2016. "All 20 'Rules for the History of Philosophy.'" History of Philosophy without Any Gaps (website). December 31. https://historyofphilosophy.net/rules-history-philosophy.

Allais, Lucy. 2016. "Kant's Racism." *Philosophical Papers* 45:1–36.

Allcott, Hunt. 2011. "Social Norms and Energy Conservation." *Journal of Public Economics* 95:1082–95.

Arendt, Hannah. 1963. *Eichmann in Jerusalem*. New York: Penguin.

Aristotle. (4th c. BCE) 1928. *Metaphysica*. Translated by W. D. Ross. Vol. 7 of *The Works of Aristotle*. Oxford: Oxford University Press.

Aristotle. (4th c. BCE) 1995. *Politics, Books I and II*. Translated by T. J. Saunders. Oxford: Oxford University Press.

Armitage, David. 2004. "John Locke, Carolina, and the *Two Treatises of Government*." *Political Theory* 32:602–627.

Arpaly, Nomy. 2003. *Unprincipled Virtue*. Oxford: Oxford University Press.

Arpaly, Nomy, and Zach Barnett. 2017. "Philosophy: Truth or Dare?" *The View from the Owl's Roost* (blog). September 28. https://theviewfrom theowlsroost.com/2017/09/28/philosophy-truth-or-dare.

Asimov, Isaac. 1950. *I, Robot*. New York: Random House.

Asimov, Isaac. 1976. *Bicentennial Man*. Herts, UK: Victor Gollancz.

Aspy, Denholm J., Paul Delfabbro, and Michael Proeve. 2015. "Is Dream Recall Underestimated by Retrospective Measures and Enhanced by Keeping a Logbook? A Review." *Consciousness and Cognition* 33:364–74.

Ayer, A. J. 1967. *Metaphysics and Common Sense*. San Francisco: Freeman Cooper.

Ayres, Ian, Sophie Raseman, and Alice Shih. 2013. "Evidence from Two Large Field Experiments That Peer Comparison Feedback Can Reduce Residential Energy Usage." *Journal of Law, Economics, and Organization* 29:992–1022.

Barnhart, Robert K. 1988. *The Barnhart Dictionary of Etymology*. New York: H. W. Wilson.

Baron, Robert A. 1997. "The Sweet Smell of . . . Helping: Effects of Pleasant Ambient Fragrance on Prosocial Behavior in Shopping Malls." *Personality and Social Psychology Bulletin* 23:498–503.

Basl, John. 2013. "The Ethics of Creating Artificial Consciousness." *APA Newsletter on Philosophy and Computers* 13 (1): 23–29.

Batson, C. Daniel. 2016. *What's Wrong with Morality?* Oxford: Oxford University Press.

Baumrind, Diana. 1971. "Current Patterns of Parental Authority." *Developmental Psychology* 4:1–103.

Bazargan, Mohsen, Marian Makar, Shahrzad Bazargan-Hejazi, Chizobam Ani, and Kenneth E. Wolf. 2009. "Preventive, Lifestyle, and Personal Health Behaviors among Physicians." *Academic Psychiatry* 33:289–295.

Benatar, David. 2006. *Better Never to Have Been*. Oxford: Oxford University Press.

Bentham, Jeremy. (1781) 1988. *The Principles of Morals and Legislation*. New York: Prometheus.

Bernasconi, Robert. 2011. "Kant's Third Thoughts on Race." In *Reading Kant's Geography,* edited by S. Elden and E. Mendieta, 291–318. Albany: State University of New York Press.

Berridge, Kent C., and Morten L. Kringelbach. 2013. "Neuroscience of Affect: Brain Mechanisms of Pleasure and Displeasure." *Current Opinion in Neurobiology* 23:294–303.

Bicchieri, Cristina. 2017. *Norms in the Wild*. Oxford: Oxford University Press.

Bicchieri, Cristina, and Erte Xiao. 2009. "Do the Right Thing: But Only If Others Do So." *Journal of Behavioral Decision Making* 22:191–208.

Blair, James, Derek Robert Mitchell, and Karina Blair. 2005. *The Psychopath*. Malden, MA: Blackwell.

Blanken, Irene, Niels van de Ven, and Marcel Zeelenberg. 2015. "A Meta-analytic Review of Moral Licensing." *Personality and Social Psychology Bulletin* 41:540–558.

Block, Ned. (1978) 2007. "Troubles with Functionalism." In *Consciousness, Function, and Representation*, 63–101. Cambridge, MA: MIT Press.

Block, Ned. (2002) 2007. "The Harder Problem of Consciousness." In N. Block, *Consciousness, Function, and Representation*, 397–433. Cambridge, MA: MIT Press.

Bloom, Paul. 2013. *Just Babies*. New York: Penguin.

Bloomfield, Paul, ed. 2008. *Morality and Self-Interest*. Oxford: Oxford University Press.

Boddy, Kimberly K., Sean Carroll, and Jason Pollack. 2016. "De Sitter Space without Quantum Fluctuations." Unpublished manuscript, last modified February 22, 2016. arXiv:1405.0298.

Boltzmann, Ludwig. 1897. "Zu Hrn. Zermelo's Abhandlung 'Ueber die mechanische Erklärung irreversibler Vorgänge.'" *Annalen der Physik* 296 (2): 392–398.

Bondi, Hermann. (1952) 1960. *Cosmology*. 2nd ed. Cambridge: Cambridge University Press.

Bonnefon, Jean-François, Azim Shariff, and Iyad Rahwan. 2016. "The Social Dilemma of Autonomous Vehicles." *Science* 352 (6293):1573–1576. https://www.doi.org/10.1126/science.aaf2654.

Borges, Jorge Luis. (1962) 2007. *Labyrinths*. Translated by D. A. Yates and J. E. Irby. New York: New Directions.

Bostrom, Nick. 2003. "Are We Living in a Computer Simulation?" *Philosophical Quarterly* 53:243–255.

Bostrom, Nick. 2014. *Superintelligence*. Oxford: Oxford University Press.

Bostrom, Nick, and Eliezer Yudkowsky. 2014. "The Ethics of Artificial Intelligence." In *Cambridge Handbook of Artificial Intelligence*, edited by K. Frankish and W. M. Ramsey, 316–334. Cambridge: Cambridge University Press.

Bradbury, Robert J. 1997–2000. "Matrioshka Brains." Unpublished manuscript, accessed July 4, 2018. https://www.gwern.net/docs/ai/1999-bradbury-matrioshkabrains.pdf.

Bramble, Ben. 2016. "A New Defense of Hedonism about Well-Being." *Ergo* 3 (4). http://dx.doi.org/10.3998/ergo.12405314.0003.004.

Brink, David O. 1989. *Moral Realism and the Foundations of Ethics*. Cambridge: Cambridge University Press.

Brown, Ryan P, Michael Tamborski, Xiaoqian Wang, Collin D. Barnes, Michael D. Mumford, Shane Connelly, and Lynn D. Devenport. 2011. "Moral Credentialing and the Rationalization of Misconduct." *Ethics & Behavior* 21:1–12.

Bruner, Jerome. 1987. "Life as Narrative." *Social Research* 54:11–32.

Bryson, Joanna J. 2010. "Robots Should Be Slaves." In *Close Engagements with Artificial Companions*, edited by Y. Wilks, 63–74. Amsterdam: John Benjamins.

Bryson, Joanna J. 2018. "Patiency Is Not a Virtue: Intelligent Artifacts and the Design of Ethical Systems." *Ethics and Information Technology* 20:15–26.

Burge, Tyler. 1979. "Individualism and the Mental." *Midwest Studies in Philosophy* 4:73–121.

Carlin, George. 1972. "The Seven Words You Can Never Say on Television." Transcript (annotated). Accessed July 4, 2018. https://genius.com/George-carlin-the-seven-words-you-can-never-say-on-television-annotated.

Carroll, Sean. 2010. *From Eternity to Here*. New York: Penguin Random House.

Carroll, Sean. 2017. "Why Boltzmann Brains Are Bad." Unpublished manuscript, last modified February 2, 2017. arXiv:1702.00850.

Carruthers, Peter. 1996. *Language, Thought and Consciousness*. Cambridge: Cambridge University Press.

Carruthers, Peter. 2018. "The Problem of Animal Consciousness." *Proceedings and Addresses of the American Philosophical Association* 92:179–205.

Cartwright, Nancy. 2015. "Philosophy of Social Technology: Get on Board." *Proceedings and Addresses of the American Philosophical Association* 89:98–116.

Casebeer, William D. 2003. *Natural Ethical Facts*. Cambridge, MA: MIT Press.

Chalmers, David J. 1996. *The Conscious Mind*. Oxford: Oxford University Press.

Chalmers, David J. (2003) 2010. "*The Matrix* as Metaphysics." In *The Character of Consciousness*, 455–494. Oxford: Oxford University Press.

Chalmers, David J. 2017. "The Virtual and the Real." *Disputatio* 9 (46): 309–352.

Chase, Ronald. 2002. *Behavior and Its Neural Control in Gastropod Molluscs*. Oxford: Oxford University Press.

Chomanski, Bartek. 2018. "Could There Be Scattered Subjects of Consciousness?" *Phenomenology and the Cognitive Sciences.* Published ahead of print, August 8. https://doi.org/10.1007/s11097-018-9591-x.

Christie, Richard, and Florence L. Geis. 1970. *Studies in Machiavellianism.* New York: Academic.

Churchland, Paul M. 1981. "Eliminative Materialism and the Propositional Attitudes." *Journal of Philosophy* 78:67–90.

Cialdini, Robert B., Linda J. Demaine, Brad J. Sagarin, Daniel W. Barrett, Kelton Rhoads, and Patricia L. Winter. 2006. "Managing Social Norms for Persuasive Impact." *Social Influence* 1:3–15.

Cialdini, Robert B., Raymond R. Reno, and Carl A. Kallgren. 1990. "A Focus Theory of Normative Conduct: Recycling the Concept of Norms to Reduce Littering in Public Places." *Journal of Personality and Social Psychology* 58:1015–1026.

Clark, Andy. 2008. *Supersizing the Mind.* Oxford: Oxford University Press.

Clot, Sophie, Gilles Grolleau, and Lisette Ibanez. 2013. "Self-Licensing and Financial Rewards: Is Morality for Sale?" *Economics Bulletin* 33:2298–2306.

Colón, A. R., and P. A. Colón. 2001. *A History of Children.* Westport, CT: Greenwood.

Confucius. (5th c. BCE) 2003. *The Analects.* Translated by E. Slingerland. Indianapolis: Hackett.

Conway, Paul, and Johanna Peetz. 2012. "When Does Feeling Moral Actually Make You a Better Person? Conceptual Abstraction Moderates Whether Past Moral Deeds Motivate Consistency or Compensatory Behavior." *Personality and Social Psychology Bulletin* 38:907–919.

Cooper, Joel. 2007. *Cognitive Dissonance.* Los Angeles: Sage.

Cornelissen, Gert, Michael R. Bashshur, Julian Rode, and Marc Le Menestrel. 2013. "Rules or Consequences? The Role of Ethical Mind-Sets in Moral Dynamics." *Psychological Science* 24:482–488.

Crawford, Lyle. 2013. "Freak Observers and the Simulation Argument." *Ratio* 26:250–264.

Crisp, Roger. (2001) 2017. "Well-Being." In *Stanford Encyclopedia of Philosophy*, Fall 2017 ed., last revised September 6, 2017. https://plato .stanford.edu/archives/fall2017/entries/well-being.

Cuda, Tom. 1985. "Against Neural Chauvinism." *Philosophical Studies* 48: 111–127.

Damon, William. 1988. *The Moral Child*. New York: Simon & Schuster.

Darling, Kate. 2016. "Extending Legal Protection to Social Robots: The Effects of Anthropomorphism, Empathy, and Violent Behavior toward Robotic Objects." In *Robot Law*, edited by R. Calo, A.M. Froomkin, and I. Kerr. Glos, UK: Edward Elgar. https://papers.ssrn.com/sol3/papers.cfm ?abstract_id=2044797.

Darling, Kate. 2017. "'Who's Johnny?' Anthropomorphic Framing in Human-Robot Interaction, Integration, and Policy." In *Robot Ethics 2.0*, edited by P. Lin, G. Bekey, K. Abney, and R. Jenkins. Oxford: Oxford University Press. https://papers.ssrn.com/sol3/papers.cfm?abstract_id =2588669.

Davenport, Matthew, and Ken D. Olum. 2010. "Are There Boltzmann Brains in the Vacuum? Unpublished manuscript, last revised August 4, 2010. arXiv:1008.0808.

Davidson, Donald. 1987. "Knowing One's Own Mind." *Proceedings and Addresses of the American Philosophical Association* 61:441–458.

De Simone, Andrea, Alan H. Guth, Andrei Linde, Mahdiyar Noorbala, Michael P. Salem, and Alexander Vilenkin. 2010. "Boltzmann Brains and the Scale-Factor Cutoff Measure of the Multiverse." *Physical Review D* 82 (6):063520-1–30.

de Waal, Frans. 1996. *Good Natured*. Cambridge, MA: Harvard University Press.

Dennett, Daniel C. 1991. *Consciousness Explained*. Boston: Little, Brown.

Dennett, Daniel C. 1992. "The Self as a Center of Narrative Gravity." In *Self and Consciousness*, edited by F. Kessel, P. Cole, and D. Johnson, 103–115. Hillsdale, NJ: Erlbaum.

Dennett, Daniel C. 1996. *Kinds of Minds*. New York: Basic.

Dennett, Daniel C. 2005. *Sweet Dreams*. Cambridge, MA: MIT Press.

Descartes, René. (1641) 1984. "Meditations on First Philosophy." In *The Philosophical Writings of Descartes*, vol. 2, translated by J. Cottingham, R. Stoothoff, and D. Murdoch, 1–62. Cambridge: Cambridge University Press.

Dimeo, Nate. 2008. "Iconoclastic Comic George Carlin Dies at 71." *NPR: Morning Edition*, radio transcript, June 23. https://www.npr.org/2008/06/23/91791901/iconoclastic-comic-george-carlin-dies-at-71.

Dretske, Fred. 1988. *Explaining Behavior*. Cambridge, MA: MIT Press.

Dretske, Fred. 1995. *Naturalizing the Mind*. Cambridge, MA: MIT Press.

Egan, Greg. 1994. *Permutation City*. London: Millennium.

Egan, Greg. 1997. *Diaspora*. London: Millennium.

Ellenberg, Jordan S. 2013. "Do We Really Underestimate How Much We'll Change? (Or: Absolute Value Is Not Linear!)." *Quomodocumque* (blog). January 5. https://quomodocumque.wordpress.com/2013/01/05/do-we-really-underestimate-how-much-well-change-or-absolute-value-is-not-linear/.

Epictetus. (1st c. CE) 1944. *Discourses and Enchiridion*. Translated by T. W. Higginson. Roslyn, NY: Walter J. Black.

Eskine, Kendall J., Natalie A. Kacinik, and Jesse J. Prinz. 2011. "A Bad Taste in the Mouth: Gustatory Disgust Influences Moral Judgment." *Psychological Science* 22:295–299.

Estrada, Daniel. 2017. "Robot Rights. Cheap, Yo!" *Made of Robots*, episode 1 (May 24). URL: https://www.madeofrobots.com/2017/05/24/episode-1-robot-rights-cheap-yo/.

Faye, Emmanuel. (2005) 2009. *Heidegger*. Translated by M. B. Smith. New Haven, CT: Yale University Press.

Fehr, Beverley, Deborah Samsom, and Delroy L. Paulhus. 2013. "The Construct of Machiavellianism: Twenty Years Later." In *Advances in Personality Assessment*, vol. 9, edited by Charles D. Spielberger and James N. Butcher, 77–116. Hillsdale, NJ: Erlbaum.

Feldman, Fred. 2004. *Pleasure and the Good Life*. Oxford: Oxford University Press.

Ferguson, R. Brian. 2013a. "Pinker's List: Exaggerating Prehistoric War Mortality." In *War, Peace, and Human Nature*, edited by D. P. Fry, 112–131. Oxford: Oxford University Press.

Ferguson, R. Brian. 2013b. "The Prehistory of War and Peace in Europe and the Near East." In *War, Peace, and Human Nature*, edited by D. P. Fry, 191–240. Oxford: Oxford University Press.

Festinger, Leon. 1957. *A Theory of Cognitive Dissonance*. Stanford, CA: Stanford University Press.

Feynman, Richard P., and Ralph Leighton. 1985. *"Surely You're Joking, Mr. Feynman": Adventures of a Curious Character*. Edited by E. Hutchings. New York: W. W. Norton.

Fiala, Brian, Adam Arico, and Shaun Nichols. 2012. "The Psychological Origins of Dualism." In *Creating Consilience*, edited by E. Slingerland and M. Collard, 88–109. Oxford: Oxford University Press.

Fischer, John Martin. 1994. "Why Immortality Is Not So Bad." *International Journal of Philosophical Studies* 2:257–270.

Fischer, John Martin. 1997. "Death, Badness, and the Impossibility of Experience." *Journal of Ethics* 1:341–53.

Fischer, John Martin. 2005. "Free Will, Death, and Immortality: The Role of Narrative." *Philosophical Papers* 34:379–403.

Fischer, John Martin, and Benjamin Mitchell-Yellin. 2014. "Immortality and Boredom." *Journal of Ethics* 18:353–72.

Flanagan, Owen, Hagop Sarkissian, and David Wong. 2008. "Naturalizing Ethics." In *Moral Psychology*, vol. 1, edited by W. Sinnott-Armstrong, 1–26. Cambridge, MA: MIT Press.

Frank, Erica, and Carolina Segura. 2009. "Health Practices of Canadian Physicians." *Canadian Family Physician* 55 (8): 810–811.e7.

Frankfurt, Harry G. (1986) 2005. *On Bullshit*. Princeton, NJ: Princeton University Press.

Frankfurt, Harry G. 2004. *The Reasons of Love*. Princeton, NJ: Princeton University Press.

Frege, Gottlob (1884) 1953. *The Foundations of Arithmetic*. Translated by J. L. Austin. New York: Philosophical Library.

Frege, Gottlob. (1918) 1956. "The Thought: A Logical Inquiry," translated by P. T. Geach. *Mind* 65:289–311.

Gaiman, Neil (1996) 1998. "The Goldfish Pool and Other Stories." In *Smoke and Mirrors*, 72–107. New York: HarperCollins.

Gazzaniga, Michael S. 2005. "Forty-Five Years of Split-Brain Research and Still Going Strong." *Nature Reviews Neuroscience* 6:653–659.

Garson, Justin. 2016. "Two Types of Psychological Hedonism." *Studies in History and Philosophy of Biology and Biomedical Sciences* 56:7–14.

George, Susan, Janice Hanson, and Jeffrey L. Jackson. 2014. "Physician, Heal Thyself: A Qualitative Study of Physician Health Behaviors." *Academic Psychiatry* 38:19–25.

Glausser, Wayne. 1990. "Three Approaches to Locke and the Slave Trade." *Journal of the History of Ideas* 51:199–216.

Gleick, James. 1987. *Chaos: Making a New Science*. New York: Penguin.

Goff, Philip. 2017. *Consciousness and Fundamental Reality*. Oxford: Oxford University Press.

Goldstein, Noah J., Robert B. Cialdini, and Vladas Griskevicius. 2008. "A Room with a Viewpoint: Using Social Norms to Motivate Environmental Conservation in Hotels." *Journal of Consumer Research* 35:472–482.

Gómez, José María, Miguel Verdú, Adela González-Megías, and Marcos Méndez. 2016. "The Phylogenetic Roots of Human Lethal Violence." *Nature* 538:233–237.

Gordon, Peter E. 2014. "Heidegger in Black." *New York Review of Books*, October 9. http://www.nybooks.com/articles/2014/10/09/heidegger-in -black/.

Gosling, Samuel D., Oliver P. John, Kenneth H. Craik, and Richard W. Robins. 1998. "Do People Know How They Behave? Self-Reported Act

Frequencies Compared with On-Line Codings by Observers." *Journal of Personality and Social Psychology* 74:1337–1349.

Gott, J. Richard. 2008. "Boltmann Brains—I'd Rather See Than Be One." Unpublished manuscript, last revised February 2, 2008. arXiv:0802.0233.

Green, Peter. (1972) 2013. *Alexander of Macedon*. Berkeley: University of California Press.

Greene, Brian. 2011. *The Hidden Reality*. New York: Vintage.

Griffin, James. 1979. "Is Unhappiness Morally More Important Than Happiness?" *Philosophical Quarterly* 29:47–55.

Haidt, Jonathan. 2012. *The Righteous Mind*. New York: Random House.

Hall, Lars, Petter Johansson, and Thomas Strandberg. 2012. "Lifting the Veil of Morality: Choice Blindness and Attitude Reversals on a Self-Transforming Survey." *PLOS ONE* 7 (9): e45457.

Hanh, Thich Nhat. (1998) 2015. *The Heart of Buddha's Teaching*. New York: Harmony.

Hansen, Thomas. 2012. "Parenthood and Happiness: A Review of Folk Theories versus Empirical Evidence." *Social Indicators Research* 108 (1):29–64.

Hegel, G. F. W. (1807) 1977. *Phenomenology of Spirit*. Translated by A. V. Miller. Oxford: Oxford University Press.

Herbst, Chris M., and John Ifcher. 2016. "The Increasing Happiness of U.S. Parents." *Review of the Economics of the Household* 14:529–551.

Herodotus (5th c. BCE) 2017. *The Essential Herodotus*. Translated by W. A. Johnson. Oxford: Oxford University Press.

Heschel, Susannah. 2003. "Orange on the Seder Plate." In *The Women's Passover Companion*, edited by S. C. Anifeld, T. Mohr, and C. Spector, 70–77. Woodstock, VT: Jewish Lights.

Hilbert, Martin, and Priscila López. 2011. "The World's Technological Capacity to Store, Communicate, and Compute Information." *Science* 332:60–65.

Hume, David. (1740) 1978. *A Treatise of Human Nature*. Edited by L. A. Selby-Bigge and P. H. Nidditch. Oxford: Oxford University Press.

Hume, David. (1751) 1975. "Enquiry Concerning the Principles of Morals." In *Enquiries Concerning Human Understanding and Concerning the Principles of Morals*, 3rd ed., edited by L. A. Selby-Bigge and P. H. Nidditch, 168–346. Oxford: Oxford University Press.

Hurlburt, Russell T. 1979. "Random Sampling of Cognitions and Behavior." *Journal of Research in Personality* 13:103–111.

Hurlburt, Russell T. 2011. *Investigating Pristine Inner Experience*. Cambridge: Cambridge University Press.

Hurlburt, Russell T., and Eric Schwitzgebel. 2007. *Describing Inner Experience? Proponent Meets Skeptic*. Cambridge, MA: MIT Press.

Hursthouse, Rosalind, and Glen Pettigrove. (2003) 2017. "Virtue Ethics." In *Stanford Encyclopedia of Philosophy*, Winter 2016 ed., last revised December 8, 2016. https://plato.stanford.edu/archives/win2016/entries/ethics-virtue.

Ivanhoe, Philip J. (1990) 2002. *Ethics in the Confucian Tradition*. Indianapolis: Hackett.

James, Aaron. 2012. *Assholes: A Theory*. New York: Penguin.

Jarausch, Konrad H., and Gerhard Arminger. 1989. "The German Teaching Profession and Nazi Party Membership: A Demographic Logit Model." *Journal of Interdisciplinary History* 20:197–225.

Jiang, Yuan, Michael K. Ong, Elisa K. Tong, Yan Yang, Yi Nan, Quan Gan, and Teh-wei Hu. 2007. "Chinese Physicians and Their Smoking Knowledge, Attitudes, and Practices." *American Journal of Preventive Medicine* 33:15–22.

Johansson, Petter, Lars Hall, Sverker Sikström, Betty Tärning, and Andreas Lind. 2006. "How Something Can Be Said about Telling More Than We Can Know: On Choice Blindness and Introspection." *Consciousness and Cognition* 15:673–692.

John, Oliver P., and Richard W. Robins. 1993. "Determinants of Inter-judge Agreement on Personality Traits: The Big Five Domains,

Observability, Evaluativeness, and the Unique Perspective of the Self." *Journal of Personality* 61:521–551.

Johnson, Robert, and Adam Cureton. (2004) 2016. "Kant's Moral Philosophy." In *Stanford Encyclopedia of Philosophy*, Spring 2018 ed., last revised July 7, 2016. https://plato.stanford.edu/archives/spr2018/entries/kant-moral.

Johnson, Susan C. 2003. "Detecting Agents." *Philosophical Transactions of the Royal Society B* 358:549–559.

Jones, Daniel N., and Delroy L. Paulhus. 2014. "Introducing the Short Dark Triad (SD3): A Brief Measure of Dark Personality Traits." *Assessment* 21:28–41.

Jordan, Jennifer, Elizabeth Mullen, and J. Keith Murnighan. 2011. "Striving for the Moral Self: The Effects of Recalling Past Moral Actions on Future Moral Behavior." *Personality and Social Psychology Bulletin* 37:701–713.

Kahneman, Daniel, Alan B. Krueger, David A. Schkade, Norbert Schwarz, and Arthur A. Stone. 2004. "A Survey Method for Characterizing Daily Life Experience: The Day Reconstruction Method." *Science* 306:1776–1780.

Kahneman, Daniel, and Gary Klein. 2009. "Conditions for Intuitive Expertise: A Failure to Disagree." *American Psychologist* 64:515–526.

Kammerer, François. 2015. "How a Materialist Can Deny That the United States Is Probably Conscious—Response to Schwitzgebel." *Philosophia* 43:1047–1057.

Kant, Immanuel. (1764) 2007. "Observations on the Feeling of the Beautiful and Sublime." In *Anthropology, History, and Education*, edited by H. Wilson and G. Zöller, 18–62. Cambridge: Cambridge University Press.

Kant, Immanuel (1775) 2007. "Of the Different Races of Human Beings." In *Anthropology, History, and Education*, edited by H. Wilson and G. Zöller, 82–97. Cambridge: Cambridge University Press.

Kant, Immanuel (1781/1787) 1998. *Critique of Pure Reason*. Edited and translated by P. Guyer and A. W. Wood. Cambridge: Cambridge University Press.

Kant, Immanuel (1785) 1996. "Groundwork of the Metaphysics of Morals," translated by M. J. Gregor. In *Practical Philosophy*, edited by M. J. Gregor, 37–108. Cambridge: Cambridge University Press.

Kant, Immanuel (1797) 1996. "The Metaphysics of Morals," translated by M. J. Gregor. In *Practical Philosophy*, edited by M. J. Gregor, 353–604. Cambridge: Cambridge University Press.

Karlin, Beth, Joanne F. Zinger, and Rebecca Ford. 2015. "The Effects of Feedback on Energy Conservation: A Meta-analysis." *Psychological Bulletin* 141:1205–1227.

Kay, Margaret P., Geoffrey K. Mitchell, and Christopher B. Del Mar. 2004. "Doctors Do Not Adequately Look after Their Own Physical Health." *The Medical Journal of Australia* 181:368–370.

Karpel, Ari. 2014. "How to Be Prolific: Guidelines for Getting It Done from Joss Whedon." Fast Company (website). January 9. https://www.fastcompany.com/1683167/how-to-be-prolific-guidelines-for-getting-it-done-from-joss-whedon.

Kesey, Ken. 1962. *One Flew over the Cuckoo's Nest*. New York: Penguin.

Kirk, Robert. (2003) 2015. "Zombies." In *Stanford Encyclopedia of Philosophy*, Summer 2015 ed., last revised March 16, 2015. https://plato.stanford.edu/archives/sum2015/entries/zombies.

Kohlberg, Lawrence. 1981. *The Philosophy of Moral Development*. San Francisco: Harper & Row.

Kornblith, Hilary. 1998. "The Role of Intuition in Philosophical Inquiry: An Account with No Unnatural Ingredients." In *Rethinking Intuition*, edited by M. R. DePaul and W. Ramsey, 129–141. Lanham, MD: Rowman and Littlefield.

Kriegel, Uriah. 2011. "Two Defenses of Common-Sense Ontology." *Dialectica* 65:177–204.

Kruger, Justin, and David Dunning. 1999. "Unskilled and Unaware of It: How Difficulties in Recognizing One's Own Incompetence Lead to Inflated Self-Assessments." *Journal of Personality and Social Psychology* 77:1121–1134.

Kurzweil, Ray. 2005. *The Singularity Is Near*. New York: Penguin.

LaBerge, Stephen, and Howard Rheingold. 1990. *Exploring the World of Lucid Dreaming*. New York: Ballantine.

Ladyman, James, and Don Ross. 2007. *Every Thing Must Go: Metaphysics Naturalized*. Oxford: Oxford University Press.

Lake, Brenden M., Tomer D. Ullman, Joshua B. Tenebaum, and Samuel J. Gershman. 2017. "Building Machines That Learn and Think like People." *Behavioral and Brain Sciences* 40:e253. https://doi.org/10.1017/S0140525X16001837.

Landy, Justin F., and Geoffrey P. Goodwin. 2015. "Does Incidental Disgust Amplify Moral Judgment? A Meta-analytic Review of Experimental Evidence." *Perspectives on Psychological Science* 10:518–536.

Langford, Simon, and Murali Ramachandran. 2013. "The Products of Fission, Fusion, and Teletransportation: An Occasional Identity Theorist's Perspective." *Australasian Journal of Philosophy* 91:105–117.

Langlois, Judith H., Lisa Kalakanis, Adam J. Rubenstein, Andrea Larson, Monica Hallam, and Monica Smoot. 2000. "Maxims or Myths of Beauty? A Meta-analytic and Theoretical Review." *Psychological Bulletin* 126:390–423.

Lau, Joe, and Max Deutsch. (2002) 2014. "Externalism about Mental Content." In *Stanford Encyclopedia of Philosophy*, Fall 2018 ed., last revised January 22, 2014. https://plato.stanford.edu/archives/fall2018/entries/content-externalism/.

Leaman, George. 1993. *Heidegger im Kontext*. Hamburg: Argument-Verlag.

Leary, Timothy. (1988) 2003. *Musings on Human Metamorphoses*. Berkeley, CA: Ronin.

LeCun, Yann, Yoshua Bengio, and Geoffrey Hinton. 2015. "Deep Learning." *Nature* 521:436–44.

Levin, Janet (2004) 2013. "Functionalism." In *Stanford Encyclopedia of Philosophy*, Winter 2016 ed., last revised July 3, 2013. https://plato.stanford.edu/archives/win2016/entries/functionalism.

Lewis, David K. 1986. *On the Plurality of Worlds*. Malden, MA: Blackwell.

Lilienfeld, Scott O., and Brian P. Andrews. 1996. "Development and Preliminary Validation of a Self-Report Measure of Psychopathic Personality Traits in Noncriminal Populations." *Journal of Personality Assessment* 66:488–524.

Locke, John. (1689) 2016. *Second Treatise of Government and A Letter Concerning Toleration*. Edited by M. Goldie. Oxford: Oxford University Press.

Lorenz, Edward U. 1972. "Predictability: Does the Flap of a Butterfly's Wings in Brazil Set Off a Tornado in Texas?" Address to the American Association for the Advancement of Science, Washington, DC, December 29. https://www.ias.ac.in/describe/article/reso/020/03/0260-0263.

Margolis, Rachel, and Mikko Myrskylä. 2011. "A Global Perspective on Happiness and Fertility." *Population and Development Review* 37:29–56.

Mazar, Nina, and Chen-Bo Zhong. 2010. "Do Green Products Make Us Better People?" *Psychological Science* 21:494–98.

McDowell, John. 1985. "Values and Secondary Qualities." In *Morality and Objectivity: A Tribute to J. L. Mackie*, edited by Ted Honderich, 110–29. Abingdon, Oxon, UK: Routledge.

McFarland, Matt. 2017. "California Is Officially Embracing the Self-Driving Car." CNN Tech, March 10. https://money.cnn.com/2017/03/10/technology/california-dmv-self-driving-car/index.html.

McGeer, Victoria. 1996. Is "Self-Knowledge" an Empirical Problem? Renegotiating the Space of Philosophical Explanation." *Journal of Philosophy* 93:483–515.

McKay, Thomas, and Michael Nelson. (2010) 2014. "Propositional Attitude Reports: The De Re/De Dicto Distinction." In *Stanford Encyclopedia of Philosophy*, Spring 2014 ed., last revised October 5, 2010. https://plato.stanford.edu/entries/prop-attitude-reports/dere.html.

McKinsey, Michael. 1991. "Anti-individualism and Privileged Access." *Analysis* 51:9–16.

Melton, Wayne Rollan. 2009. *How to Eliminate Fear of Global Economic Recession and Terrorism*. Reno, NV: Fix Bay.

Meltzoff, Andrew N., Rechele Brooks, Aaron P. Shon, and Rajesh P. N. Rao. 2010. "'Social' Robots Are Psychological Agents for Infants: A Test of Gaze Following." *Neural Networks* 23:966–972.

Mengzi. (4th c. BCE) 2008. *Mengzi*. Translated by B. W. Van Norden. Indianapolis: Hackett.

Metzinger, Thomas. 2003. *Being No One*. Cambridge, MA: MIT Press.

Miernowski, Jan. 2016. "Montaigne on Truth and Skepticism." In *The Oxford Handbook of Montaigne*, edited by P. Desan, 544–561. New York: Oxford University Press.

Mikkelson, David, and Dan Evon. (2007) 2017. "Al Gore's Home Energy Use." Snopes.com. https://www.snopes.com/fact-check/al-gores-energy -use/.

Miller, Joshua D., and W. Keith Campbell. 2008. "Comparing Clinical and Social-Personality Conceptualizations of Narcissism." *Journal of Personality* 76:449–476.

Millikan, Ruth Garrett. 1984. *Language, Thought, and Other Biological Categories*. Cambridge, MA: MIT Press.

Millikan, Ruth Garrett. 2010. "On Knowing the Meaning: With a Coda on Swampman." *Mind* 119:43–81.

Mills, Charles W. 2005. "Kant's *Untermenschen*." In *Race and Racism in Modern Philosophy*, edited by A. Valls, 169–193. Ithaca, NY: Cornell University Press.

Montaigne, Michel de. (1580/1595) 1957. *The Complete Essays*. Translated by D. M. Frame. Stanford, CA: Stanford University Press.

Moody-Adams, Michele M. 1997. *Fieldwork in Familiar Places*. Cambridge, MA: Harvard University Press.

Moore, Andrew (2004) 2013. "Hedonism." In *Stanford Encyclopedia of Philosophy*, Winter 2013 ed., last modified October 17, 2013. https:// plato.stanford.edu/archives/win2013/entries/hedonism.

Moore, G. E. 1922. *Philosophical Studies*. London: Kegan, Paul, Trench, Trubner.

Moore, G. E. 1925. "A Defence of Common Sense." In *Contemporary British Philosophy*, edited by J. H. Muirhead, 191–223. London: Allen & Unwin.

Moore, G. E. 1953. *Some Main Problems of Philosophy*. London: Allen & Unwin.

Moore, G. E. 1957. "Visual Sense Data." In *British Philosophy in Mid-century*, edited by C. A. Mace, 130–137. London: Allen & Unwin.

Moravec, Hans. 1999. "Rise of the Robots." *Scientific American* 781 (6): 124–35.

Mozi (5th c. BCE) 2013. *Mozi: A Study and Translation of the Ethical and Political Writings*. Translated by J. Knoblock and J. Riegel. Berkeley, CA: Institute of East Asian Studies, University of California.

Murdock-Perriera, Lisel Alice, and Quentin Charles Sedlacek. 2018. "Questioning Pygmalion in the Twenty-First Century: The Formation, Transmission, and Attributional Influence of Teacher Expectancies." *Social Psychology of Education* 21:691–707.

Mullen, Elizabeth, and Benoît Monin. 2016. "Consistency versus Licensing Effects of Past Moral Behavior." *Annual Review of Psychology* 67:363–385.

Müller-Lauter, Wolfgang. (1971) 1999. *Nietzsche: His Philosophy of Contradictions and the Contradictions of His Philosophy*. Translated by D. J. Parent. New York: de Gruyter and University of Illinois Press.

Nagel, Thomas. 1979. *Mortal Questions*. Cambridge: Cambridge University Press.

Neander, Karen. 1996. "Swampman meets Swampcow." *Mind & Language* 11:118–129.

Nietzsche, Friedrich. (1887) 1998. *On the Genealogy of Morality*. Translated by M. Clark and A. J. Swensen. Indianapolis: Hackett.

Nozick, Robert. 1974. *Anarchy, State, and Utopia*. New York: Basic.

O'Toole, Garson. 2014. "You Just Chip Away Everything That Doesn't Look like David." Quote Investigator. Last modified June 22, 2014. https://quoteinvestigator.com/2014/06/22/chip-away/.

Oizumi, Masafumi, Larissa Albantakis, and Giulio Tononi. 2014. "From the Phenomenology to the Mechanisms of Consciousness: Integrated Information Theory 3.0." *PLOS Computational Biology* 10 (5): e1003588. https://doi.org/10.1371/journal.pcbi.1003588.

Parfit, Derek. 1984. *Reasons and Persons*. Oxford: Oxford University Press.

Paulhus, Delroy L., and Kevin M. Williams. 2002. "The Dark Triad of Personality: Narcissism, Machiavellianism, and Psychopathy." *Journal of Research in Personality* 36:556–63.

Petersen, Steve. 2012. "Designing People to Serve." In *Robot Ethics*, edited by P. Lin, K. Abney, and G. A. Bekey, 283–298. Cambridge, MA: MIT Press.

Piaget, Jean. (1932) 1975. *The Moral Judgment of the Child*. Translated by M. Gabain. New York: Free Press.

Pichler, Alois. 2007. "The Interpretation of the *Philosophical Investigations*: Style, Therapy, *Nachlass*." In *Wittgenstein and His Interpreters*, edited by G. Kahane, E. Kanterian, and O. Kuusela, 123–144. Malden, MA: Blackwell.

Pinkard, Terry. 2000. *Hegel: A Biography*. Cambridge: Cambridge University Press.

Pinker, Steven. 2011. *The Better Angels of Our Nature*. New York: Penguin.

Popper, Karl (1945) 1994. *The Open Society and Its Enemies*. Princeton, NJ: Princeton University Press.

Priest, Graham, Francesco Berto, and Zach Weber. (1998) 2018. "Dialetheism." In *Stanford Encyclopedia of Philosophy*, Fall 2018 ed., last revised June 22, 2018. https://plato.stanford.edu/archives/fall2018/entries/dialetheism.

Putnam, Hilary. 1975. "The Meaning of 'Meaning.'" In *Philosophical Papers*, vol. 2, 215–271. Cambridge: Cambridge University Press.

Putnam, Hilary. 1981. *Reason, Truth, and History*. Cambridge: Cambridge University Press.

Quoidbach, Jordi, Daniel T. Gilbert, and Timothy D. Wilson. 2013. "The End of History Illusion." *Science* 339:96–98.

Railton, Peter. 1986. "Moral Realism." *Philosophical Review* 95:163–207.

Reck, Erich. 2005. "Frege on Numbers: Beyond the Platonist Picture." *Harvard Review of Philosophy* 13 (2): 25–40.

Reid, Thomas. (1774–1778) 1995. "Materialism." In *Thomas Reid on the Animate Creation*, edited by P. Wood, 30–56. University Park: Pennsylvania State University Press.

Reid, Thomas. (1788) 2010. *Essays on the Active Powers of Man*. Edited by K. Haakonssen and J. A. Harris. University Park: Pennsylvania State University Press.

Richards, J. G. 1999. "The Health and Health Practices of Doctors and Their Families." *New Zealand Medical Journal* 112:96–99.

Ringer, Fritz K. 1969. *The Decline of the German Mandarins*. Hanover, NH: University Press of New England.

Roache, Rebecca. 2015. "Rebecca Roache on Swearing." *Philosophy Bites* (podcast), March 29. http://philosophybites.com/2015/03/rebecca-roache-on-swearing.html.

Roache, Rebecca. 2016. "Naughty Words." *Aeon*, February 22. https://aeon.co/essays/where-does-swearing-get-its-power-and-how-should-we-use-it.

Roese, Neal J., and Kathleen D. Vohs. 2012. "Hindsight Bias." *Perspectives on Psychological Science* 7:411–426.

Rosenthal, Robert, and Lenore Jacobson. (1968) 1992. *Pygmalion in the Classroom*. Norwalk, CT: Crown House.

Rousseau, Jean-Jacques. (1762) 1979. *Emile*. Translated by A. Bloom. New York: Basic.

Rousseau, Jean-Jacques (1769) 1995. *The* Confessions *and Correspondence, including the Letters to Malesherbes* (Vol. 5, Collected Writings of Rousseau), edited by C. Kelly, R. D. Masters, and P. G. Stillman, translated by C. Kelly, 1–550. Hanover, NH: University Press of New England.

Rust, Joshua, and Eric Schwitzgebel. 2015. "The Moral Behavior of Ethicists and the Power of Reason." In *Advances in Experimental Moral Psychology*, edited by H. Sarkissian and J. C. Wright, 91–108. London: Bloomsbury.

Sacks, Oliver. 1985. *The Man Who Mistook His Wife for a Hat.* London: Duckworth.

Sarna, Linda, Stella Aguinaga Bialous, Karabi Sinha, Qing Yang, and Mary Ellen Wewers. 2010. "Are Health Care Providers Still Smoking? Data from the 2003 and 2006/2007 Tobacco Use Supplement-Current Population Surveys." *Nicotine and Tobacco Research* 12:1167–1171.

Schiller, Henry Ian. 2018. "Phenomenal Dispositions." Synthese. Published ahead of print, September 5. https://doi.org/10.1007/s11229-018 -01909-9.

Schnall, Simone, Jonathan Haidt, Gerald L. Clore, and Alexander H. Jordan. 2008. "Disgust as Embodied Moral Judgment." *Personality and Social Psychology Bulletin* 34:1096–109.

Schneider, Susan. 2019. *Artifical You: AI and the Future of Your Mind.* Princeton, NJ: Princeton University Press.

Schroeder, Timothy. 2004. *Three Faces of Desire.* Oxford: Oxford University Press.

Schultz, P. Wesley, Jessica M. Nolan, Robert B. Cialdini, Noah J. Goldstein, and Vladas Griskevicius. 2007. "The Constructive, Destructive, and Reconstructive Power of Social Norms." *Psychological Science* 18:429–434.

Schwitzgebel, Eric. 1999. "Gradual Belief Change in Children." *Human Development* 42:283–96.

Schwitzgebel, Eric. 2007. "Human Nature and Moral Education in Mencius, Xunzi, Hobbes, and Rousseau." *History of Philosophy Quarterly* 24:147–168.

Schwitzgebel, Eric. 2009. "Do Ethicists Steal More Books?" *Philosophical Psychology* 22:711–25.

Schwitzgebel, Eric. 2011. *Perplexities of Consciousness.* Cambridge, MA: MIT Press.

Schwitzgebel, Eric. 2012. "Self-Ignorance." In *Consciousness and the Self,* edited by J. Liu and J. Perry, 184–197. Cambridge: Cambridge University Press.

Schwitzgebel, Eric. 2013. "My Boltzmann Continuants." *The Splintered Mind* (blog). June 6. http://schwitzsplinters.blogspot.com/2013/06/my -boltzmann-continuants.html.

Schwitzgebel, Eric. 2014a. "A Theory of Jerks." *Aeon*, June 4. https://aeon. co/essays/so-you-re-surrounded-by-idiots-guess-who-the-real-jerk-is.

Schwitzgebel, Eric. 2014b. "The Crazyist Metaphysics of Mind." *Australasian Journal of Philosophy* 92:665–682.

Schwitzgebel, Eric. 2014c. "Tononi's Exclusion Postulate Would Make Consciousness (Nearly) Irrelevant." *The Splintered Mind* (blog). July 16. https://schwitzsplinters.blogspot.com/2014/07/tononis-exclusion-post ulate-would-make.html.

Schwitzgebel, Eric. 2015a. "If Materialism Is True, the United States Is Probably Conscious." *Philosophical Studies* 172:1697–721.

Schwitzgebel, Eric. 2015b. "The Dauphin's Metaphysics." *Unlikely Story* no. 12. http://www.unlikely-story.com/stories/the-dauphins-metaphysics -by-eric-schwitzgebel.

Schwitzgebel, Eric. 2015c. "The Tyrant's Headache." *Sci Phi Journal* no. 3: 78–83.

Schwitzgebel, Eric. 2016a. "Is the United States Phenomenally Conscious? Reply to Kammerer." *Philosophia* 44:877–883.

Schwitzgebel, Eric. 2016b. "Fish Dance." *Clarkesworld* no. 118 (July). http://clarkesworldmagazine.com/schwitzgebel_07_16.

Schwitzgebel, Eric. 2017. "1% Skepticism." *Noûs* 51:271–290.

Schwitzgebel, Eric. 2018a. "Death, Self, and Oneness in the Incomprehensible Zhuangzi." In *The Oneness Hypothesis*, edited by P. J. Ivanhoe, O. J. Flanagan, V. S. Harrison, S. Sarkissian, and E. Schwitzgebel, 321–339. New York: Columbia University Press.

Schwitzgebel, Eric. 2018b. "Is There Something It's Like to Be a Garden Snail?" Unpublished manuscript. http://www.faculty.ucr.edu/ ~eschwitz/SchwitzAbs/Snails.htm.

Schwitzgebel, Eric. 2019. "Aiming for Moral Mediocrity." *Res Philosophica*.

Schwitzgebel, Eric. Forthcoming. "Kant Meets Cyberpunk." *Disputatio*.

Schwitzgebel, Eric, and R. Scott Bakker. 2013. "Reinstalling Eden." *Nature* 503:562.

Schwitzgebel, Eric, and Jonathan E. Ellis. 2017. "Rationalization in Moral and Philosophical Thought." In *Moral Inferences*, edited by J.-F. Bonnefon and B. Tremoliere, 170–190. East Sussex, UK: Psychology Press.

Schwitzgebel, Eric, and Mara Garza. 2015. "A Defense of the Rights of Artificial Intelligences." *Midwest Studies in Philosophy* 39:98–119.

Schwitzgebel, Eric, and Mara Garza. Forthcoming. "Designing AI with Rights, Consciousness, Self-Respect, and Freedom." In *The Ethics of Artificial Intelligence*, edited by S. M. Liao. New York: Oxford University Press.

Schwitzgebel, Eric, and Alan T. Moore. 2015. "Experimental Evidence for the Existence of an External World." *Journal of the American Philosophical Association* 1:564–582.

Schwitzgebel, Eric, and Joshua Rust. 2014. "The Moral Behavior of Ethics Professors: Relationships among Self-Reported Behavior, Expressed Normative Attitude, and Directly Observed Behavior." *Philosophical Psychology* 27:293–327.

Schwitzgebel, Eric, and Joshua Rust. 2016. "The Behavior of Ethicists." In *A Companion to Experimental Philosophy*, edited by J. Sytsma and W. Buckwalter, 225–233. Malden, MA: Wiley Blackwell.

Schwitzgebel, Ralph K. 1965. *Streetcorner Research*. Cambridge, MA: Harvard University Press.

Schwitzgebel, Ralph K., and Robert W. Taylor. 1980. "Impression Formation under Conditions of Spontaneous and Shadowed Speech." *Journal of Social Psychology* 110:253–63.

Searle, John R. 1980. "Minds, Brains, and Programs." *Behavioral and Brain Sciences* 3:417–457.

Searle, John R. 1984. *Minds, Brains, and Science*. Cambridge, MA: Harvard University Press.

Searle, John R. 1992. *The Rediscovery of the Mind*. Cambridge, MA: MIT Press.

Sedikides, Constantine, and Aiden P. Gregg. 2008. "Self-Enhancement: Food for Thought." *Perspectives on Psychological Science* 13:102–116.

Sextus Empiricus. (ca. 200 CE) 1994. *Outlines of Skepticism*. Translated by J. Annas and J. Barnes. Cambridge: Cambridge University Press.

Sezer, Hafize, Nuran Guler, and R. Erol Sezer. 2007. "Smoking among Nurses in Turkey: Comparison with Other Countries." *Journal of Health, Population, and Nutrition* 25:107–111.

Shaikh, Raees A., Asia Sikora, Mohammad Siahpush, and Gopal K. Singh. 2015. "Occupational Variations in Obesity, Smoking, Heavy Drinking, and Non-adherence to Physical Activity Recommendations: Findings from the 2010 National Health Interview Survey." *American Journal of Industrial Medicine* 58:77–87.

Shelley, Mary (1818) 1965. *Frankenstein*. New York: Signet.

Shepperd, James A., William M. P. Klein, Erika A. Waters, and Neil D. Weinstein. 2013. "Taking Stock of Unrealistic Optimism." *Perspectives on Psychological Science* 8 (4): 395–411.

Silver, David, Aja Huang, Chris J. Maddison, Arthur Guez, Laurent Sifre, George van den Driessche, Julian Schrittwieser, et al. 2016. "Mastering the Game of Go with Deep Neural Networks and Tree Search." *Nature* 529:484–489.

Singer, Peter. (1975) 2009. *Animal Liberation*. New York: HarperCollins.

Singer, Peter. 2009. *The Life You Can Save*. New York: Random House.

Sinnott-Armstrong, Walter. (2003) 2015. "Consequentialism." In *Stanford Encyclopedia of Philosophy*, Winter 2015 ed., last revised October 22, 2015. https://plato.stanford.edu/archives/win2015/entries/consequentialism.

Skinner, B. F. (1948) 1972. *Walden Two*. New York: Macmillan.

Sluga, Hans. 1993. *Heidegger's Crisis*. Cambridge, MA: Harvard University Press.

Smart, R. N. 1958. "Negative Utilitarianism." *Mind* 67 (268): 542–543.

Smith, Derek R., and Peter A. Leggat. 2007. "Tobacco Smoking by Occupation in Australia: Results from the 2004 to 2005 National Health Survey." *Journal of Occupational and Environmental Medicine* 49:437–445.

Snodgrass, Melinda M., and Robert Scheerer. 1989. "The Measure of a Man." *Star Trek: The Next Generation*. Season 2, episode 9.

Sober, Elliott, and David Sloan Wilson. 1998. *Unto Others*. Cambridge, MA: Harvard University Press.

Sparrow, Robert. 2004. "The Turing Triage Test." *Ethics and Information Technology* 6:203–213.

Sperber, Dan. 2010. "The Guru Effect." *Review of Philosophy and Psychology* 1:583–592.

Spinoza, Benedict de. (1677) 1994. *Ethics*. Translated by E. Curley. New York: Penguin.

Squier, Christopher, Vicki Hesli, John Lowe, Victor Ponamorenko, and Natalia Medvedovskaya. 2006. "Tobacco Use, Cessation Advice to Patients and Attitudes to Tobacco Control among Physicians in Ukraine." *European Journal of Cancer Prevention* 15:548–563.

Stangneth, Bettina. 2014. *Eichmann before Jerusalem*. New York: Penguin.

Steinhart, Eric. 2014. *Your Digital Afterlives*. New York: Palgrave.

Stich, Stephen. 1983. *From Folk Psychology to Cognitive Science*. Cambridge, MA: MIT Press.

Strawson, Galen. 2006. *Consciousness and Its Place in Nature*. Edited by A. Freeman. Exeter, UK: Imprint Academic.

Strawson, P. F. 1985. *Skepticism and Naturalism*. New York: Columbia University Press.

Susewind, Moritz, and Erik Hoelzl. 2014. "A Matter of Perspective: Why Past Moral Behavior Can Sometimes Encourage and Other Times Discourage Future Moral Striving." *Journal of Applied Social Psychology* 44:1722–1731.

Taylor, Shelley E., and Jonathon D. Brown. 1988. "Illusion and Well-Being: A Social Psychological Perspective on Mental Health." *Psychological Bulletin* 103:193–210.

Tegmark, Max. 2014. *Our Mathematical Universe*. New York: Random House.

Timmer, Erika, Gerben J. Westerhof, and Freya Dittmann-Kohli. 2005. "'When Looking Back on My Past Life I Regret . . .': Retrospective Regret in the Second Half of Life." *Death Studies* 29: 625–644.

Tversky, Amos, and Daniel Kahneman. 1991. "Loss Aversion in Riskless Choice: A Reference Dependent Model." *Quarterly Journal of Economics* 107:1039–61.

Tversky, Amos, and Daniel Kahneman. 1992. "Advances in Prospect Theory: Cumulative Representation of Uncertainty." *Journal of Risk and Uncertainty* 5:297–323.

Vazire, Simine. 2010. "Who Knows What about a Person? The Self-Other Knowledge Asymmetry (SOKA) Model." *Journal of Personality and Social Psychology* 98:281–300.

Vedantam, Shankar. 2017. "Can Robots Teach Us What It Means to Be Human?" *Hidden Brain* (podcast), July 10. https://www.npr.org/templates/transcript/transcript.php?storyId=536424647.

Velleman, J. David. 2005. "The Self as Narrator." In *Autonomy and the Challenges to Liberalism*, edited by J. Christman and J. Anderson, 56–76. Cambridge: Cambridge University Press.

Wallace, David. 2015. "Recurrence Theorems: A Unified Account." *Journal of Mathematical Physics* 56:022105. https://www.doi.org/10.1063/1.4907384.

Ware, Bronnie. 2011. *Top Five Regrets of the Dying*. Carlsbad, CA: Hay House.

Weinberg, Jonathan M., Chad Gonnerman, Cameron Buckner, and Joshua Alexander. 2010. "Are Philosophers Expert Intuiters?" *Philosophical Psychology* 23:331–355.

Weizenbaum, Joseph. 1976. *Computer Power and Human Reason*. San Francisco: Freeman.

Wheatley, Thalia, and Jonathan Haidt. 2005. "Hypnotically Induced Disgust Makes Moral Judgments More Severe." *Psychological Science* 16:780–84.

Williams, Bernard. 1973. *Problems of the Self*. Cambridge: Cambridge University Press.

Wilson, Erin Faith. 2017. "17 Antigay Leaders Exposed as Gay or Bi." *The Advocate*, November 21. https://www.advocate.com/politics/2017/11/21/17-antigay-leaders-exposed-gay-or-bi.

Wolf, Susan. 1982. "Moral Saints." *Journal of Philosophy* 79:419–439.

Wolfram, Stephen. 2002. *A New Kind of Science*. Champaign, IL: Wolfram Media.

Xunzi. (3rd c. BCE) 2014. *Xunzi*. Translated by E. Hutton. Princeton, NJ: Princeton University Press.

Yablo, Stephen. 1987. "Identity, Essence, and Indiscernibility." *Journal of Philosophy* 84:293–314.

Yankovic, Weird Al. 2006. *Straight outta Lynwood*. Los Angeles: Volcano Entertainment.

Young, Julian. 1997. *Heidegger, Philosophy, Nazism*. Cambridge: Cambridge University Press.

Zawidzki, Tadeusz. 2013. *Mindshaping*. Cambridge, MA: MIT Press.

Zhuangzi. (4th c. BCE) 2009. *The Essential Writings*. Translated by B. Ziporyn. Indianapolis: Hackett.

Index